Teaching Language Minority Students in the Multicultural Classroom

ROBIN SCARCELLA

PRENTICE HALL REGENTS, Upper Saddle River, New Jersey 07458

Library in Congress Cataloging-in-Publication Data

Scarcella, Robin C.
　　Teaching language minority students in the multicultural classroom
　/ Robin C. Scarcella.
　　　p.
　　Includes bibliographical references.
　　ISBN 0-13-851825-4 (pbk.)
　　　1. English language—Study and teaching—Foreign speakers.
　2. English language—Study and teaching—United States.
　3. Intercultural education—United States. 4. Minorities—
　Education—United States. 5. Education, Bilingual—United States.
　I. Title.
　PE1128.A2S3 1990
　428.007—dc20
　　　　　　　　　　　　　　　　　　　　　　　　　　90-31799
　　　　　　　　　　　　　　　　　　　　　　　　　　CIP

Editorial/production supervision and
　interior design: Noël Vreeland Carter
Cover design: Ray Lundgren Graphics, Ltd.
Manufacturing buyer: Ray Keating

©1990 by Prentice Hall Regents
Prentice-Hall, Inc.
A Simon & Schuster Company
Upper Saddle River, New Jersey 07458

Printed in the United States of America
10

Permissions appear on page xv which constitutes a continuation
of the Copyright page.

ISBN 0-13-851825-4

Prentice-Hall International (UK) Limited, *London*
Prentice-Hall of Australia Pty. Limited, *Sydney*
Prentice-Hall Canada Inc., *Toronto*
Prentice-Hall Hispanoamericana, S. A., *Mexico*
Prentice-Hall of India Private Limited, *New Delhi*
Prentice-Hall of Japan, Inc., *Tokyo*
Simon & Schuster Asia Pte. Ltd., *Singapore*
Editora Prentice-Hall do Brasil, Ltda., *Rio de Janeiro*

Contents

Preface

This book is for content-area teachers who instruct students who, though lacking in English proficiency, have been placed into classes where the ability to communicate fluently in nativelike English is often assumed. In most cities in the United States, teachers desire information about students of diverse cultural backgrounds. Teachers also clamor for advice concerning how language minority students who are non-native speakers of English can continue their acquisition of English while they simultaneously pursue mastery of content areas.

In recognition of the need to provide teachers with information concerning language minority students of diverse cultural backgrounds, the present volume discusses strategies for culturally responsive education. Drawing from the fields of second language development, teaching, and testing, as well as from those of education and cross-cultural communication, I suggest practical ways to provide students with an environment which will further their English language development and help them to learn in content areas. My own teaching experience at the elementary, secondary, adult education and university levels is reflected in all chapters. Relevant teaching techniques—suggested by leaders in their fields—are presented throughout the book.

Perhaps I should emphasize at this point that this book is not an effort to replace bilingual education programs with all-English instruction. Let me make it clear here that I advocate bilingual education programs. Such programs can teach students that their first languages are resources rather than liabilities. The student's native language is invaluable in teaching basic content areas. Yet, given the large number of students of diverse langauge backgrounds in many of today's classrooms and the absence of qualified bilingual instructors, more and more language minority students are being mainstreamed into classes which assume full English proficiency, often before these students are ready to handle the language demands. Too often, I have seen the results: the students cannot understand their content classes, and their acquisition of English slows or even halts.

The question may arise of why a mainstream author from the United States should write a book concerning educating diverse cultural groups. Wouldn't it be better if Korean writers wrote about teaching Korean children and Latino writers wrote about teaching Latino children? After all, we can never really walk in someone else's shoes. True. Readers should keep in mind my own mainstream American orientation when reading this book. Yet, given the absence of a book which provides information about many different cultures from the positive perspective of a mainstream educator who specializes in second language development, I felt it important that I write the present volume.

Due to space limitation, I have not been able to address the needs of all cultural groups in this volume. Instead, I have focused on Cambodians, Chinese, Koreans, Laotians, Mexican-Americans, Puerto Ricans and Vietnamese, currently among the most numerous groups of language minority students in the United States. Although the publishers have encouraged me to address the needs of Hawaiians, native Americans, African Americans, Cubans and others, I have not done so, feeling that since I could not begin to address the richness of all cultural groups in one book, I was wisest to address those groups whose students I have taught over the past twenty years, and whose values I therefore feel familiar enough with to discuss in a positive light from the perspective of a mainstream teacher and administrator. To members of those groups that I have not discussed, I apologize.

This book will not answer all the questions that educators have when teaching in multicultural classrooms. Clearly, national reforms are needed to create educational equity for all cultural groups. However, such reforms will take time. Hopefully, the information contained here will provide teachers with practical ideas for immediately improving the education of the language minority students enrolled in their classes now.

Robin Scarcella
Irvine, California
August 26, 1989

Acknowledgments

This book could not have been written without the valuable comments and suggestions of teachers, administrators and researchers. I am particularly indebted to those who shared their insights on cultural values: Richard Liao (for Chinese), Sary Song (for Cambodians), Chunok Lee (for Koreans), and Norma de la Torre, Laura Enriquez and Regina Marquez (for Latinos). In addition, I am grateful to the students in my courses at the University of California at Irvine and to the teachers in the Santa Ana Unified School District who provided me with opportunities to organize my ideas and test earlier versions of the manuscript. I am also indebted to Katherine Watson for her critical and insightful comments and suggestions on every chapter of this volume, to Joyce Neu for her thorough reviews of several chapters, and to Tina Carver, Gordon Johnson and Anne Riddick of Prentice-Hall Regents for their guidance. I wish to thank as well, Noël Vreeland Carter and Donald N. Unger. Special thanks are also due to Joan Bissell. I also thank Rita Peterson, who initially inspired this book. Finally, I thank my husband, Lou Scarcella for his patience and support.

Introduction

In the past decade, classrooms across the United States have radically changed. The influx of Latino and Asian refugees and immigrants has given our classrooms a multicultural hue. At the same time that increased numbers of non-English speaking students have enrolled in our schools, bilingual education programs have witnessed major budgetary reductions. Teachers have suddenly found that they are faced with teaching a population of students of unfamiliar cultures and languages. These instructors are often ill-prepared to provide their language minority students, who are non-native English speakers, with the type of language-rich and culturally sensitive environment needed for them to foster their learning and to develop their English skills. While a growing number of books discuss the content-area instruction of language minority students (see, for example, Mohan 1986, Cantoni-Harvey 1987, and Enright and McCloskey 1988), these works do not provide adequate information concerning diverse cultural groups.

The lack of information concerning cultural diversity is unfortunate. Our economic and political survival now depends on the strength of our ties with other nations. Educators who promote multicultural schooling are contributing to the success of language minority students and to the security and economic interests of the United States.

To avoid confusion, it is important to clarify terms at the beginning of this volume. I use the term *cultural group* interchangeably with *ethnic group* to refer to a group which shares "a common ancestry, culture, history, tradition and sense of peoplehood and that is a political and economic interest group" (Banks 1988, p. 8). The term *language minority student* is used to refer to a non-native English-speaking student who lacks full proficiency in English. I use the term *Latino* in reference to individuals of Latin American heritage. The term *Mexican-American* is used to refer to those persons who arrived in the United States from Mexico fewer than ten years ago, while the term *Chicano* is used to refer to individuals of Mexican heritage who have lived in the United States for more than ten years (or for several generations) and who are striving to achieve political, social, and educational equality in the United States. The word *Asian* is used to refer to persons who have recently immigrated to the United States

vii

from Asian countries (including Japan, Kampuchea [Cambodia], Korea, Laos, the People's Republic of China, the Philippines, Samoa and Thailand and Vietnam), while *Asian-American* refers to those individuals of Asian heritage who have lived in the United States for more than ten years or who were born here. Included in this last category are individuals whose families immigrated to the United States generations ago. Finally, I should explain that I use the terms *middle-American* and *mainstream American* interchangeably to refer to anyone in the United States *of any race or religion* who shares middle-class values and traditions.

The present book has many purposes. One goal of this book is to put in one place the information on language minority instruction which may be helpful to content-area teachers. Currently, information about language minority students is scattered in books in disparate fields. This volume integrates information from second language acquisition and pedagogy, bilingual education, multicultural education, ethnography of education and critical pedagogy. Second language researchers (such as Ellis 1986, Krashen 1981, and McLaughlin 1987) want to know how learners can best acquire a second language. By contrast, second language pedagogues are interested in creating methods and approaches which facilitate language development in the classroom (see, for instance, Larsen-Freeman 1986 and Richard-Amato 1988). Bilingual educators (such as Cummins and Swain 1986) are primarily concerned with the ways in which learners develop two languages. The primary goal of multicultural education as discussed by Banks (1981, 1987, 1988; see also Garcia 1982, Gollnick and Chinn 1986 and Kendall 1983), is then to create a school environment which fosters *pluralism*, that is, one in which members of specific diverse cultural groups have equal educational opportunities, where cultural differences and similarities are valued, and where students are presented with cultural alternatives.[1] Ethnographers of education (such as Heath 1983, Philips 1983, and Spindler and Spindler 1987) also contribute to our knowledge of cultural groups in the United States through, for instance, their observations of the ways in which specific groups raise and educate children. While there is no set implementation or application of critical pedagogy, those involved in this field view the educational problems of language minority students as manifestations of social and political inequities and injustices rather than merely a function of the educator's lack of sensitivity to the students' needs or the inherent problems of the students (see, for example, Freire 1973, 1983, 1985, and Giroux 1983, 1985, 1988; for useful application of critical pedagogy to language minority education, see Cummins 1989, Darder 1989, and Skutnabb-Kangas and Cummins 1988). All these fields have contributed information directly related to the instruction which we provide to our language minority students.

A second important goal of this volume is to describe certain principles for teaching language minority students so as to achieve culturally responsive education. By *principles* I mean here general guidelines or rules of thumb. These principles are based on the conceptual framework proposed by Cummins (1989) and the theoretical work of Long (1983), Krashen (1981), Swain (1986), Wong-Fillmore (1983) and others. They are listed below.

1. *Know your students.*
   Educators need to understand who their students are and the types of schooling which appeal to them;

2. *Understand language development.*
   Educators need to understand the factors affecting language development;

3. *Make your lessons comprehensible.*
   Educators need to provide students with lessons that they will understand;

4. *Encourage interaction.*
   Educators need to offer students opportunities to use language purposefully;

5. *Appeal to varying learning styles.*
   Teachers need to respond to their learners in culturally-sensitive ways and to encourage learning style flexibility;

6. *Provide effective feedback.*
   Teachers need to give students culturally-responsive feedback;

7. *Test fairly.*
   The pedagogical assessment procedures need to be culturally sensitive;

8. *Encourage minority parent participation.*
   Minority parent participation needs to be an integral part of the students' learning;

9. *Appreciate cultural diversity.*
   Educators need to understand their students' cultures;

10. *Incorporate your students' language and cultures.*
    Educators need to incorporate their minority students' languages and cultures into the school curriculum; and

11. *Reduce prejudice.*
    Educators need to implement policies, procedures and activities which are explicitly designed to reduce prejudice.

The volume is organized around these eleven principles. While these principles do not provide teacher-proof solutions to the problems facing language minority students, they do provide a basis for improving their education.

Chapter 1, *Establishing the Rationale*, explains the underlying reasons for the principles. In this chapter, I analyze why language minority students so frequently fail in mainstream American schools. A discussion of the causes of language minority student academic failure leads logically to a consideration of those principles which are needed to guide educational reforms in order to reverse the pattern of minority student school failure. The remaining chapters in the volume address these principles.

Principle 1: Know your students.

Considerable research shows that dramatic improvements can result when teachers understand their students. It is important that those who teach language minorities have more than a superficial knowledge of their students' lives. The following remark, made by a language minority student who is reflecting upon her school experiences, accentuates this point:

> I think it would have helped me a lot if the teachers just *knew* more about me.
>   (reported in Ovando and Collier 1986, p. 15)

Chapter 2, *Getting to Know Language Minority Students*, provides information about the linguistically and culturally diverse populations of students in our classrooms. It begins by describing the characteristics of these students and outlining explanations for their academic successes and failures. In addition, it describes important federal legislation affecting the education these students receive and the different educational programs available to them. Clearly, the information contained in this chapter is not intended to be complete. Rather, it is given as an introduction to the fundamental concepts teachers must know to address the needs of their language minority students.

Principle 2: Understand language development.

Significant improvements in language minority education also occur when teachers know about language development. Chapter 3, *Understanding Second Language Acquisition*, examines those factors which foster successful second language learning. Such factors include reduced instruction in mechanical grammatical exercises and drills and increased emphasis on real communication instead.

Principle 3: Provide comprehensible lessons.

In line with understanding language development, teachers must provide students of diverse English proficiencies with comprehensible lessons in English. Simply put, when students do not understand their teachers, they do not learn, no matter what may be the subject area. Teachers who instruct language minority students must have available a variety of techniques for ensuring that their students receive comprehensible input (Krashen 1981). Cultural gaps which prevent learners from understanding classroom lessons also need to be addressed. Chapter 4, *Providing Comprehensible Lessons*, is devoted to a discussion of the strategies which teachers can use to make their lessons more comprehensible to language minority students.

Principle 4: Encourage interaction.

Teachers in multicultural classrooms frequently lament their students' inability to communicate effectively because of limited English proficiency. Unfortunately, these same teachers often fail to encourage interaction in their classrooms. It is not enough for learners to be exposed to comprehensible input. In order for learners to maximally benefit from this input, they must use it to interact purposefully. A number of researchers (including Wells 1986 and Lindfors 1980) have argued that learning emerges from interaction. Likewise, the Bullock report, which emphasizes the importance of interaction, states that "talking and writing are a means to learning" (p. 50). The following characteristics of a pedagogy which enable students to use language in interaction are summarized by Cummins (1989):

- genuine dialogue between student and teacher in both oral and written modalities;
- guidance and facilitation rather than control of student learning by the teacher;
- encouragement of student-student talk in a collaborative learning context;
- encouragement of meaningful use of language by students rather than correctness of surface forms;
- conscious integration of language use and development with all curricular content rather than teaching language and other content as isolated subjects;
- focus on developing higher level cognitive skills rather than on factual recall;
- task presentation that generates intrinsic rather than extrinsic motivation. (p. 64)

Interaction helps language minority students to personalize the language input they receive, to attain knowledge, and also to share multicultural experiences (Cummins 1986, 1989). In classrooms without such interaction, the students' experiences are often excluded from the curriculum (Cummins 1989). Chapter 5, *Encouraging Interaction in the Multicultural Classroom*, suggests ways to create classrooms which maximize the language minority students' opportunities to interact. In addition, it suggests specific activities that teachers can use to foster effective interaction among students of diverse cultural groups.

Principle 5: Appeal to diverse learning styles.

Successful instruction for language minority students in multicultural classrooms also demands pedagogy which appeals to diverse learning styles. Chapter 6, *Appealing to a Variety of Learning Styles*, focuses on such learning styles as the gestalt, analytic, visual, auditory, cooperative, independent, and competitive. In this chapter, I use the term, *learning style* to refer to cognitive and interactional patterns which affect the ways in which learners perceive, remember and think. I do not advocate assessing student learning styles, labeling them, and employing specific instructional practices with specific students. Instead, I suggest ways to varying teaching approaches to appeal to a wide variety of learning styles and encouraging students to try out new learning behaviors.

Principle 6: Provide effective feedback.

Educators who work with language minority students also need to give their students effective feedback. By *feedback*, I mean the teachers' responses to their students' efforts to communicate. Chapter 7, *Providing Effective Feedback*, concerns the feedback teachers give their students. The perception of feedback varies widely across cultures. For example, many groups of Latinos generally expect more positive feedback than do their native English-speaking peers, while some Asians interpret as too effusive and insincere the positive feedback of their mainstream American instructors. In this chapter, different perceptions of feedback are discussed and strategies are given to help teachers provide culturally responsive feedback.

Principle 7: Test fairly.

The massive over-representation of language minority children in classes for the learning disabled and language impaired, reported by Mercer (1973), Cummins (1984) and others, underscores the importance of employing culturally sensitive assessment procedures in multicultural classrooms. Unfortunately, most assessment procedures traditionally reflect middle American values and priorities. Language minority children often fare poorly on the tests used in our schools. Chapter 8, *Testing in Culturally Responsive Ways*, covers information concerning the avoidance of cultural bias in evaluating and placing students. Strategies are given which validly assess the abilities of learners from diverse cultural backgrounds.

Principle 8: Encourage minority parent participation.

Dramatic changes in the education of language minority children can take place when minority parents are actively involved in their students' schooling. A variety of studies has demonstrated that when parents and schools collaborate, children become more interested in their learning at school. Many parents of minority students have high academic aspirations for their children (Wong-Fillmore 1983), but they may not know how to participate in their children's schooling, they may feel intimidated by the educational system, or they may even be excluded from participating (Cummins 1989). Chapter 9, *Interacting with Parents*, focuses on parental input in the schooling of children. This chapter is primarily intended for teachers of elementary and secondary students. Strategies for interacting effectively with language minority parents are suggested.

Principle 9: Appreciate cultural diversity.

Chapter 10, *Appreciating Cultural Diversity in the United States*, provides teachers with information concerning the histories, problems, values, and educational backgrounds of what are currently among the most numerous groups of language minority students in the United States. These include Cambodians; Chinese from Hong Kong, the People's Republic of China, Taiwan, and Vietnam; Filipinos; Hmong; Koreans; Mexican-Americans; and Vietnamese. I have taught these particular groups for many years, and can discuss their diverse histories and values from the positive perspective of a mainstream America. (For information concerning those cultural groups I was unable to discuss in this volume, refer to the recommended readings at the end of Chapter 10.) Although ethnographers of education encourage teachers to research the values and problems of their students so that teachers can respond in culturally sensitive ways, educators often lack the time, resources or ability to do this. The information contained in this chapter should help teachers recognize the rich cultural resources that their language minority students bring to our schools.

Principle 10: Incorporate your students' languages and cultures.

Educators who incorporate their students' languages and cultures into the curriculum are more successful than those who do not. For convincing arguments, see for example, Cummins 1989 and Crawford 1989. As Cummins cogently argues, "It is important to emphasize that schools can play a significant role in encouraging children to develop their L1 (first language) proficiency even in situations where bilingual education or heritage (after-school)-language teaching is not possible" (p. 60). Chapter 11, *Incorporating Your Students Languages and Cultures*, discusses major strategies for utilizing the linguistic and cultural talents of language minority students in content-area classrooms.

Principle 11: Reduce prejudice.

Educational reforms are futile unless teachers can reduce the prejudice pervading our schools. Prejudice will not disappear by itself. Educators need to implement strategies and activities explicitly designed to reduce it. Suggestions for purging prejudice from our curricula and classrooms are given throughout this volume.

The various chapters in this volume share one unifying focus: effectively teaching language minority students from diverse cultural backgrounds in content-area classes. The principles suggested are a response to the unique educational needs, aspirations, and goals of students with limited English proficiency.

This book is intended for elementary teachers, junior high school and high school teachers, as well as for instructors in higher education. Educational administrators should also find the volume useful. In writing this book, I have kept a variety of ages in mind.

Clearly, the reader will consider some suggestions more appropriate for adults and others more appropriate for children.

It would be naive of me to believe that the principles I have suggested here can help all language minority students succeed in our schools. They cannot. Before educational equity can be achieved, the current political, social, and economic structure of the United States will undoubtedly need to be changed. In the meantime, I hope that the principles described here will further stimulate improvements in the education that language minority students receive.

NOTES

[1]Multicultural education is in direct opposition to the *melting pot* or assimilationist ideology prevalent at the end of the 19th century. This ideology held that cultural groups should assimilate and become a part of mainstream American society. Cultural differences were thought best to melt away and to create a new, stronger society. Interestingly, Lucas (1981) points out that many language minority students (including Latino groups) were never allowed to approach the melting pot. These groups were segregated; if they did come near to the pot, they were most likely placed under it, and were burned by the flames. (See also Cummins 1989.)

Permissions

The author gratefully acknowledges the following publishers and companies for permission to reprint copyrighted materials:

Aspen Publishers, Inc. for use of Table 9–1 and excerpts from L.-R. Cheng, 1987, ASSESSING ASIAN LANGUAGE PERFORMANCE: GUIDELINES FOR EVALUATING LIMITED-PROFICIENCY STUDENTS, Rockville, Maryland: An Aspen Production.

National Education Association for the tables on pages 120 and 128 from B. Cox, and M. Ramirez, 1981, "Cognitive Styles: Implications For Multiethnic Education." J. Banks (ed.) EDUCATION IN THE 1980'S; Washington, D.C.: National Education Association.

Longman Group UK Ltd. for use of figures appearing on page 56 from J. Cummins and M. Swain, 1986, BILINGUALISM IN EDUCATION; London: Longman.

Addison-Wesley for Table 10–1 from L. Damen, 1988, CULTURE LEARNING: THE FIFTH DIMENSION IN THE LANGUAGE CLASSROOM; Reading, Massachusetts: Addison-Wesley and to quote from D. S. Enright and M. McClosky, 1988, INTEGRATING ENGLISH: DEVELOPING ENGLISH LANGUAGE AND LITERACY IN THE MULTILINGUAL CLASSROOM, Reading, Massachusetts: Addison-Wesley.

Center for Applied Lingistics for the use of Table 3-1 from G. Valdes-Fallis, 1981, "Code-switching and the Classroom Teacher; Language in Education: Theory and Practice," 4:16. Washington, D.C.: Center for Applied Linguistics.

Harper & Row, Publishers, Inc. for use of a chart from PSYCHOLINGUISTICS by Evelyn Hatch, Copyright © 1983 by Newbury House, a division of Harper & Row, Publishers, Inc. Reprinted by permission of the publisher. Also thanks to them for use of the excerpt from RAISING SILENT VOICES by Henry Trueba, Copyright © 1989 by Newbury House, a division of Harper & Row, Publishers, Inc. Reprinted by permission of the publisher.

Crane Publishing Company for use of the table appearing on pages 41–42 from J. Crawford, 1989, BILINGUAL EDUCATION: HISTORY, POLITICS, THEORY AND PRACTICE; Trenton, New Jersey: Crane Publishing Company.

California Association for Bilingual Education for use of the cartoon on page 14 from J. Cummins, 1989, EMPOWERING LANGUAGE MINORITY STUDENTS, Sacramento: California Association for Bilingual Education.

Resources for Teachers, Inc. for the use of an excerpt from Spencer Kagan, 1989, COOPERATIVE LEARNING: RESOURCES FOR TEACHERS; San Juan Capistrano: Resources for Teachers, Inc.

CHAPTER ONE

Establishing the Rationale

Cultural diversity has become more the norm than the exception in the United States. As Cortes (1986) notes, between 1970 and 1980, the United States population increased by 11.6 percent; however, the four major ethnic minority groups grew even more remarkably. The African-American population rose by 17.8 percent, the Latino by 61 percent, the Native American by 71 percent and the Asian-American by 233 percent. Evans (1987) points out that the number of students for whom English is not a native language has also dramatically risen in the last decade and, from all indications, this number will continue to grow. "The major contributing factors are continuing sizable immigration from Asia and Latin America and the fact that the average age of ethnic minorities is about five years less than the national average. The latter translates into a larger percentage being in or entering the most active child-bearing years" (Cortes 1986, p. 10). Figure 1–1 gives the proportions of language minorities in the United States in 1980.

As suggested by Figure One, many schools currently have student bodies that are composed of more than one-fourth minority populations. More than 50% of the Los Angeles Unified School District (kindergarten through second grade) is composed of just one cultural group: Latinos. Most certainly, the nation's schools have developed a multicultural hue.

This trend will continue into the future. The number of language minority students enrolled in our schools is predicted to rise. According to Oxford et al. (1981), the number of students who lack English proficiency, (aged four to 18), estimated to be 3.6 million in 1978, will rise to 5.2 million by the year 2000.

These demographic trends make it imperative for teachers to understand their students and to respond to them in culturally sensitive ways. Working with and knowing about different cultural groups is not simply political liberalism. Rather, because of our multicultural nation, it has become a necessity to interact effectively with diverse groups. These groups bring to our schools a valuable multilingual, multicultural resource which enriches education. As Cummins (1989) argues:

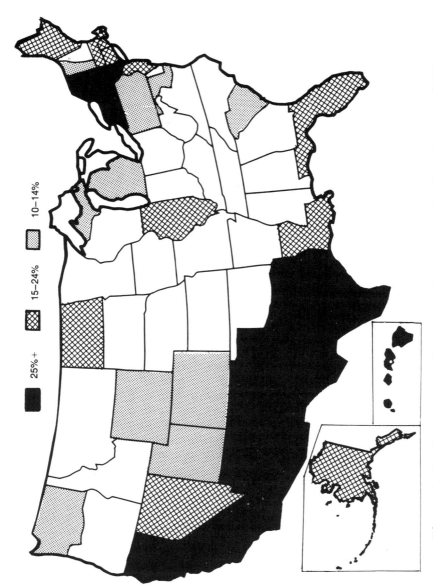

Figure 1–1: Proportions of Language Minorities in the United States: 1980

Educators who promote children's bilingual skills are contributing to a linguistically-competent nation, and to its security and economic interests, far more than those who attempt to eradicate these language skills. Eradicating children's linguistic talents contributes only to the creation of a nation of *monolinguistic bumpkins* (in the words of former Education Secretary Terrell Bell) that is internationally isolated and subject to mutual misunderstanding with other nations. (p. 129)

In short, English monolingualism is bad for our economy, national security, and international communications.

Understanding the Success and Failure of Language Minority Students

Although language minority students often enter our schools bilingual and bicultural and are therefore intellectually *gifted*, many of them fail in our schools. Approximately one-third of our nation's children are academically *at risk.* The majority of these children are non-native speakers of English. Before we can implement educational changes which prevent language minority students from failing in our schools, we must first understand why they fail (Cummins 1989). Numerous explanations have been offered to explain the differential academic success of language minority students. My summary of these explanations relies heavily on the insightful work of Trueba (1989).

Teacher Prejudice

One explanation for the differential success experienced by the language minority students in our classrooms is prejudice.[1] The failure of many of our language minority students is not the fault of their cultural group, but rather the fault of prejudice, reflected in the way middle-American teachers treat them. For example, in analyzing teacher attitudes in South Texas, Meadowcroft and Foley (1978) found that some teachers held false stereotypes about Mexican culture. They believed that all Mexicans encourage low achievement, laziness, lack of discipline, and unwise use of money. Like it or not, prejudiced teachers are not prevented from obtaining teaching credentials in the United States.

In a well-known study, Spindler and Spindler (1982) document the case of Roger Harker (a pseudonym), a middle-class, mainstream-American teacher who taught children of diverse cultural backgrounds. The teachers who worked with Roger Harker considered him an excellent, well-organized instructor who was sensitive to the needs of his students. What follows are Roger Harker's evaluations of the children in his classroom:

> He [Roger Harker] ranked highest on all dimensions, including personal and academic factors, those children who were most like himself—Anglo, middle to upper middle social class, and, like him, ambitious (achievement oriented). He also estimated that these children were the most popular with their peers and were the leaders of the classroom group. His knowledge about the individual children, elicited without recourse to files or notes, was distributed in the same way. He knew significantly more about the children culturally like himself (on items concerned with home background as well as academic performance), and least about those culturally different. . . . He most frequently called on, touched, helped and looked directly at the children culturally like himself. He was never mean or cruel to the other children. It was almost as though they weren't there. (Spindler and Spindler 1982, p. 26)

Interestingly, Roger Harker's young students evaluated each other quite differently than he did. The non-middle-American students viewed several of Harker's *star* mainstream American pupils as *teacher's pets*. They often considered those non-middle-American children to whom Harker gave negative ratings as *leaders*. Not surprisingly, many students felt their teacher was unfair.

This example underscores the pervasiveness of prejudice and its sweeping, though subtle, effect on classroom instruction. Roger Harker was unaware of his own prejudice. Unfortunately, most of us are equally unaware of our prejudices. Such favoritism clearly thwarts some language minority students' efforts to achieve academic success in our schools. In Cummins' (1988) words,

> There is usually no intent to discriminate on the part of educators; however, their intentions with minority students are mediated by a system of unquestioned assumptions that reflect the values and priorities of the dominant middle-class culture. It is in these interactions that minority students are educationally disabled. (p. 132)

Rosenthal and Jacob's (1968) classic volume, *Pygmalion in the Classroom*, reports research which demonstrates just how important teacher expectations are. As a part of this research, a group of teachers were told that the particular students they taught had received exceptionally high scores on intelligence tests. In reality, the students they taught were of various abilities. While their teachers never explicitly told their students that they were bright, their behaviors conveyed to these students their high expectations. By the end of the experiment, the children's actual scores on standardized tests reflected their teachers' expectations. The results indicated that the children had indeed become exceptionally bright. What Rosenthal and Jacob's research demonstrates is that if teachers believe that their students have high potential, and treat them as though they have this potential, then, after a while, the students will rise to meet their teachers' expectations. This is known as the *self-fulfilling prophecy.* It should be pointed out that Eliza, in Shaw's *Pygmalion,* claimed that she only became a lady when Colonel Pickering began to *treat* her as one. Unfortunately, a number of studies report that many teachers do not treat their minority learners as intelligent students, and, perhaps as a result, their minority students fail in their classes. (For a review of these studies, see Garcia 1982; see also Rist 1970.)

Implications

Clearly, teachers must know their students, recognize their own prejudices and combat these prejudices. They can have high expectations for all students. They can critically evaluate their own treatment of these students and validate all students' cultural and linguistic identities through the subtle messages they convey to them.[2]

Home/School Discontinuities

Home/school discontinuities are also believed to result in the academic failure of many language minority students. This explanation holds that the language and cultural differences between the middle-American school culture and the language minority students' home culture are so great that they prevent language minority students from attaining academic success. Teachers who find this hypothesis appealing, frequently lament that they are unable to deal with the diverse cultures they find in their classrooms and complain about the many communication difficulties which occur as they try to instruct their non-native English students. One reason that communication difficulties occur so frequently in classrooms where language minority students are instructed by middle-American teachers is that the language minority students and their native English-speaking teachers do not share the same understanding of what *ought to* comprise classroom behavior. Inaccurate character judgments sometimes arise as a result. Consider the example below. (Bracketing indicates interruptions.)

Anousheh: Teacher, my teacher. Try come here.
Teacher: I can't. I'm working with Billy.
Anousheh: (interrupting) I need your help.

Like many middle-Americans, the teacher assumes that interruptions are impolite (Zimmerman and West 1975). In this exchange, the teacher incorrectly concludes that Anousheh is rude. However, rather than associating rudeness with her student's speech behavior, the teacher associates rudeness with Anousheh. Such reasoning is unfortunate for Anousheh, who comes from a part of Iran where interruptions may be associated with friendliness and active involvement in classroom activities. Unfortunately, once character judgments are formed, people generally stick to them, even to the point of ignoring considerable discrepancies between their own expectations and others' behaviors.

In a now classic study, Philips (1970, 1972, 1974, 1983) investigated the repeated failure of Warm Spring Indian children to perform on a par with their white peers. Philips identified several important differences between the conversational styles employed in the children's homes and schools. At home, there were no authority figures. Yet at school, their teachers expected the Warm Spring Indian children to participate in teacher-controlled activity. At home, questions did not demand immediate answers. Yet at school, teachers encouraged students to answer all questions immediately. Because the Warm Spring Indian children did not fulfill their teachers' expectations, the children were viewed as uncooperative and disrespectful.

Following Philips, Mohatt and Erickson (1981) compared two classes of Native American children on an Odawa reservation in Ontario, Canada. One class was taught by a Native American and the other by a white instructor. Mohatt and Erickson found that the white instructor tended to monitor the children's interaction on a more continual basis, providing the children with constant correction and even employing the *spotlighting* approach, singling out specific children and calling on them to answer questions from across the room. Although both teachers were considered competent and effective by the researchers, the Native American's interactional style was more familiar to the students and, perhaps as a consequence, the students felt more comfortable with this teacher.

Weeks (1983) investigated the mismatch between the classroom interactional styles of Native American children and their white middle-American peers. When compared to middle-American children, Yakima children were found to have guessed at fewer answers, paused longer before answering questions, and never interrupted. According to Weeks, the *deficiencies* in language which some white teachers attributed to their Yakima students were merely *differences* in interactional styles.

Sato (1981) examined communication difficulties of a different sort, those which occur in the language classroom. Her study focused on cultural patterns of participation observable in aspects of the students' turn-taking and interruption behavior. The participants of her study were two groups of students and their instructors in English as a Second Language classes. Nineteen of the students were Asian and twelve were non-Asian. Sato found that the Asian students took significantly fewer speaking turns than their non-Asian classmates. Their patterns of participation seemed to prevent them from taking an active part in the classroom.

In a nine-year ethnographic study, Heath (1982, 1983) focused on child language and teacher training in two communities in North Carolina, Roadville (a white working-class community) and Trackton (a black working-class community). Heath states, "The different ways children learned to use language were dependent on the ways each community structured their families, defined the roles which community members could assume, and played out their concepts of childhood that guided child socialization" (1983, p. 3). During the time of Heath's study, desegregation in the South became a legislative mandate and, for the first time, blacks and whites found themselves working and studying side by side. Heath's ethnography explains why students and teachers had difficulty understanding one another, why questions which customarily received answers were not answered, and why habitual ways of communicating did not always work. Although Heath does not link communication difficulties to discrete language or cultural differences, her research suggests that patterns of communication which are successful in some English-speaking communities fail in those in which alternative patterns are employed.

Numerous other studies cite mismatches between school and home cultures which are hypothesized to interfere with the education of language minority students. (See Chapter 5.) However, despite the excellent body of research on the topic, home/school discontinuities alone cannot explain the differential academic success of language minority students. The fact remains that many groups of language minority students have attained considerable academic success in the United States despite large differences in the expectations of their teachers and families. Some groups of language minority students seem more capable of overcoming the negative outcomes of home/school discontinuities than others.

Implications

Teachers need to understand their own behaviors and their students' behaviors and to avoid stereotyping. As suggested by Banks (1988) and others, this may require "antiracist workshops and courses for teachers as well as an examination of the total environment, to determine ways in which racism can be reduced, including curriculum materials, teacher attitudes and school norms" (p. 96). Teachers also need to create environments where students feel safe enough to try out new behaviors. To smooth the transition between the students' home culture and the school culture, educators need to incorporate teaching behaviors which are congruent with their students' behaviors, and to teach their students new conduct when the students are ready to learn it. Specific suggestions for reducing the negative consequences of home/school discontinuities are discussed in Chapter 5.

Learning Style Discontinuities

Related to the home/school discontinuities explanation is the *learning style discontinuities* explanation. In brief, according to this explanation, traditional mainstream classrooms, which rely heavily on competition and place little value on cooperative work, "provide a bias in favor of the achievement and values of majority [mainstream] students who are generally more competitive in their social orientation than are minority students" (Kagan 1989, 2:9). Whereas many mainstream teachers favor competition as a means of motivating students, as discussed in Chapter 6, many Latino and Asian-American groups more easily attain academic success in cooperative learning environments.

Implications

Dramatic improvements in the academic achievement of language minority students result when their teachers understand their learning styles and incorporate these learning styles into everyday classroom teaching. For example, Kagan (1989) reports that the incorporation of cooperative learning techniques has resulted in significant improvements in the test scores of Latino and Asian students. He states:

> Although high achieving students spend considerable time in cooperative learning working with weaker students, they achieve as well or better than if they were working on their own all of the time. Apparently, as they teach they learn. Alternatively, it may be that if learning allows them to teach, if it empowers them, they may be more motivated to learn. (2:9)

Language Attitudes and Linguistic Prejudice

A similar explanation for the academic failure of language minority students concerns language attitudes. When students have lived in the United States for a long period, they usually acquire a variety (or dialect) of English. Often, this variety is not the so-called *standard* English which has been codified in dictionaries and grammars and used by teachers at school.

Students may also code-switch (that is, switch between two languages). Ovando and Collier (1985) give these as typical examples of code-switching, used by a Mexican-American child to a peer: "*Andale, pues. [hurry up, then]* I don't know" and "Gimme the ball, *que le voy a decir a la maestra.* [I'm going to tell the teacher about this]" (p. 131). Most linguists view code-switching as a complex skill which increases the students' ability to communicate effectively with bilingual speakers (Valdes-Fallis 1981).

People are often judged on the basis of their language or language variety and code-switching. Ethnocentrism, "the view that one's own way of life is superior to all others" (Fishman 1989, p. 18) can develop into racism. Language attitudes (or the evaluative reactions toward language) can reflect this racism. For example, Hermann Gauch, a Nazi scientist, claimed:

> The Nordic race alone can emit sounds of untroubled clearness, whereas among non-Nordics the pronunciation is . . . like noises made by animals, such as barking, sniffing, snoring, squeaking

. . . That birds can learn to talk better than other animals is explained by the fact that their mouths are Nordic in structure. (quoted in Mosse 1966, p. 225)

Unfortunately, the language attitudes which teachers hold toward their students' language varieties and code-switching may interfere with their students' academic success. (For useful discussions of language attitude, see, for instance, Fasold 1984; Milroy and Milroy 1985; and Ryan and Giles 1982.) When language minority students use nonstandard varieties of a language or code-switching, conclusions are often made about their academic abilities and aptitudes. This process is sometimes called *linguistic prejudice,* the habit of arriving at conclusions about a person's social status on the basis of his or her speech. People tend to evaluate others' intelligence, personality and educational background on the basis of speech characteristics alone. Teachers' attitudes toward nonstandard language varieties may affect the extent to which those teachers encourage minority students to interact in their classes, and may eventually lead to the students' low academic achievement. For example, in a study by Ramirez, Arce-Torres and Politzer (1978), teachers admitted that they rated nonstandard speech varieties and speech varieties charcterized by code-switching lower than standard English as contributing to likelihood of achievement in school.[3]

The attitudes held by teachers may reinforce the negative attitudes already held by students toward their own nonstandard dialects of English or standard and nonstandard dialects of their native languages. Unfortunately, students often find that their teachers disapprove of nonstandard dialects. Many dialects, such as certain varieties of Spanish and Chicano English spoken in the Southwest, are often stigmatized. If language minority students become ashamed of their native languages or the English dialects they speak, they may decide they do not like to speak these languages: eventually they may refuse to speak in their native tongues. Consider the example below.

Linda (Mexican-American): I know how to speak Spanish—my grandmother taught me but I don't like to.

The stigmatized minority language may alternatively come to serve as a marker of personal, group, and cultural solidarity (see Fishman 1989 and Giles 1979). In this case, students may decide not to identify with speakers of standard English and may even cease any attempts to use the standard variety. Instead, they may prefer to use their primary language and/or a nonstandard dialect of English.

As Finnegan and Besnier (1989) point out, teachers cannot simply ask their students to switch to standard English, as patterns of language use are intimately tied to students' personal identities.

Asking people to change their customary language patterns is not like asking them to try on different sweaters; it is asking them to take on a new identity and espouse the values associated with speakers of a different dialect. The principal reason that nonstandard dialects are so hearty, so resistant to the urgings of education, is simply that language varieties are deeply entwined with the identities of their speakers. (Finnegan and Besnier 1989, p. 511)

It is important to keep in mind that no dialect is more grammatical than another; all dialects of English have complete grammatical systems. To think that a nonstandard dialect of English is inferior to standard American English is erroneous. All dialects have rules for what can and cannot be said, and a construction may be ungrammatical in a nonstandard dialect of English just as readily as it can be in Standard American English.

Implications

Schools can minimize negative attitudes toward the native languages of minority students. All students, including middle-American, can develop linguistic tolerance and understand the prejudice underlying the formation of rigid ethnolinguistic stereotypes based on language. (Specific strategies for reducing prejudice are discussed in Chapter 5.) Students can become *bidialectal.* That is, they can learn to use two dialects, their native one and the standard one which is spoken in the school. The teachers' job is not to denigrate their students' dialects but to help their students acquire *school English*, the dialect of English found in their textbooks. Teachers can show students when it is appropriate to use school English and when it is more appropriate to use their native dialects.

There are positive ways to deal with nonstandard dialects in the multicultural classroom. Cummins (1989), for example, suggests that when a nonstandard word comes up in class, the teacher:

> . . . go around the class to see what other words (in different dialects) children have for the object or idea. In this way, students soon realize the need for a standard form of the language in order to facilitate communication between different groups whose native dialects are different. Children also realize that the nonstandard varieties are appropriate and valid within the contexts in which they are typically used and that there is no need to replace the nonstandard form with the standard. The teacher's orientation should be to add the standard form to the child's linguistic repertoire while encouraging continued use of the nonstandard forms in contexts in which they are appropriate. (pp. 24–25)

Cummins further argues that "provision by the teacher of explicit information about conventions of standard language (e.g., spelling, grammar) is appropriate and can be useful in the context of tasks to which students are committed. When students want the final product to conform to these conventions, they will be motivated to acquire these conventions" (p. 25). Persistent error correction by the instructor and explicit teaching solely of the standard dialect outside any communicative context are likely to raise the students' anxieties and lower the students' self-esteem.

Above all, teachers must respect the rights of language minority students to maintain their own languages. In 1974, the National Council of Teachers of English in the United States adopted a resolution which guarantees this right. It states:

> We affirm the students' right to their own patterns and varieties of language—the dialects of their nurture or whatever dialects in which they find their own identity and style. . .We affirm strongly that teachers must have the experience and training that will enable them to respect diversity and uphold the right of students to their own language. (p. 252)

The rights of language minority students to speak their own words have not always been upheld. Cazden and Dickenson (1981) give a poignant example of this. They describe an exhibit of Native American children's art which was shown throughout the United States in 1974. Among the striking drawings and paintings, a few pieces of writing were also displayed. One of the writings, by an Apache child in Arizona, is particularly memorable:

> Have you ever hurt
>   about baskets?
> I have, seeing my grandmother weaving
>   for a long time.
> Have you ever hurt about work?
> I have, because my father works too hard
>   and he tells how he works.
> Have you ever hurt about school?
> I have, because I learned a lot of words
>   from school,
> And they are not my words. (pp. 457–8)

As Cazden and Dickenson point out, students of all ages do learn *words* in school. But all too often, this happens in situations where their own *words* are corrected and denigrated.

Socio-Economic Status

Another explanation frequently used to explain the academic failure of language minority students concerns their socioeconomic status (SES). Clearly, teachers who do not share the SES of their students are less likely to understand these students. Even worse, they may have lower expectations for students of a lower SES than their own. Trueba (1989) states:

> Undoubtedly, poverty and lower social status have clear implications for participation in educational institutions and for making use of other public services. . . Perhaps income determines not only the knowledge and experiences of children but also the way in which these children are treated in public institutions. (p. 15)

If teachers equate low socioeconomic levels with low intelligence, they might have lower expectations of those students whom they believe to be poor. The students might then live up to their teachers' expectations and fail in our schools.

Although SES alone may not be able to explain the differential success of members of diverse cultural groups in the United States, the resources that language minority students possess certainly affect their education. For example, many students may not have writing material or books to prepare for class. Others may live in such cramped living quarters that they are unable to find a quiet place to study. Yet others may live in a part of a city where gangs prevent them from getting to class safely. Still others may come to class hungry. Some may never arrive because their work interferes with their schooling. As illustrated by the example below, the stress experienced by those living in poverty and its effect on education cannot be underestimated.

> Once I was here the hardest problem was the financial instability. We didn't have anyone after my mother went back to El Salvador. Only my brother and me and we couldn't support ourselves. My brother went to work and night school. His salary is not enough for both of us. It's hard to handle and that makes me think about dropping out of school, too. It is hard to go on like this. It is not a good idea to go back to our country, but if I don't have an education it will always be hard here. I worry so much about money I think I have to leave school. Cesar Menjivar, 11th grade Salvadoran student, Public Testimony, San Francisco. (Reported in Olsen 1988, pp. 89–90)

As discussed above, many immigrant families are poor. Olsen (1988) points out,

> . . . even those who were skilled and well employed in their native land often face employment barriers here in the United States. Pressure to help with family survival falls on all members. Children are sometimes needed to work, often because they learn English quicker and are better able to find jobs than the adults in their family. Further increasing the financial burden, many families try to send money back to relatives in the homeland to help out or provide the means for them to immigrate. (p. 31)

SES undoubtedly affects our language minority students' success in school. Yet, many students of a low SES do succeed in our nation's schools.

Implications

Teachers can help their students overcome socio-economic barriers to education by becoming advocates for their students. They can provide community services to them. They can also help older students improve their socioeconomic status by finding them jobs which contribute to their intellectual development. For instance, in one successful high school program, students are given tutoring positions which pay good wages, increase the students' self-esteem and increase their knowledge. As one high-achieving high school student explains, "If it weren't for this tutoring job, I'd be flipping hamburgers at McDonald's."

Inadequate Pedagogy

The pedagogy itself has been blamed for the academic failure of language minority students. It is frequently criticized for being inappropriate for language development. As seen in the following example, the language used by teachers is sometimes too difficult for our students to understand and sometimes too easy. In this example, a college-bound senior describes the type of language input she received in her classes.

> When I first came here to grade school the teachers thought I would have a lot of problems and they ended up putting me in a reading class a couple of grades below what I could read. I think it was a Dick and Jane book. In high school, now, some of the teachers talk real slow, like I don't understand or something, but then others . . . Well, it seems like it's always either below my knees or above my head! . . . (reported in Ovando and Collier 1985, p. 11)

Researchers, such as Cummins (1989) and Ada (1986, 1988), also suggest that much instruction confines students to a form of *learned helplessness,* in which the teacher exclusively controls the lesson and imparts knowledge to the students. This model is referred to by Freire (1973, 1985) as the *banking* model and by Barnes (1976) and Wells (1986) as the *transmission* model. As Cummins (1989) points out, transmission models eliminate the students' experiences and therefore fail to acknowledge the students' cultural identities. He states, "The message to the student is the same: to survive in this society your identity must be eradicated and your community must not threaten the power and privilege of the dominant group" (p. 56). To illustrate this point, he provides a graphic description of the transmission model in his depiction of assembly workers actively filling young minds with facts that must later be regurgitated whole. (See cartoon.)

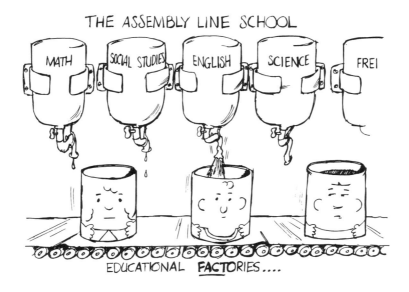

THE ASSEMBLY LINE SCHOOL

EDUCATIONAL **FACTORIES**....

From Cummins 1989, p. 71

Implications

Clearly, pedagogical changes are called for. Teachers need to understand second language development, provide their students with comprehensible lessons, encourage meaningful interaction, and incorporate the students' languages and cultures into the curriculum. They need to collaborate with their students in such a way that their students' interests and experiences are validated.

Unfair Assessment Procedures

Culturally-biased assessment procedures are often used to prevent language minority students from taking the academic courses needed to succeed in our schools. Historically, they were used to incorrectly place large numbers of Latino children into special education classes. More recently, they are being used to incorrectly identify language minority students as learning disabled or language impaired (Cummins 1989). Such assessment procedures unquestionably thwart the academic progress of language minority students. Cummins (1984, 1989) convincingly argues that diagnostic conclusions based on the majority of assessments are logically impossible. He states:

To challenge the disabling of minority students, the assessment must focus on the extent to which children's language and culture are incorporated within the school program, the extent to which educators collaborate with parents in a shared enterprise, and the extent to which children are encouraged to use language (both L1 and L2) actively within the classroom to amplify their experiences in interaction with other children and adults. (1989, p. 66)

Implications

Teachers must assess fairly and place students in classes which will enhance their opportunities to succeed in our schools. In short, as Cummins (1986) suggests, they must become advocates of their students. (See Chapter 7.)

Language Minority Parents

Research has repeatedly demonstrated the necessity of involving parents in their children's schooling (see, for instance, Becker and Epstein 1982, Boger, Richter and Paolucci 1986). Cummins (1986, 1989) maintains that the success of an educational program designed for minority students can be determined by the extent to which minority parents participate in their children's schooling.

Language minority parents are often blamed for failing to involve themselves in their children's education. Although most minority parents do have high academic expectations for their children, the fact remains that many feel intimidated by our schools. Others are reluctant to participate in our schools because they are not encouraged to do so. Still others are unfamiliar with the functions that schools serve and their own expected participation in their children's schooling.

Implications

To validate the cultural and linguistic identities of language minority students, teachers must join forces with their students' families. This can be accomplished effectively through home literacy programs (such as that described by Ada 1988), community services (such as those described by Ashworth 1985), and school-sponsored activities (such as those suggested by Baker 1983, and Enright and McCloskey 1988). Above all, confirming the identities of our students can be achieved by understanding that academic failure is not, as Jensen (1973) and others have suggested, related to cultural deficits concerning the home socialization process. Chapter 9 considers specific ways to involve language minority parents in the schooling of their children.

Stress

Language minority students frequently suffer from stress which can interfere with their academic success. As illustrated in the following example, language minority students often experience continuous pressures from the push-and-pull of living between two cultures.

> At home my parents speak Chinese. At school, my friends speak English. I don't think the Chinese students like me because I hang around with Americans. They tease me and I can't stop them. (Chinese-American student, born in the United States)

Added to the stress of being caught between two cultures is the pressure which grows out of the animosity between late arrivals (language minority students who have lived in the United States for more than ten years or even decades) and recent arrivals (language minority students who have only recently arrived in the United States). The example below illustrates this difficulty.

> There is so much discrimination and hate. Even from kids from Mexico who have been here longer. They don't treat us like brothers. They hate even more. It makes them feel more like natives. They want to be American. They don't want to speak Spanish to us, they already know English and how to act. If they're with us, other people will treat them more like wetbacks, so they try to avoid us. 9th grade Mexican boy, immigrated six months previous. (Reported in Olsen 1988, p. 36)

On top of all this, language minority students often find they have taken on new ways of acting which the older members of their families do not understand. They may become more direct and straightforward with their opinions than is generally acceptable in their home cultures, and may even argue with their parents. Consider the examples below.

> My family has such set values and they hold to them strongly. They hold on to the old ways. It is very difficult to explain something to them about my life now. We end up always arguing— about school, religion, how I dress, what I can and can't do. They even get mad at me for arguing. They say I shouldn't talk back. I have my family. We fight all the time. 11th grade Cambodian girl, immigrated at age 10. (Reported in Olsen 1988, p. 31)

> There is an increasing sense of separation between the parents and children, where the parents are still having some trouble adjusting to the culture, to the language, the students themselves are moving forward which sometimes includes losing their sense of their roots. There's a clash in terms of the language, the values, the backgrounds. As a result, children ask, *Why don't my parents understand what I am feeling, what my values are?*, and the parents ask *Where have my children gone wrong, why don't they understand my values, my language any longer?* Carlos Cordova, La Raza Studies, San Francisco State University. (Reported in Olsen 1988)

There are other more serious sources of stress. Olsen (1988) notes that many immigrant children have suffered war trauma and are here virtually without support. Others who are undocumented are also "at high risk for emotional stresses and problems" (p. 75). One student describes this pressure.

> I don't have immigration papers and I feel afraid of being caught. I work at night, so it's hard to study. But the main thing is being afraid. All I want is for my family to stay together and not have problems with the Migra [INS]. My uncle says we may not be able to work anymore and may have to go somewhere else. My teacher asks for my mother to sign a paper, but I am afraid to have her name in the school file. I am afraid they will deport her. 11th grade Mexican boy, immigrated at age 14. (Reported in Olsen 1988, p. 75)

In outlining some of the serious consequences of excessive and persistent stress on school children, Trueba (1989) states:

> First, it [stress] makes academic activities traumatic and the transition from one activity to another difficult to understand. Next, stress makes efforts at communication ineffective. It also makes the establishment of lasting learning relationships most difficult. Finally, stress results in the acquisition of English being painfully extended. The child never quite understands either the classroom content (which is already foreign in many aspects) or the expected behavior. This confusion causes stress that peaks when the child is forced to perform while still unfamiliar with the cultural context. (p. 24)

Trueba further suggests three ways in which language minority children cope with stress at school.

1. By withdrawing from painful encounters and isolating themselves from the world around them;
2. By compensating with excessive and anxious efforts to participate, often mimicking behaviors that are not yet fully understood (pretending to read or write, for example); and
3. By choosing to participate under protest and demonstrating their anger outwardly. (1989, p. 23)

All three ways negatively affect the children's academic progress.

Implications

It is important for teachers to appreciate the difficulties language minority students face adjusting to mainstream American schools and to create learning environments to reduce student anxiety. Community mental health professionals can become involved in training teachers to recognize the signs of war trauma, suggesting approaches to take in helping students who have been traumatized and emotionally disfigured due to war, and referring students to mental health professionals (Olsen 1988). Counseling programs can be arranged to assist students who are experiencing severe stress. (A number of excellent suggestions for these programs are offered by Brislin, Cushner, Cherrie, and Yong 1986 and Pedersen 1988.) Peer support groups and buddy systems which bring students from the same cultural background together can be formed to provide students with opportunities to share their experiences and learn that they are not alone; there are others who have also undergone similar problems. Peer support groups and buddy systems in which native and non-native English speakers are carefully matched can provide students with a climate of acceptance which tells students, "*Minority students belong here*" (Trueba 1989, p. 22). In line with the idea of counseling and peer support groups, Trueba (1989) suggests that students who are experiencing stress should be helped "to reinterpret past [negative] experiences, overcome the impact of degradation events, and engage in learning activities through personal relationships with teachers and peers" (p. 22). Teachers, too, can relieve their students' anxieties by allowing these students to observe for a period until they have the confidence to participate confidently and by providing multiple opportunities for them to succeed. In addition, they can also collaborate with parents to reduce their students' stress.

To reduce the stress of undocumented students, it is necessary to assure these students that the school plays no role in deporting those who are in the United States illegally. All those involved in educating language minority students need to be informed that "it is unacceptable to ask for documentation or to harass students and deny participation [in school programs] on the basis of being undocumented" (Olsen 1988, p. 75).

Finally, I might mention that specific programs designed to increase our students' self-esteem often simultaneously lower their anxiety. However, actual academic success may lower our students' school-related anxieties to a far greater extent than these programs. When students are given *early* and *frequent* opportunities to succeed in our schools, school-related stress often disappears.

Minority Students' Perception of Their Own Status in the United States

A different explanation of school failure concerns the language minority students' perception of their own status in the United States. Ogbu and Matute-Bianchi (1986) use this explanation when discussing the comparative academic success of Sikhs, Japanese, and Chinese relative to blacks and Latinos. They suggest that students from some cultural groups, observing the discrimination around them, simply stop trying to succeed in middle-American schools. These individuals believe that the cards are stacked against them and hold little hope of ever participating in the social, economic and political institutions of this nation. They suffer from feelings of helplessness, powerlessness and inferiority. (See also Ogbu 1978, 1987.)

Implications

Freire (1985) offers some solutions to this problem. He contends that students should bear the burden of defining the sources of their powerlessness and making effective life changes. Like Freire, Banks (1988) suggests that cultural minorities "will be able to liberate themselves from psychological and physical oppression only when they know how and why the myths about them emerged and were institutionalized and validated by the scholarly community and the mass media" (p. 186). He further suggests that teachers help marginalized cultural groups improve their ability to make reflective decisions and take social action. According to Banks, students need experience "obtaining and exercising power" (p. 186).

Along similar lines, Giroux (1988) suggests that teachers empower students "with the skills and knowledge needed to address injustices and to be critical actors committed to developing a world free of oppression and exploitation" (p. xxxiv).

Power Relations: Institutional Racism

In line with this explanation, a theme of much current research is that the causes of language minority students' academic failure are rooted in institutional racism, mirrored in the power relations between middle-American and minority groups. As Cummins (1988) puts it, "As societal institutions, schools tend to reflect the values and priorities of the dominant group and to reproduce the status and power differences between class and ethnic groups that are so evident in the broader society" (p. 130). Chomsky (1979, 1981) convincingly argues that the dominant classes often attempt to control the thoughts and actions of those living in the United States. Arguably, the way that they do this is by controlling the schools.

Consistent with this line of reasoning, Heath (1983) explains that no amount of books or public services would have improved the Trackton children's success in school. This is partially because "successful completion of composition and advanced grammar classes in high school would not have secured better-paying jobs for its residents" (Romaine 1984, p. 252). This explanation suggests that language minority students fail in our schools because these institutions typically reflect the power relations between middle-American and minority groups in our society. Consequently, language minority students do not develop confidence in their cultural identities and academic abilities.

Implications

The work of Freire (1973, 1985), Cummins (1989), Ada (1986, 1988) and Wallerstein (1983) suggests some pedagogical solutions to the problem of institutional racism. These include: helping students become conscious of their problems, encouraging them to think about these problems critically, and encouraging minority community and parent involvement in student education.

Undoubtedly, there are many reasons language minority students fail to attain success in our schools. Those discussed are summarized in Table 1–1 below.

Table One implies that, in many cases, teachers and administrators can take specific actions to help their students overcome obstacles to their academic progress. The Jaime Escalantes of this nation are creating innovative programs that increase the students' desire to learn, develop the students' self-confidence and enhance the students' academic performance. Successful programs for language minority students are based on the firm belief that *every* student can learn and that it is the school's responsibility to make sure that everyone succeeds. In these programs, pedagogy is employed which is consistent with theories of language development, parent involvement is encouraged, and the students' home cultures and primary languages are incorporated into the curriculum (Cummins 1989). In cases of institutional racism, however, teachers have more difficulty controlling the factors affecting their language minority students' schooling and must therefore work more diligently to overcome negative factors.

Conclusion

The explanations of student academic failure logically lead to principles for reversing this failure. In the introduction, I discussed these principles. They are listed below.

1. Know your students.
2. Understand language development.
3. Make lessons comprehensible.
4. Encourage interaction.
5. Appeal to varying learning styles.
6. Provide effective feedback.
7. Test fairly.
8. Encourage minority parent participation.
9. Appreciate cultural diversity.
10. Incorporate students' languages and cultures.
11. Reduce prejudice.

Clearly, the implementation of these principles will vary according to the situational context.

Table 1–1
Explanations for the Academic Failure
of Language Minority Students

Explanations	Principles	Intervention
Teacher Prejudice	Know your students.	Be aware of prejudice and combat it.
Home/School Discontinuities	Appreciate cultural diversity.	Understand home/school continuities and avoid stereotyping.
Learning Style Discontinuities	Appeal to varying learning styles.	Incorporate the learning styles of your students into daily classroom instruction.
Language Attitudes	Understand language development. Incorporate students' languages and cultures.	Be sensitive to linguistic prejudice; avoid stereotyping on the basis of speech; appreciate the varieties of language spoken by your students.
Socio-economic Status	Know your students.	Understand how socio-economic status affects your students; when possible, provide community services to your students; help working students improve their own socio-economic status by providing them with jobs which contribute to their intellectual development.
Ineffective Pedagogy	Provide comprehensible lessons. Encourage interaction. Incorporate the languages and cultures of your students.	Use pedagogy designed to maximize the success of language minority students.

(continued)

Table 1–1
Continued

Explanations	Principles	Intervention
Unfair Tests	Test fairly.	Become advocates for language minority students.
Minority Parents	Involve minority parents.	Collaborate with language minority parents.
Stress	Know your students. Reduce racism. Test fairly. Incorporate the languages of your students into the curriculum. Involve minority parents.	Implement specific programs and procedures designed to lower the learners' anxieties.
Students' Perception Of Their Own Status In the United States	Understand cultural diversity. Incorporate the languages and cultures of your students into the curriculum. Reduce racism.	Use empowerment strategies (discussed by Cummins 1989) which enable students to bear the burden of defining the sources of their power-lessness and make effective life changes.
Institutional Racism	Test fairly. Involve minority parents.	Help students achieve educational equity.

ACTIVITIES AND DISCUSSION QUESTIONS

1. Observe a language minority student's participation in a variety of classroom activities. Describe the student's interaction patterns with the teacher. Does the student have the English proficiency necessary to communicate well? If not, does the student try to *pass* as a more competent speaker of English? How do you explain the student's classroom interaction patterns?

2. Describe three specific instances in which communication break-downs could occur in middle-American/language minority student classroom interaction. Have you ever experienced such communication breakdowns? What can teachers do to alleviate them?

3. It is sometimes said that teachers are in a unique position to eradicate the pernicious beliefs the children of the poor may have about their own powerlessness and inferiority. For example, some argue that teachers can educate children about the importance of completing a formal education and are in a position to teach these children the ways and means of taking advantage of what institutions and opportunities do exist to help the poor with educational, medical, and family expenses.

   To what extent do you believe that teachers can change the beliefs of the children of the poor concerning their feelings of powerlessness in the United States?

4. What are some concrete steps teachers can take to help language minority students of low socioeconomic levels succeed in schools in the United States?

5. Observe a mainstream American teacher instruct students of diverse cultural backgrounds. How does the teacher appeal to his or her students' different learning styles?

RECOMMENDED READING

ASHWORTH, M. 1985. *Beyond Methodology: Second Language Teaching and the Community.* Cambridge: Cambridge University Press. Chapter Four contains a particularly useful description of the national policies affecting second language instruction.

CUMMINS, J. 1989. *Empowering Minority Students.* Sacramento: California Association of Bilingual Education. Reviews what is known about language proficiency, language learning, bilingualism, and academic learning among minority students; proposes a model for understanding why some groups of students fail and a framework of interventions required to reverse the pattern of minority student academic failure.

MCKAY, S., and WONG, S. L. (eds.) 1988. *Language Diversity: Problem or Resource?* Cambridge: Harper and Row Publishers. Provides a social and educational perspective on recent immigrant language minorities. Particular focus is on Asian and Latino groups.

OVANDO, C., and COLLIER, V. 1986. *Bilingual and ESL Classrooms.* New York: McGraw-Hill. Provides a description of the special needs of bilingual and ESL students, the role of language and culture in the classroom, federal and state legislation affecting language minority student education, methods of teaching in ESL and bilingual education programs. It outlines useful strategies for building effective school-community relations.

SKUTTNABB-KANGAS, T., and CUMMINS, J. (eds) 1988. *Minority Education.* Clevedon: Multilingual Matters. Analyzes issues regarding the education of language minority students in industrialized nations. A central theme of the book is that the causes of the language minority students' difficulties are rooted in the power relations between the dominant and subordinate groups in society rather than in the students; presents case studies which illustrate how minority students can empower themselves.

TRUEBA, H. T. 1989. *Raising Silent Voices: Educating the Linguistic Minori-*

ties for the 21st Century. Cambridge: Harper and Row. Examines the language, culture and schooling of language minority children, the legislation affecting these children, and the role of school administrators in implementing programs for linguistic minorities. The book is especially useful to administrators who are involved in multicultural teacher-training programs.

NOTES

1. By prejudice, I mean here the tendency to respond in a negative way toward members of different cultural groups.

2. To increase the teachers' appreciation of their students, some pedagogues suggest that teachers become ethnographers (see for instance, Cazden 1982 and Enright and McCloskey 1988). Heath (1982) defines the goal and essential features of ethnography as follows:

> The goal of ethnography is to describe the ways of living of a social group, a group in which there is in-group recognition of the individuals living and working together as a social group. By becoming a participant in the social group, an ethnographer attempts to record and describe the overt, manifest, and explicit behaviors and values and tangible items of the society and structures and functions of cultural components, before attempting to recognize patterns of behavior that may be covert, ideal and implicit to members of the culture. Ethnographers attempt to learn the conceptual framework of members of the society and to organize materals on the basis of boundaries understood by those being observed instead of using a predetermined system of categories established before the participant-observation. (p. 34)

The tools of ethnography include interviewing, collecting life histories, studying written documents pertaining to the history of the group and collecting samples of language of all types, including narratives, songs and myths. Other researchers, such as Banks (1988), advise teachers to experience the various stages of ethnicity their students do, through role playing in hypothetical situations. Still others advise teachers to examine the critical incidents their students encounter. (See Brislin, Cushner, Cherrie and Yong 1986.) In an interesting approach presented by Trueba (1989; see also Spindler 1982), teachers are helped to understand their own interaction patterns and their students' through reflective analysis of videotaped classroom interaction.

3. It is not only teachers, however, but students too who have linguistic prejudices. In studies of language attitudes of children, Day (1982) found that children over age ten develop negative stereotypes based on language. Ovando and Collier (1986) give this example of linguistic prejudice, which comes from a middle-American child:

> Laurie: I know. There's a girl in my class who all she does is speak Spanish and she's so dumb! All she does is copy my work.

CHAPTER TWO

Getting to Know
Language Minority Students

Most educators agree that it is essential to know who it is we teach. Knowing our language minority students minimally involves understanding their personal characteristics—including their language backgrounds, socioeconomic levels, acculturation patterns, and resident status in the United States. It also entails understanding the political and historical context of their schooling.

First Language Backgrounds

Table 2–1, provides estimated numbers of people aged five and older who in 1980 reported speaking languages other than English at home. (The languages are listed in order of speaker population.)

Socioeconomic Status

Language minority students represent all socioeconomic levels. Some are better off than their mainstream American peers. Yet, many others "come from sociocultural groups which have and continue to be the recipients of varying degrees of socioeconomic marginality and racial or ethnic discrimination" (Ovando and Collier 1985, p. 6). Many language minority students have had to adjust to a different socioeconomic level than they had in their home countries.

LEP [limited English proficient] students often bring with them to the schools a change in their socioeconomic status. Sometimes such students come from relatively well-educated middle-class families who have to undergo some alterations economically and socially until they get themselves on their feet in the United States. Many language minority students, depending on the economic conditions, undergo social adjustments because of the change in the way in which they fit into society. This can be the case whether the family has moved from a higher socioeconomic

Table 2-1
Estimated Numbers of People, Ages Five and Older, Who
Speak Languages Other Than English at Home, by Age Group
and Language: 1980 (Numbers in Thousands)

Language	Total	Age Group 5-17	18-24	25-44	45-66	+65
Total	**23,060**	**4,568**	**3,146**	**7,095**	**4,978**	**3,273**
Spanish	11,116	2,952	1,913	3,756	1,847	648
Italian	1,618	147	112	302	543	515
German	1,587	192	166	401	404	424
French	1,551	223	204	467	398	259
Polish	821	41	35	120	344	281
Chinese	631	114	83	251	129	53
Filipino	474	63	50	225	88	48
Greek	401	66	46	118	118	55
Portuguese	352	68	42	109	87	46
Japanese	336	34	29	110	119	45
American Indian or Alaska native	333	93	54	104	56	27
Yiddish	316	19	13	33	77	174
Korean	266	60	33	132	33	8
Asian Indian	243	44	25	147	23	5
Arabic	218	37	44	84	36	17
Vietnamese	195	64	35	73	18	4
Hungarian	179	11	10	33	64	62
Russian	173	19	14	46	43	51
Serbo-Croatian	150	19	10	37	47	38
Dutch	148	16	15	40	45	33
Czech	122	5	4	18	43	53
Ukranian	121	9	9	24	47	32
Norwegian	112	6	6	15	28	57
Persian	107	18	31	44	19	3
Armenian	101	14	11	26	29	21
Swedish	100	7	6	15	20	52
Slovak	88	2	2	7	34	42
Thai	85	22	13	45	4	1
Lithuanian	73	3	3	10	26	30
Finnish	69	3	32	10	25	29
Other languages	973	197	126	294	193	162

Note: Detail may not add to total because of rounding.
Source: 1980 Census of Population (Bureau of the Census 1984)

status in the country of origin to a lower status in the United States or is experiencing upward mobility. (Ovando and Collier 1985, p. 7)

Rural versus Urban Areas

Teachers also need to know whether their language minority students come from urban or rural areas. Through their exposure to television and news media, for example, residents of urban areas may be more familiar with mainstream American values than their rural counterparts from the same country. While language minority students may share certain characteristics of language and culture with other students who come from the same country, they may differ in their values as well as in their understanding of how the institutions of the United States function, depending on whether they come from urban or rural areas.

Previous Schooling

Teachers must understand their students' previous schooling. The nature of the language minority students' educational background depends upon a number of factors, including socioeconomic level, country of origin, rural vs. urban area, and sociopolitical characteristics of their nation. (See Chapter 10.)

Patterns of Acculturation

To better understand our language minority students, teachers must also understand their home cultures and how the students have adapted to the United States. Culture has been described in many ways. Indeed, over thirty years ago, Kroeber and Klockholn (1954) identified 160 definitions. Hall (1959) suggested that culture is the sum total of the ways of life of a people. If we adopt this definition of culture, then it ought to include "learned behavior, patterns, attitudes, and material things" (Nine-Curt 1976, p. 4) as well as "all the aspects of one society; how its people behave, feel and interact" (Donoghe and Kunkle 1979, p. 82). It determines such things as "how adults and children greet one another, what gestures they employ, how they view the concept of time, their perceptions of authority, and the social relations they develop" (Evans 1987, p. 10).[1] It also reflects the existing social, economic, and political context.

Assimilation into a new culture involves the complete absorption of minority groups into the dominant group and quite often the loss of the values and behavioral patterns remaining from their native culture. *Acculturation*, however, involves the adaptation of minority cultures to the dominant culture, which entails developing an understanding of the beliefs, emotions and behaviors of the new culture. Acculturation is an important concept for understanding second language acquisition because it has been hypothesized that successful language learning is more likely when learners acculturate (Ellis 1986) and that most language minority students fail to attain proficiency in English when they do not acculturate (Schumann 1978, 1980, 1986). (This discussion of acculturation only begins to describe a very complex process. For excellent theoretical discussion, refer to Kim 1988.)

Several researchers have described the four stages which have been identified in the normal acculturation process. Acculturation should not be viewed as an either/or phenomenon but as the continuous process by which the language minority student adapts to the United States. Thus, while the stages of acculturation are described here, it is important for the reader to keep in mind that the process is a continuous one, having stages not at all discrete. Recent arrivals to the United States seem particularly affected by the first stages of this process. In the first stage of acculturation, language minority students generally feel a type of euphoria mixed with the excitement of being in the United States. This is sometimes referred to as the *honeymoon* or *streets of gold* stage. Next, language minority students, who have recently arrived in the United States move into the second stage, that of *culture shock.* The term, *culture shock,* refers to the point at which frustration peaks, and language minority students begin to feel fearful. Damen (1987) notes that their fears are often compounded if they are refugees "who cannot go back home" (p. 226). Brown (1980, 1986) refers to this state as *anomie* (see also Srole 1956), a state in which students begin to adapt to the target culture, while often simultaneously losing some of their native culture.

The third stage represents the beginning of the students' recovery from frustration. The pressure is still felt but they are beginning to gain control over problems which previously seemed like major stumbling blocks. Toward the end of this stage, students begin to fully adjust to the new culture. Lambert (1967) hypothesizes that language minority students are readily *teachable* and master the English language quite easily during this period. (See also Brown 1986 and Acton 1979.) The fourth stage brings complete acculturation. "Under normal circumstances, people who become acculturated pass through all the stages at varying rates, though they do not progress smoothly from one stage to the next and may regress to previous stages" (Richard-Amato 1988, p. 6).

The full acculturation process probably occurs most thoroughly among young language minority students who have had an opportunity to attend schools in the United States and who anticipate participating in the mainstream. "It does not work as well for those who are isolated and denied access, the segregated, those who are older, and those who expect to return to the home country" (Kitano and Daniels 1988, p. 33).

Different cultural groups follow different acculturation patterns; some assimilate very quickly, while others maintain their own cultural identity. There is also considerable individual variation among members of cultural groups. A variety of factors affects the extent to which people acculturate. Olsen (1988, p. 18) cites the following:

- nation of origin;
- reasons for coming to the United States;
- age at which immigrated;
- degree of prior schooling;
- extent of economic deprivation and resources brought with the family in their immigration;
- difficulties in the journey;
- extent of life disruption and trauma due to war;
- immigration status (official refugee, legal or undocumented).

Other factors which may affect the language minority students' ability to adjust to the United States include the students' previous exposure to English and other languages, experiences living in other countries, the extent of family separation caused by immigration; the proximity of the United States to the students' homeland; the status of the students' cultural group; the amount of discrimination faced by the students, and the degree to which the students' cultural group desires to maintain *cultural solidarity* and *identity.* In line with these factors, Conklin and Lourie (1983) discuss a host of factors which are hypothesized to affect language maintenance and language shift. Like Olsen's factors, these elements may also be related to student acculturation in the United States. They are listed in Table 2–2.

Schumann (1978) discusses other considerations in acculturation. For instance, he asks whether, in relation to middle-Americans, the language minority students' cultural group is politically, culturally, technically or economically dominant, non-dominant, or subordinate. He also asks whether the integration patterns of the two groups are congruent and what the attitudes of the two groups are towards each other. He argues that the answers to such questions can explain the language minority students' success or failure in learning English.

Teachers will note that the students' ages will affect the rate and success of their acculturation. Children who are born in the United States sometimes have an easier time adjusting to the United States than their older grandparents. When is the optimal time for our students to acculturate to life in the United States? For Brown (1986), it is the young who are best able to fully acculturate. According to Robinson (1985), the optimum age for cultural acquisition depends upon what is being acquired. She states: "While selective perceptual patterns and basic levels of representation may be optimally transmitted during childhood, other aspects of culture such as identification and group affiliation may optimally be acquired during adolescence, as the learner enters a biological transition to adulthood" (p. 47). She suggests that adolescence is a critical period for cultural instruction aimed at developing positive attitudes towards and identification with other people as well as lessening insularity. She hastens to add, however, that while perceptual patterns may be easily acquired in childhood, and group affiliation in adolescence, these may

Table 2–2
Factors Encouraging Language Retention and Language Loss

Language Retention	Language Loss
Political, social and demographic factors	
Large number of speakers living in concentration (ghettos, reservations, ethnic neighborhoods, rural speech islands)	Small number of speakers, dispersed among speakers of other languages
Recent arrival and/or continuing immigration	Long, stable residence in the United States
Geographical proximity to the homeland; ease of travel to the homeland	Homeland remote and inaccessible
High rate of return to the homeland; Homeland language community still intact	Low rate or impossibility of return to the homeland (refugees, Native Americans)
Occupational continuity	Occupational shift, especially from rural to urban
Vocational concentration: employment where co-workers share language background; employment within the language community (stores serving the community, traditional crafts, homemaking, etc.)	Vocations in which some interaction with English or other languages is required; speakers dispersed by employers
Low social and economic mobility in mainstream occupations	High social and economic mobility in mainstream occupations
Low level of education, leading to low social and economic mobility; but educated and articulate community leaders, familiar with the English-speaking society and loyal to their own language community	Advanced level of education, leading to social and economic mobility; education that alienates and Anglifies potential community leaders
Nativism, racism and ethnic discrimination as they serve to isolate a community and encourage identity only with the ethnic group rather than the nation at large	Nativism, racism and ethnic discrimination as they force individuals to deny their ethnic identity in order to make their way in society
Cultural Factors	
Mother tongue institutions, including schools, churches, clubs, theatres, communications, media.	Lack of mother-tongue institutions, from lack of interest or lack of resources
Religious and/or cultural ceremonies requiring command of the mother tongue	Ceremonial life institutionalized in another tongue or not requiring active use of mother tongue

(continued

Table 2-2
Continued

Language Retention	Language Loss
Ethnic identity strongly tied to language; nationalistic aspirations as a language group; mother tongue the homeland national language	Ethnic identity defined by factors other than language, as for those from multilingual countries or language groups spanning several nations; low level of nationalism
Emotional attachment to mother tongue as a defining characteristic of ethnicity, or self	Ethnic identity, sense of self, derived from factors such as religion, custom, race rather than shared speech
Emphasis on family ties and position in kinship or community network	Low emphasis on family or community ties; high emphasis on individual achievement
Emphasis on education, if in mother tongue or in community-controlled schools, or used to enhance awareness of ethnic heritage; low emphasis on education otherwise	Emphasis on education and acceptance of public education in English
Culture unlike Middle-American society	Culture and religion congruent with Middle-American society

Linguistic Factors

Standard, written variety as mother tongue	Minor, nonstandard, and/or unwritten variety as mother tongue
Use of Latin alphabet in mother tongue, making reproduction inexpensive and second language literacy relatively easy	Use of non-Latin writing system in mother tongue, especially if it is unusual, expensive to reproduce, or difficult for bilinguals to learn
Mother tongue of international status	Mother tongue of little international importance
Literacy in mother tongue, used for exchange within the community and with homeland	No literacy in mother tongue; illiteracy
Some tolerance for loan words, if they lead to flexibility of the language in its new setting	No tolerance for loan words, if no alternate ways of capturing new experience evolve; too much tolerance of loans, leading to mixing [the first and second languages] and eventual language loss

Adapted from: Conklin, N. and M. Lourie, 1983. *A Host of Tongues.* New York: The Free Press.

be modified throughout life. It is wise to promote a positive identification with culturally diverse groups at all age levels.

Many language minority students have fully acculturated to the United States, while others have not. This means that teachers should never assume that all students from a particular culture will act in any stereotypical pattern. For instance, a Japanese student who has lived in the United States from birth may have fully acculturated. Like her middle-American peers, this student may interrupt her teacher to ask questions, and she may love McDonald's. Another Japanese student who has lived in the United States all her life may choose to associate only with Japanese and to retain her Japanese identity. Teachers should also realize that many students whose families have lived in the United States for decades (even those born in the United States) still experience English language difficulties. Their English language problems are not indicative of their intellectual potential. Rather, they suggest the students' lack of exposure to and interaction with native English speakers in academic contexts. (Refer to Chapter 3.)

Resident Status

It is also critical that educators know the resident status of their students. International students, immigrants and refugees generally follow different acculturation patterns (Pedersen 1988). International students who come to the United States only for a short time period generally undergo cultural shock as well as the first stages of acculturation. Yet, these students have a different mentality from that of students who plan to make their lives here in the United States. Immigrant and refugee students generally come to the United States in search of better opportunities and plan to stay here to obtain them. Although both immigrants and refugees may have the same ultimate goal, refugee students often will have come for survival purposes and without much preparation. Until such refugees have settled down and gained economic stability, their major goal is simply to survive. In contrast, immigrants will generally have come out of choice, after having made extensive preparations. The children of all three of these groups often come without having been consulted about their move. Frequently, these children never wanted to leave their native lands.

In many cases, language minority students are descendants of the original, indigenous populations of the land, who lost their freedom and land to invaders. At least 206 native American languages are spoken in the United States (Crawford 1989). "A major cause of school failure among Indians, and among other language minorities as well, is the students' inadequate foundation in either [standard] English or the native language" (p. 144). Recognizing this problem, in 1978, Congress extended the definition of *limited English proficient* to include native American children.

Numerous language minority students have entered the United States without documentation.

Mexican immigration is believed to be largely undocumented and uncontrolled; there are no accurate statistics or numbers. Many Central American immigrants are also undocumented, and applications for refugee status or political asylum are seldom granted. Because the largest wave of Central American immigrants has been in the past five years, they are not eligible for Amnesty, under provisions of the 1986 immigration law. Most immigrants from Vietnam, Laos, Cambodia, and Thailand have been granted official refugee status. There is believed to be a substantial number of people from other Asian countries who either entered illegally or came in with a temporary visa and remained after it expired.

(Olsen 1988, p. 27)

Political and Historical Backgrounds

Clearly, it is impossible to understand language minority students without understanding their political and historical backgrounds. For example, the current political situation in Korea, the relations between Korea and the United States, the Korean War, and the domination of Korea by Japan all have some effect on the Korean language minority students we find in our classes today.

Perhaps most important, racism, past and present, suffered by language minority groups affects their educations today. The United States has a history of racism against certain cultural groups. The "eradication of identity was an explicit goal of most residential and missionary schools for native Americans" (Cummins 1989, p. 8). Like native Americans, Latinos have also been "conquered, subjugated, and regarded as inherently inferior for generations by members of the dominant Anglo group" (Cummins 1989, p. 8). Asians too have been discriminated against in this nation. For excellent descriptions of the political and historical backgrounds of language minority students, refer to Crawford 1989, Cummins 1989, Fishman 1989, and Ogbu and Matute-Bianchi 1986. (See also Chapter 9.)

Recognizing the importance of reducing prejudice against language minority students, federal legislation was created to improve their schooling. This legislation has not always been successful.

While it is important that teachers understand the legal rights of their language minority students, only a basic introductory overview of the federal legislation affecting language minority students is given here. For other resources which provide greater detail on this subject, refer to the references.

Before discussing the legislation, it might be useful to clarify the terms *Limited English Proficiency (LEP)*, *Potential English Proficient (PEP)*, and *English as a Second Language (ESL)*. When the legislation refers to second language learners who are not fully proficient in English, it often uses the terms, LEP (limited English proficient), or ESL (English as a second language), or, more recently, PEP (Potential English Proficient).

Federal Legislation Affecting the Education of Language Minority Students

In the 1960's, concern for language minority students from low socioeconomic levels led to the Bilingual Education Act of 1968 (which later became Title VII of the Elementary and Secondary Education Act). This act was aimed largely at Latinos and Native Americans. It states, "no person shall be subjected to discrimination on the basis of race, color, or national origin." It requires schools to take *affirmative steps* to provide children who are not native English speakers with the language skills needed to participate effectively in our schools.

The first memorandum concerning language minority students with limited English skills was issued by the Office for Civil Rights on May 25, 1970. It recommended the following means of compliance with Title VI of the Civil Rights Acts:

1. Where inability to speak and understand the English language excludes national origin-minority group children from effective participation in the educational program offered by a school district, the district must take affirmative steps to rectify the language deficiency in order to open its instructional program to these students.

2. School districts must not assign national origin-minority group students to classes for the mentally retarded on the basis of criteria which essentially measure or evaluate English language skills; nor may school districts deny national origin-minority group children access to college preparatory courses on a basis directly related to the failure of the school system to inculcate English language skills.

3. Any ability grouping or tracking system employed by the school system to deal with the special language skill needs of national origin-minority group children must be designed to meet such language skill needs as soon as possible and must not operate as an educational dead-end or permanent track.

4. School districts have the responsibility to adequately notify national origin-minority group parents of school activities which are called to the attention of other parents. Such notice in order to be adequate may have to be provided in a language other than English (United States Office for Civil Rights, 1970)

In 1974, the Bilingual Education Act was revised to create a greater range of programs for a larger number of children. Yet, even with state and federal governments spending substantial amounts on bilingual education, only one out of ten children with limited English was receiving any bilingual services in 1980. Unfortunately, the budget cuts in the 1980s have reduced that proportion even further. Fishman (1981) laments that the Bilingual Education Act "was primarily an act for the Anglification of non-English speakers and not an act for Bilingualism" (p. 518). He explains that under this act, transitional bilingual programs were created which only use the language minority children's primary languages until the children have acquired enough English to be instructed in English only.

One of the most famous tests of language rights in the United States was the *Lau vs. Nichols* case. "The case originated in 1970, when a San Francisco poverty lawyer, Edward Steinman, learned that a client's child was failing in school because he could not understand the language of instruction. Steinman filed a class action suit on behalf of Kinney Lau and 1,789 other Chinese students in the same predicament" (Crawford 1989, p. 35). The claim was made that these language minority students were being denied the right to equal educational opportunities because they could not benefit from the all-English instruction their schools provided. The case went to the United States Supreme Court, where on January 21, 1974, it was ruled that the failure of the school district to provide appropriate language instruction to LEP children prevented them from participating in the educational program and hence violated their right to educational opportunity as guaranteed by the Constitution of the United States and by the State of California. The court stated:

> There is no equality of treatment merely by providing students with the same facilities, textbooks, teachers, and curriculum; for students who do not understand English are effectively foreclosed from any meaningful education.

To implement the Lau decision, the Office of Civil Rights established broad guidelines for instructional programs for *LEP* children. These guidelines, called the *Lau Remedies,* prescribed various types of bilingual/multicultural programs for elementary schools and ESL programs for secondary schools. While the Supreme Court's decision did not specifically call for bilingual programs, many districts responded to it by creating them. Consequently, the number of bilingual programs increased. One of the most important aspects of the Lau Remedies is assessment. The first step in establishing special services for LEP students is the identification of all students who can be categorized as limited or non-English speaking and/or achieving below grade level. The remedies specify that students be identified by means of a home-language questionnaire, a parent interview (in grades K–8), or a student interview (in grades 9–12). Those students who have difficulties communicating in English are entitled to special services. The assessment is completed through proficiency testing in both English and the student's primary language. The Lau Remedies also recommend ongoing evaluation of students in all content-area classes. The Lau Remedies have frequently been criticized, since definitions are not clearly specified, and the Office of Civil Rights has failed to enforce its requirements.

Despite such criticisms, the Lau decision has affected the language instruction of language minority children across the nation.

> Throughout the late 1970s, the federal Office for Civil Rights (OCR) continued to monitor school districts' performance in serving language minority children. Where it found violations, OCR required districts to initiate bilingual education programs and other changes under the Lau Remedies. By 1980, it had negotiated 359 Lau plans to remedy past discrimination, enabling many LEP children to receive special help for the first time. (Crawford 1989, p. 41).

A number of school districts were cited for civil rights violations. "The schools of Alhambra, California, for example, had no bilingual education and only minimal ESL instruction in 1977, when OCR cited the district for multiple civil rights violations. Ten years later, the district had 120 bilingual classrooms, featuring instruction in Spanish, Vietnamese, Cantonese and Mandarin" (Crawford 1989, p. 41).

In 1978, the original Bilingual Education Act, Title VIII, was reauthorized, but with *Non-English Speaking* (NES) and *Limited-English Speaking* (LES) changed to *Non-English Proficient* (NEP) and *Limited English Proficient* (LEP). This was done to emphasize the recent concern for teaching and testing language proficiency. As Enright and McCloskey (1988) correctly point out, the terms have a negative meaning, since they indicate that the students are somehow limited or insufficient and fail to recognize the students' true linguistic talents as second language learners. For this reason, the term Potential English Proficient (PEP) is often used.

Other national court cases such as Plyler vs. Doe (1982 United States Supreme Court) held that children who are not citizens of the United States cannot be denied elementary or secondary education. As a result of this Supreme Court decision, the state of Texas was required to educate the children of undocumented, illegal workers from Mexico. (For more detailed discussion of the legislation affecting language minority students, refer to Ashworth 1985, Crawford 1989, Trueba 1989, Wolfson 1989, and Wong 1988.)

Educational Programs Available to Language Minority Students

Content-area teachers must understand the previous schooling their language minority students have received in the United States. Before entering content-area classes, many language minority students participate in bilingual and ESL programs. In the following, I discuss the major pedagogical approaches used in bilingual education and the various types of programs implemented in the United States. This discussion is intended to provide only a brief overview of bilingual education. See the recommended reading listed at the end of this chapter.)

Bilingual Programs

The United States Office of Education (1971) defined bilingual programs as:

> . . . the use of two languages, one of which is English, as mediums of instruction for the same pupil population in a well-organized program which encompasses all or part of the curriculum and includes the study of the history and culture associated with the mother tongue. A complete program develops and maintains the children's self-esteem and a legitimate pride in both cultures.

Approaches

The preferred approach used in many bilingual elementary and secondary classrooms is the *preview/review* technique, in which the content of the lesson is previewed in one language, and the body of the lesson is presented in the other language. A bilingual teacher may provide the lesson by him or herself, or two teachers may teach the lesson together. For example, when the approach is used by one bilingual instructor, the teacher summarizes the main points of the lesson in the students' primary language. Next, the body of the lesson is taught in English and then followed up with a review of the most important points of the lesson in the students' primary language. When the preview/review technique is used in team-teaching, one teacher presents a brief overview of the lesson in English, and the second teacher gives the bulk of the lesson in the students' primary language. Then, the English-medium teacher summarizes the lesson in English. In a less popular approach, sometimes called the *Alternate Language Method* or *Flip-Flop Method*, a lesson is presented in the primary language on one day and in English the next. Much less effective are the *Concurrent Method* and the *Direct Translation Method*. In these methods, the teacher frequently provides instant translation of everything said, often switching from one language to the next language within the same lesson. These methods or approaches are not effective, since the students typically tune out when the teacher is using the unfamiliar language and instead simply wait to hear the language they will understand (Legarreta 1979).[2]

Types of Bilingual Programs

Several types of bilingual programs are currently in use in the United States. These include transition programs, enrichment programs, and two-way bilingual programs.

(1) Early-Exit Transition Programs.   These programs provide some instruction in the language minority students' native language to help them keep up in school subjects, while they study English in programs designed for ESL students. The goal in these programs is to

provide just enough first language skills for students not to *fall be-hind* in subject areas. Most transition programs are considered compensatory. Students are prepared to enter classrooms where full English proficiency is assumed, usually within two to three years. Students who complete these transition programs generally lack the competence to compete well with native English-speaking peers. In describing these programs, Crawford (1989) states:

> . . .the legal definition of TBE [transitional bilingual education] is broad, requiring only that some amount of native language and culture be used, along with ESL instruction. Programs may stress native-language development, including initial literacy, or they may provide students with nothing more than the translation services of bilingual aides. Contrary to public perceptions, studies have shown that English is the medium of instruction from 72 to 92 percent of the time in TBE programs. (p. 175)

(2) Late-Exit Enrichment (Maintenance) Programs. The goal in these programs is to provide students with instruction which aids the development of advanced primary language skills. Such instruction is based on research described by Crawford (1989):

- Early childhood is not the optimum age to acquire a second language; older children and adults are *more efficient language students.* Thus, the sense of urgency in introducing English to non-English speaking children and the concern about postponing children's exit from bilingual programs are misplaced.
- Language is not a unified skill, but a complex configuration of abilities...Language used for conversational purposes is quite different than language used for school learning, and the former develops earlier than the latter.
- Because many skills are transferable to a second language, time spent learning in the native language...is not time lost in developing English or other subjects. To the contrary, a child with a strong foundation in the first language will perform better in English over the long term.
- Reading should be taught in the native language, particularly for children who, on other grounds, run the risk of reading failure. Reading skills acquired in the native language will transfer readily and quickly to English, and will result in higher ultimate reading achievement in English.
- There is no cognitive cost in the development of bilingualism in children. Very possibly, bilingualism enhances children's thinking skills.

(Refer to Chapter 3 for further discussion.) The goal of enrichment bilingual programs is *additive bilingualism,* that is, continued development of the child's first and second languages. Additive bilingualism contrasts sharply with *subtractive bilingualism,* which attempts to replace the child's native language with the second language as soon as possible.

In 1980, the California Department of Education attempted to implement maintenance bilingual programs which were consistent with current research on bilingual education. Called *Case Studies* in *Bilingual Education*, a curriculum was developed which was based on the principles listed below.

Basic Principles of the Case Studies Project

These theoretical principles and their practical implications are adapted from *Basic Principles for the Education of Language Minority Students: An Overview*, and reprinted in Crawford (1989, p. 129).

1. For bilingual students, the development of proficiencies in both the native language and English has a positive effect on academic development.
2. Language proficiency is the ability to use language for both basic communicative tasks and academic purposes.
3. For limited-English-proficient students, reaching the threshold of native-language skills necessary to complete academic tasks forms the basis for similar proficiency in English.

Implications

- Students are provided substantial amounts of instruction in and through the native language.
- Initial reading classes and other cognitively demanding subjects are taught in the native language.
- Sufficient texts and supplementary materials are available in the native language.
- A sufficient number of well-trained teachers with high levels of native language proficiency are available to provide instruction.
- Teachers avoid mixing English and the native language during instruction.
- Teachers accept regional and nonstandard varieties of the native language.

4. Acquisition of basic communicative competency in a second language is a function of comprehensible second language instruction and a supportive environment.

Implications

- Comprehensible second language input is provided through both ESL classes and sheltered English instruction in academic content areas [sheltered English instruction is discussed below].

- Subjects are selected in which the cognitive demands are low to average when content areas are used to provide comprehensible English input.
- ESL instruction is communication-based rather than grammar-based and is characterized by the following: (a) content is based on the students' communicative needs; (b) instruction makes extensive use of contextual clues; (c) the teacher uses only English, but modifies speech to students' level and confirms their comprehension; (d) students are permitted to respond in their native language when necessary; (e) the focus is on language function of content, rather than grammatical form; (f) grammatical accuracy is promoted not by correcting errors overtly, but by providing more comprehensible input; and (g) students are encouraged to respond spontaneously and creatively.
- Opportunities for comprehensible English input are provided for LEP students when grouped by language proficiency and when interacting with fluent English-speaking peers.

5. The perceived status of students affects the interaction between teachers and students and among students themselves. In turn, student outcomes are affected.

Implications

- Teachers use positive interactions in an equitable manner with both language majority and language minority students.
- Language majority and language minority students are enrolled in content-area classes in which cooperative learning strategies are used.
- Language majority students are enrolled, whenever possible, in classes designed to develop second language proficiency in the minority language(s) represented in the school.
- Administrators, teachers, and students use the minority language(s) represented in the school for noninstructional purposes.

The Case Studies curriculum was developed on the hypothesis that strong first language skills transfer readily from the child's native language into English and that considerable time (approximately four years or more) is needed to develop strong first language skills. The success of maintenance bilingual programs is well-documented, (for a detailed report of student scores in Case Studies schools, see Krashen and Biber 1988).

(3) Two-Way Bilingual Programs. Two-way bilingual programs offer a means of encouraging bilingualism among both language minority and majority students. Including students from both language groups creates a learning environment that fosters sustained contact

for both groups in a second language. Lindholm (1987), provides the following guidelines for two-way bilingual programs.

Criteria for Effective Two-Way Bilingual Education

1. *Long-term treatment.* A program must last four to six years for students to achieve bilingual proficiency.

2. *Optimal input in two languages.* Second language input, provided through language arts and subject-matter instruction, must be comprehensible, that is, adjusted to students' level; relevant, so as to stimulate student interest; sufficient in quantity; and challenging, so that it requires students to *negotiate meaning.*

3. *Focus on academic subjects.* Children need more than language development. The curriculum should emphasize concept development as well, beginning in the second language for English speakers, in the native language for minority students.

4. *Integration of language arts into the curriculum.* Sheltered instruction alone has failed to produce native-like proficiency in the second language; students also need instruction in formal language arts. Linguistic structures are best mastered in connection with subject-matter instruction, rather than through isolated grammar exercises.

5. *Separation of languages for instruction.* Sustained periods of monolingual instruction promote linguistic development better than concurrent approaches that mix languages during the same lesson.

6. *Additive bilingual environment.* Enrichment approaches, in which children acquire a second language without abandoning their mother tongue, lead to higher levels of bilingual proficiency, along with improved self-esteem and more favorable attitudes toward other cultures.

7. *Balance of language groups.* To ensure equity in the classroom, as well as maximum interaction among language minority children, the two groups should be mixed in roughly equal proportions. The ratio should never slip below 2/3 to 1/3.

8. *Sufficient use of minority language.* At least 50 percent of instruction should be conducted in the minority language, both to provide English-speaking students optimal input and to ensure that minority students develop cognitive-academic language proficiency in their native tongue.

9. *Opportunities for speech production.* To become proficient in a second language, children need opportunities to practice orally with native speakers, preferably including exer-

cises on which language-minority and language-majority students can collaborate.

10. *Administrative support.* Bilingual programs should be treated equitably within a school for many reasons; one important reason for this is the negative language status implications that would otherwise be communicated to students.

11. *Empowerment objective of instruction.* Breaking with the authoritarian transmission model in which teachers impart and children receive knowledge, instruction should be a dialogue in which students learn to think for themselves rather than simply memorize information.

12. *High-quality teachers.* Teachers need to be competent bilinguals, whether or not they respond only in the target language, so they can respond to children's needs and provide comprehensible input.

13. *Home-school collaboration.* Especially for language-minority students, parental involvement is essential to reinforce children's native language development and to communicate high expectations about academic achievement.

(reported in Crawford 1989, p. 167).

Strong evidence suggests that language minority children fare better in bilingual programs than they do in English-only programs. Ashworth (1985), for example, states:

> If young children are required to learn new concepts in a language in school which is foreign to them, they will be able neither to grasp the explanations offered, nor to use language to expand and refine those concepts. If thinking skills are delayed while children struggle to learn the second language, their intellectual development will be retarded. As language skills developed in one language can be transferred to another language, vernacular language teaching can assist both cognitive and linguistic development. In addition, struggling to learn at an early age in another group's language does not engender pride in one's own ethnicity, a factor which may contribute to low achievement. (p. 13)

Research indicates that students in bilingual programs do not fall behind in subject matter. Instead, these students develop self-esteem, avoid culture conflict, and, when allowed to achieve high levels of proficiency in both their first and second languages, they even enjoy cognitive advantages. (See, for example, Crawford 1989; Cummins 1986, 1989; Hakuta 1986; and Krashen and Biber 1988; refer to Wolfson 1989 for a balanced discussion of the advantages and disadvantages of bilingual education programs. For further discussion, see Chapter 3.)

English as a Second Language

Bilingual programs are not possible where there are not enough qualified bilingual teachers or where too many students speak different primary languages. In many schools, a number of different cultural groups are represented. In Orange County, California, for example, students from more than forty language backgrounds attend elementary schools. Clearly, in such cases, bilingual education is not always feasible, and a reasonable alternative is ESL. Numerous ESL approaches and programs have been created for language minority children who have not yet acquired English. Brief descriptions follow. (Other authors have examined these approaches and programs in greater detail. For further discussion, refer to the recommended reading.)

Approaches

In recent years, many comprehension-based approaches have been developed. These include such approaches as *Total Physical Response* (Asher 1982) and the *Natural Approach* (Krashen and Terrell 1983), which emphasize the importance of providing comprehensible English input. In Total Physical Response, teachers give their students commands and model physical movements used to carry out these commands. In the Natural Approach, instruction is carefully planned and geared for the students' English proficiency levels. Teachers frequently use pictures, manipulatives, drawings, and simple explanations to make sure their students understand their lessons. More communicative approaches are also widely used in ESL classes. These approaches have a variety of names, including the *Interactive/Experiential Approach* (Cummins 1989), *Integrated Language Teaching* (Enright and McCloskey 1988), *Whole Language* (Edelsky, Draper and Smith 1983, Heald-Taylor 1989), and *Cooperative Learning* (Kagan 1989). They provide students with numerous opportunities to use input to communicate purposefully in a wide variety of situations.

Types of ESL Programs

Just as there are a variety of approaches to ESL instruction, there are also a variety of ESL programs. For children, the following classes are frequently offered:

1. *Full-day ESL classes.* In these classes, all the students lack proficiency in English. They remain in ESL classes until their teachers feel they are ready to be mainstreamed into classes in which native English proficiency is assumed.
2. *Half-day ESL classes.* In these classes, the students spend half the day in an ESL class and half in all-English, content-area classes (where native English proficiency is assumed)

and/or in transition or Sheltered English classes (see following).

3. *Pullout ESL classes.* In these classes, ESL students are withdrawn from their regular all-English content-area classes for one or more periods a week for special ESL instruction in small groups. However, these classes can hinder academic success, since students may miss valuable classroom instruction. (See Richard-Amato 1988 for a detailed description of these programs.)

4. *Sheltered English classes.* In these ESL classes, the students study the same content that is covered in all-English classes, but the language component is adapted to suit their English proficiency level. For a specific subject, students are grouped by proficiency level and teachers instruct by using strategies which make their English comprehensible to the students. (These strategies are discussed in Chapter 3.)

After students gain English skills, they are generally eased into classes in which native English proficiency is assumed. Krashen (1984) suggests that Sheltered English classes can serve as *transition* classes. Ideally, the students are only placed into these classes when they have acquired sufficient competence to handle content-area instruction. At first, elementary school students might be placed in such classes as physical education, music, and art and later in the social and natural sciences where greater English proficiency is assumed. Krashen (1984) suggests that when ESL learners are in the initial stages of transition, the content of the subject matter should be *cognitively undemanding,* the materials should be *context embedded,* the content-area teacher should be aware of "the students' need for comprehensible input and the atmosphere should be one of acceptance rather than rejection" (p. 222). He recommends the model given in Table 2–3.

In Krashen's model, LEP children take some courses in English while they also receive ESL instruction. So that they do not fall behind in their studies, they also take core subjects in their first language. As they become more advanced, they begin to take Sheltered

Table 2–3 Program for ESL Students*

Level	Mainstream	Sheltered	First Language
beginning	art, music, physical education	ESL	all core subjects
intermediate	art, music, physical education	ESL, math	social and natural sciences
advanced	art, music, physical education, math	ESL, social and natural sciences	enrichment
mainstream	all subjects	—	enrichment

*adapted from Krashen 1984, see also Richard-Amato 1988

English classes, in which they are given easier, more comprehensible English lessons. Finally, they are mainstreamed into English-only courses, but continue to take enrichment courses in their first language.[3] (For a description of content-based ESL models used in higher education, designed to teach ESL through such courses as political science and psychology, refer to Snow, Brinton and Wesche 1989).

To avoid confusion, it should be mentioned that Sheltered English is sometimes considered a type of *immersion* program.[4] In this type of program, the students are taught ESL through content-area courses, with an emphasis on comprehensible, that is, understandable, English input and instruction tailored to the students' English proficiency level. (For a useful review of immersion programs, see California State Department of Education 1984.)

A different alternative to *immersion* programs is *submersion* programs, sometimes called sink-or-swim plans. With these approaches, language minority students receive no assistance in understanding their lessons or learning English. Research has documented the failure of these policies. Crawford (1989), for example, states,

> Contrary to myth, immigrant children were more likely to sink than swim in English language classrooms. In 1908 just 13 percent of such students who were enrolled in New York City schools at age twelve went on to high school (as compared with 32 percent of white children whose parents were native born).

Not surprisingly, submersion programs violate the federal civil rights law because of the United States Supreme Court's Lau versus Nichols decision of 1974.

In addition to the ESL approaches outlined above, older children and adults may also benefit from these plans:

1. *English for Special Purposes (ESP).* Students take ESL courses which are designed to give them expertise in specific content areas. For example, one popular course is *English for Engineers.* Another is *English for the Medical Professions.*

2. *Vocational ESL Classes.* Like ESP courses, vocational ESL courses provide ESL students with experience using English in specific content areas. These courses, however, are particularly designed to train adults to work in vocations such as mechanics, nursing, or electronics.

3. *Adjunct ESL Classes.* These ESL classes are generally adjoined to regular college courses, such as psychology, history, or economics. (For example, students enroll in a psychology course at the same time they enroll in an adjunct section of ESL which supplements the psychology course.) The adjunct courses give ESL students additional practice in and exposure to the particular language uses of a field of study, as learned in a specific course.

Conclusion

A critical grasp of your students' backgrounds enables you to make important decisions concerning what should be taught and how it might best meet the needs of your students. This chapter outlines only the *basic* background issues teachers must know if they are to understand their language minority students. (For additional information, see the suggested readings listed at the end of this chapter.)

ACTIVITIES AND DISCUSSION QUESTIONS

1. Have you ever had to adapt to a different culture? Describe your own experience. Did you suffer from culture shock? Why or why not?

2. In this chapter, several factors which affect the ease with which language minority students adjust to the United States were discussed. (See pages 27 to 32.) In what specific ways do these factors affect acculturation? What other factors might affect acculturation?

3. Gleason (1961) notes that the Shona of Rhodesia and the Bassa of Liberia have fewer color categories than speakers of European languages, and they divide the color spectrum differently. Yet, they are able to describe other colors in the same way that English speakers might describe them. From such observations emerges what is now known as the *Sapir-Whorf hypothesis* which, in its strong version, states that language actually shapes world view. While this hypothesis has few zealous adherents, it underscores the significance of linguistic and cultural differences. How is the Sapir-Whorf hypothesis relevant to teaching language minority students? In answering this question, you will want to consider Whorf's (1954) summary of this hypothesis:

   The background linguistic system (in other words, the grammar) of each language is not merely a reproducing instrument for voicing ideas but rather is itself the shaper of ideas, the program and guide for the individual's mental activity, for his analysis of impressions, for his synthesis of his mental stock in trade. Formulation of ideas is not an independent process, strictly rational in the old sense, but is part of a particular grammar and differs, from slightly to greatly, as between different grammars. We dissect nature along lines laid down by our native languages. . . . We cut nature up, organize it into concepts, and ascribe significances as we do, largely because we are parties to an agreement to organize it this way—an agreement that holds through our speech community and is codified in the patterns of our language. (1954, pp. 212–214)

4. S. I. Hayakawa introduced a series of proposed constitutional amendments to make English the official language of the United States. Sixteen states have already made English the official language. They are: Nebraska (1920), Illinois (1969), Virginia (1981), Indiana, Kentucky, and Tennessee

(1984), California and Georgia (1986), Arkansas, Mississippi, North Carolina, North Dakota, and South Carolina (1987) and Arizona, Colorado, and Florida (1988). (Interestingly, in 1978, Hawaii recognized both English and native Hawaiian as official languages.) California's proposition which makes English an official state language follows. To what extent do you believe such propositions might affect the education of language minority students?

English as the Official Language of California
Initiative Constitutional Amendment

Section 1. Section 6 is added to Article III of the Constitution to read as follows:

SEC. 6. (a) Purpose.

English is the common language of the people of the United States of America, and the state of California. This section is intended to preserve, protect and strengthen the English language, and not to supersede any of the rights guaranteed to the people by this Constitution.

(b) English as the Official Language of California.

English is the official language of the State of California.

(c) Enforcement.

The legislature shall enforce this section by appropriate legislation. The Legislature and officials of the State of California shall take all steps necessary to insure that the role of English as the common language of the State of California is preserved and enhanced. The Legislature shall make no law which diminishes or ignores the role of English as the common language of the State of California.

(d) Personal Right of Action and Jurisdiction of Courts.

Any person who is a resident of or doing business in the State of California shall have standing to sue the State of California to enforce this section, and the Courts of record of the State of California shall have jurisdiction to hear cases brought to enforce this section. The Legislature may provide reasonable and appropriate limitations on the time and manner of suits brought under this section.

Section 2. Severability

If any provision of this section, or the application of any such provision to any person or circumstance, shall be held invalid, the remainder of this section to the extent it can be given effect shall not be affected thereby, and to this end the provisions of this section are severable.

5. Describe several concrete steps teachers can take to ease the stress which is associated with acculturation. What can teachers do to help students overcome *culture shock?*

RECOMMENDED READING

Bilingual Education

CRAWFORD, J. 1989. *Bilingual Education: History, Politics, Theory and Practice.* Trenton, New Jersey: Crane Publishing Company. A comprehensive overview of bilingual education in the United States, written by the former editor of *Education Week.*

CUMMINS, J. and SWAIN, M. 1986. *Bilingualism in Education.* London: Longman. A synthesis of recent theoretical work relating to the educational development of Canadian bilingual children from majority and minority language backgrounds. The importance of bilingualism on cognitive development is considered and the nature of language proficiency clarified.

FISHMAN, J. and KELLER, G. D. (eds.) 1982. *Bilingual Education for Hispanic Students in the United States.* New York: Teachers College Columbia. This collection of articles focuses on the goals, policies and problems of bilingual education.

KRASHEN, S. and BIBER, D. 1989. *On Course: Bilingual Education's Success in California.* Sacramento, California: California Association of Bilingual Education. The authors review numerous bilingual programs; their data suggest the characteristics of successful bilingual programs and document the academic gains which children enrolled in bilingual programs have made.

SWAIN, M. and LAPKIN, S. 1985. *Evaluating Bilingual Education: A Canadian Case Study.* Clevedon, England: Multilingual Matters. An overview of French immersion programs in Canada. Contains a comprehensive listing of reports, articles and books pertinent to immersion education in Canada and the United States.

TRUEBA, H. T. and C. BARNETT-MIZRAHI (eds.) 1979. *Bilingual Multicultural Education and the Professionals from Theory to Practice.* Cambridge: Harper and Row. Details historical, philosophical, and legal issues related to bilingual and multicultural education. Practical concerns of teachers and administrators are also addressed.

English as a Second Language

LARSEN-FREEMAN, D. 1986. *Techniques and Principles in Language Teaching.* Oxford: Oxford University Press. An overview of the most well-known

ESL methods. Useful illustrations of the methods are provided and principles underlying their use are described.

LONG, M. and RICHARDS, J. 1987. *Methodology in TESOL: A Book of Readings.* New York: Harper and Row. Presents a number of perspectives on second language and foreign language teaching; explores contemporary teaching practices consistent with current research.

RICHARD-AMATO, P. 1988. *Making It Happen: Interaction in the Second Language Classroom.* New York: Longman. The author, a teacher and administrator, as well as a teacher trainer, discusses current second language theory and ESL methods. A variety of ESL methods and approaches are covered; practical suggestions and strategies are given which can be put into immediate use.

KRASHEN, S. D. and TERRELL, T. D. 1983. *The Natural Approach: Language Acquisition in the Classroom.* Hayward: The Alemany Press. Describes the objectives, methodology, and theoretical underpinnings of the Natural Approach. Practical guidelines are given for organizing curricula, designing and managing classroom activities, and providing students with additional sources of input for language development.

RICHARDS, J. C. and RODGERS, T. S. 1986. *Approaches and Methods in Language Teaching: A Description and Analysis.* Cambridge: Cambridge University Press. Describes various methods used to teach ESL. These include Grammar Translation, the Direct Method, Situational Language Teaching, Audiolingualism, Communicative Language Teaching, the Silent Way, Community Language Learning, Total Physical Response, the Natural Approach and Suggestopedia; focuses on the theory of language and language learning behind the method, the objectives and language syllabus and the techniques and activities used in the method.

NOTES

1. In addition, the term *culture,* as employed in this book, encompasses those interpretations offered by behaviorists, functionalists, and cognitive and symbolic anthropologists. The current trend of second language educators is to view culture from behaviorist and/or functionalist perspectives. From the behaviorist's point of view, culture consists of discrete behaviors or sets of behaviors, e.g., traditions, habits or customs, as in marriage or leisure. "Culture is something which is shared and can be observed" (Robinson 1985, p. 8). Whereas behaviorists tend to focus on observable patterns of behavior, functionalists tend to focus on understanding behaviors and explaining why specific ones occur. Since the rules underlying behavior cannot be directly observed, they are inferred from the behavior.

The cognitive definition shifts attention from the observable aspects of behavior to what is *inside* the learner. What is *inside* is a means of ordering and interpreting the world, a way of organizing the input the learner receives. (The notion of culture as world view pertains to this interpretation.) According to cognitive approaches, culture does not consist of things, behavior, or emotions. Instead, it is the forms of things that people have in mind, their models of perceiving, relating, and otherwise interpreting them (Goodenough 1964). For Goodenough (1971), people may be competent in more than one culture; that is, they may have a *cultural repertoire*.

Symbolic anthropologists interpret culture as a system of symbols and meanings and question how meaning is derived. They focus on the relationship between meaning, experience and reality. "Applied to teaching culture in bilingual, second language and foreign language programs, this theory suggests that cultural understanding is an ongoing, dynamic process in which learners continually synthesize cultural inputs with their own past and present experience in order to create meaning" (Robinson 1985, p. 11).

2. Dulay and Burt (1978) summarize the problem with these approaches:

> When core subject matter is taught to LEP students in two languages at once (as in the concurrent method), or in one language after another (as in the preview-review method), students probably filter out the language they do not understand in favor of the language they do understand. In other words, much of the English used to present the same content a second time is probably tuned out, as it has no real function in the communicative situation. There would be little motivation to exert the extra effort to attend to information presented in a new language when students have either just heard it in their native language, or know that the same content will soon be presented in their native language. (p. 558)

3. Today, many pedagogues support the integration of English language into content-area instruction and advocate Sheltered English. For an interesting discussion of this approach, see Crandall (1987) and Mohan (1986). Sheltered English instruction is consistent with the *language across the curriculum* movement encouraged by the Bullock Report (1976), *A Language for Life*. The main argument of the Bullock Report is that the teaching of language should be integrated with all aspects of content-area instruction. That is, the report argues that students should be encouraged to develop reading, writing, speaking, and listening skills in all subjects. This means all content-area instructors must understand language pedagogy. However, in the multilingual, multilinguistic classroom, content-area teachers must also understand principles of successful ESL instruction. Sheltered English employs principles, which, as described by Curtain (1986), include:

- **(1)** focussing on meaning rather than on form;
- **(2)** avoiding error correction;
- **(2)** providing students with simplified English input (that is said to increase the ESL learners' ability to understand English; see Chapter 3);
- **(3)** using contextual clues to help ESL students understand lessons;
- **(4)** involving students in meaningful interaction; and
- **(5)** not forcing students to speak before they have enough English proficiency to do so willingly.

4. There is considerable confusion regarding the term, *immersion*, as it is used by different persons to refer to different programs. Many educators confuse it with the term, *submersion.* In contrast to submersion programs, which provide no language support, in immersion programs, language minority students are given considerable help in acquiring their new language. In certain regions of Canada, the term, immersion, is used to refer to the education that English-speaking children receive in classrooms where the teachers instruct in French, the children's second language. In Canadian immersion classes, the teachers are bilingual in French and English, and they are capable, therefore, of answering their students' questions when they are asked in English. In the United States, the term, immersion, is normally used to refer to content-area instruction which is tailored to the needs of language minority students who have not yet acquired English. The teachers in immersion programs in the United States may or may not speak their students' primary languages.

CHAPTER THREE

Understanding Second Language Acquisition

In the past twenty years, second language researchers have made several findings of direct relevance to the classroom instruction of language minority students. Some of these findings have enabled us to discredit erroneous beliefs about language learning which suggest, for example, that language learning is a simple matter of acquiring a new set of habits. Other findings have enabled us to identify the following key factors associated with effective second language instruction:

Key Factors Associated with Effective Second Language Instruction

1. Appreciation of the first languages and cultures of language minority students;

2. Sensitivity to the affective needs of language minority students;

3. Respect for individual differences in learning styles;

4. Sensitivity to factors affecting students' grammatical development in a second language;

5. Reduced instruction in mechanical grammatical exercises and related drills which emphasize the component parts of language;

6. Reduced instruction relying solely on comparisons of the first and second language (that is, contrastive analysis);

7. Continuous exposure to large quantities of written and spoken English which is comprehensible to language minority students;

8. Regular and substantial interaction in English for diverse purposes; and

9. The opportunity to communicate for real, personally significant purposes.

Each of these findings and their implications is discussed in the following.

Appreciation of the First Languages and Native Cultures of Students

It is imperative that teachers appreciate their students' home cultures and languages. Ideally, teachers should try to help their students maintain their first languages. Unfortunately, it is common practice even today for teachers to actively discourage their students' use of the first language. One teacher, reported in the *San Francisco Chronicle*, still charges his students a dime each time they speak their native languages. Why does this teacher feel so negatively toward the home languages of his students? Perhaps he believes that his students' English language skills suffer when they spend time using their first languages. To counter such reasoning, Cummins has proposed a series of hypotheses which suggest that learners who have strong first language skills do better in their academic skills than their peers who have weak first language skills.

Cummins' (1979) *Threshold Hypothesis* explains how first language development can aid the second language learner's academic progress. After reviewing the literature on bilingualism, Cummins suggests that in specific situations bilingualism seems to hinder academic progress, while in other situations bilingualism seems to help it. To explain these findings, Cummins proposes the existence of two different *thresholds* of language development, a lower threshold and an upper one. He suggests that ". . . there may be threshold levels of linguistic competency which a bilingual child must attain, both in order to avoid cognitive disadvantages and to allow the potentially beneficial aspects of bilingualism to influence his cognitive and academic functioning" (1978, p. 1).

Cummins argues that students must reach nativelike proficiency in at least one of their languages if they are to attain the same academic progress as their monolingual peers. Failure to gain high levels of proficiency in at least one of the two languages can impair their academic progress. Cummins refers to these lower levels of attainment as *the lower threshold*. With inadequate levels of skills in their first languages, Cummins argues that children might suffer the negative effects of *semilingualism;* that is, the loss of their first language may prevent them from mastering their second. This means that to avoid academic difficulties, a high level of proficiency in at least one of a bilingual student's two languages is necessary.

In Cummins' opinion, students can reap the benefits of bilingualism and enhance their academic functioning when they surpass the *higher threshold* of bilingual development, the levels of first and second language proficiency associated with schooling and extensive experience using both languages for a wide range of purposes. Those who reach this higher threshold level enjoy "an increased awareness of the nature of language, greater flexibility in understanding the arbitrary associates of words and referents and increased sensitivity to the interpersonal cues of language use" (McGroarty 1988, p. 301; see also Dolson 1985). Thus, for Cummins, the upper threshold is reached when the second language learner develops high levels of age-appropriate skills in each of the two languages, and, as a consequence, academic progress is enhanced and cognitive functioning improved. The lower threshold is reached when the second language learner does not develop age-appropriate skills in at least one of the two languages. As a consequence of this, neither language serves as a foundation for cognitive development and academic progress.[1]

Another hypothesis which supports the importance of maintaining the students' first language is Cummins' (1979) *Developmental Interdependence Hypothesis.* The Developmental Interdependence Hypothesis states that "the level of L2 [second language] competence which a bilingual child attains is partially a function of the type of competence the child has developed in the L1 [first language] at the time when intensive exposure to L2 [the second language] begins" (Cummins 1979, p. 233). Cummins draws support for his hypothesis from two sources, studies of minority language students which show that children who are more proficient in the first language do better academically than their peers, and reading research which demonstrates that first and second language reading skills are highly correlated.

Related to the issue of linguistic interdependence is that of the nature of bilingual proficiency. Cummins (1981) questions whether a bilingual's two languages represent two *separate underlying proficiencies* (SUP) or a *common underlying proficiency* (CUP). As shown in Figure 3–1, the CUP model maintains that proficiency in the first language easily transfers to the second language since there is a common underlying proficiency.

As illustrated in Figure 3–2 below, the SUP model maintains that proficiency in the first language is completely distinct from proficiency in the second language.

first language proficiency

----

second language proficiency

In this model, content and skills learned in the first language do not transfer into content and skills learned in the second. If a child, for example, learns the story of *Little Red Riding Hood* in her first language, her knowledge of this story does not help her to read this story in her second language. Cummins (1981) finds no research consistent with the SUP model, and he concludes that children who have exten-

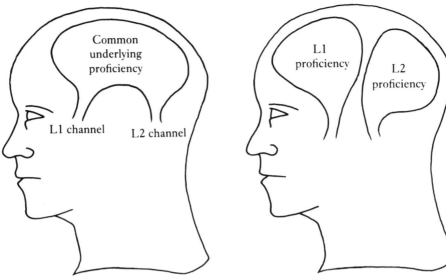

Figure 3–1 Common Underlying Proficiency

Figure 3–2 Separate Underlying Language Proficiencies

(reprinted from Cummins and Swain 1986, pgs. 83 and 81 respectively)

sive, good first language skills make better progress in school than comparable students who have not developed their first language.

Implications

While it is not possible to provide all students with bilingual classes where they are given instruction designed to maintain their first languages, there are several procedures we can follow to help our students develop and maintain pride in their first languages. First, we can encourage students to use their native languages in their homes. Second, we can create a climate in our classrooms which shows students that their first languages are valued. As Farr and Daniels (1986) explain:

> Even in a school system where the official school policy toward nonstandard dialects is unenlightened and punitive, a knowledgeable and caring teacher can not only moderate the impact of such institutional discouragement, but may even create a linguistic safe harbor, a climate of understanding and encouragement in his or her room. For students whose school experience feels like a continuous buffeting of rejection, this interlude of acceptance may be tremendously powerful. (p. 50)

(Specific means of incorporating the language minority students' cultures and languages into our classrooms are discussed in Chapter 11.) Third, when possible, we can encourage our students to maintain their native languages by studying them in *heritage classes.* In such classes, students are taught to read and write in their first languages and to appreciate the richness of their native cultures. Saturday and weekday after-school classes are often offered by members of the Chinese, Korean, Japanese, and Vietnamese communities. Chicano communities in the Southwest offer *La Escuelita,* (the little school) where elementary school children are tutored in Spanish and English.

Sensitivity to the Affective Needs of Language Minority Students

Just as teachers must appreciate their students' native languages and cultures, they must also appreciate their students' affective needs. The literature suggests that affective variables such as motivation, and interests are strongly related to successful second language development. Learning a second language can create such emotional obstacles for many learners that they simply refuse to interact with native English speakers.

Motivation plays a central role in second language development. When language minority students find that the traditions of native mainstream Americans are congruent with their own lifestyles, they are likely to be successful. Conversely, when they find that the lifestyles of middle-Americans are incongruent with their own, they usually acquire the second language slowly and may stop learning before they gain native speaker proficiency in English.[2]

To explain the role of motivation in second language acquisition, Dulay and Burt (1977) proposed the existence of an *affective filter.* (Later, Krashen [1981a, b] called this filter the *Socio-Affective Filter.*) This filter governs how much of the input gets through to a language processing mechanism. Corder (1967) claims that much of the input learners receive is not processed. He refers to that part of input which is processed as *intake.* As a result of the Socio-Affective Filter (representing the students' attitudes, beliefs, motivation and emotional states), the student is *open* or *closed* to the second language, and the input may become *intake.* Once language minority students have obtained sufficient knowledge of English to meet their communicative and emotional needs, they may stop learning. This results in what Selinker (1972) has called *fossilization,* the permanent cessation of second language acquisition. Despite the amount of English input the students receive, they fail to develop their English. Figure 3–3 depicts the role of the Socio-Affective Filter in second language acquisition.

As illustrated in Figure 3–3, the Socio-Affective *Input* Filter blocks the input from being processed, while the Socio-Affective *Output* Filter prevents the acquired competence from being performed

English Input → Second Language Acquisition Process → Output

↑   ↑

The Socio-Affective Input Filter   The Socio-Affective Output Filter

Figure 3–3   The Role of the Socio-Affective Filter in Second Language Acquisition

(Adapted from Krashen 1982)

(see also Krashen 1982). Two ESL students, Mohammed and Prof. Fujisaki, illustrate how these filters function. When Mohammed first came to the United States with his wife and newborn baby, he made excellent progress acquiring English. One day, while he was studying English, his baby was home with a middle-American babysitter and fell out the third-floor window of Mohammed's apartment complex and died. Mohammed's English ceased to develop. Krashen would explain that Mohammed's Socio-Affective Input Filter had gone up and was now preventing English input from being processed. A different case is that of Prof. Fujisaki, a well-known linguist who has lived in the United States for more than twenty years and who has had extensive experience using English in university settings. Despite his length of residence in the United States, Prof. Fujisaki still has difficulty pronouncing English *l*'s and *r*'s. Krashen would explain that Prof. Fujisaki's Socio-Affective Output Filter has been raised, thus preventing him from performing at his true level of competence. It may be that Prof. Fujisaki desires to maintain his Japanese ethnic identity by retaining some of the pronunciation features of his first language when communicating in English.

According to the Socio-Affective Filter Hypothesis, English input can only result in language development when the following affective conditions are met: motivation is high, self-confidence is strong, and anxiety is low. When students such as Mohammed and Prof. Fujisaki are *put on the defensive* (Stevick 1976), they either fail to process the input or to perform at their level of competence.

The Socio-Affective Input and Output Filters are hypothesized to be strengthened during adolescence when students pass through a period in which they become self-conscious. Elkind (1967) documents this period. During this time, he claims adolescents may have low self-esteem, experience hypersensitivity, and feel vulnerable, even falsely believing that everyone is looking at and thinking about them.

Implications

The research I have summarized suggests the importance of developing low-anxiety language learning environments for our language minority students. This means understanding our students' needs and sensitivities and avoiding procedures which raise their anxieties. Students should be encouraged to communicate when they are ready and have the competence to do so. They should never be forced to use English when they lack the skills to communicate appropriately. (Chapters 4 and 5 give additional suggestions.)

Respect for Individual Differences in Learning Styles

In line with respecting affective needs, it is also important to respect individual differences in learning styles. Although there are similarities in the ways in which students acquire their second language knowledge, there are also major differences. As Ellis (1986) puts it, "Different learners in different situations learn a second language in different ways" (p. 4). Some of the variables affecting individual differences in learning style include age and personality.

Personality variables almost always result in individual differences in language learning styles. (For a detailed discussion of preferred learning styles and preferences, see Chapter 7.) It is important to keep in mind that many different personality types characterize successful second language students.

Wong-Fillmore's (1976) study of five Spanish-speaking children acquiring English provides additional evidence that diverse learning and social styles result in different routes to second language acquisition. Wong-Fillmore studied the ways in which five Spanish monolingual five-year-olds acquired English in their first year of elementary school. She obtained information about their English language development from tape recordings and observational records of their weekly play sessions with native English-speaking friends. The results of her study showed vast differences in the ways in which the children learned English. At one extreme, for example, was Juan, who rarely spoke English during the first six weeks of the study and then suddenly began to produce English quite well, demonstrating that he had been actively, though quietly, observing the English he heard. At the other extreme was Nora, a subject who appears to have talked nonstop in English from the onset of the study. The fact that Nora appeared to be a better language learner than Juan led Wong-Fillmore to the conclusion that out-going children might be the best second language learners. More recently, however, Wong-Fillmore (1983) investigated the learning and social styles of 43 Chinese (Cantonese)-speaking and Spanish-speaking children from the beginning of kindergarten until the end of second grade. She was surprised to find that only about half of the children she identified as *good learners* in the second study were sociable or outgoing. She describes one group of successful learners as scholarly, almost wordless children, who "while not downright unsociable seldom went out of their way to be with other children" (p. 162). Wong-Fillmore concludes that "there is no single way to characterize either the good or the poor learners" (p. 161). Although many believe that extroverts make the best language learners, since they may seek out opportunities to interact with native English-speakers, this is not always the case.

Age differences also lead to individual differences in learning styles. In general, a large amount of research indicates that childen are better language acquirers than adults in the long run, but that older learners generally have an initial *head start* over children (Krashen, Long and Scarcella 1979). Thus, if we were to put a group of small children and adults in the same room and teach both groups Swahili, the adults would learn Swahili the fastest, but after a few years, the children would speak more nativelike Swahili. Neurolinguistic evidence suggests that older learners process language differently in the brain, but can still reach relatively high levels of second language proficiency. They are particularly good vocabulary learners, but often lack the ability to acquire nativelike pronunciation and grammar in the second language.

Implications

Although research has only begun to document the various routes language minority students take in becoming competent users of English, it has determined that the best teachers are able to appeal to students of a variety of ages, personalities, and motivations. This means that teachers need to consider the characteristics of their students carefully. (In Chapter 7, a number of concrete suggestions are made for appealing to students of diverse learning styles.)

Sensitivity to Factors Affecting Students' Grammatical Development in a Second Language

Teachers, struck by the numerous grammatical errors their language minority students make, frequently ask whether instruction will help to develop their language minority students' grammar. Unfortunately, it is impossible to give a simple answer to this question. Too many variables affect grammatical development in a second language. These include age, motivation, learning style, and the natural capacity to learn grammatical features. Just ten years ago, nearly all research indicated that grammar teaching had little, if any, facilitating effect on second language development. Teachers were warned to avoid such instruction altogether. However, recently, a number of studies have indicated that some grammar instruction actually improves the *rate* at which second language learners can acquire grammatical structures (for a summary of these studies, see Long 1988). A number of research findings are relevant to this discussion.

In 1981, Krashen proposed the *Natural Order Hypothesis*, which states that language minority learners tend to acquire English grammatical structures in predictable sequences, such that one linguistic structure is acquired before another. This hypothesis predicts, for example, that language minority students will acquire the morpheme *ing* before modal auxiliaries, such as *can, may, might,* and *must.* Although this hypothesis has been highly criticized (see Hatch 1983 for an excellent summary), nearly all researchers concede that language minority students go through similar stages in acquiring grammatical structures. Long and Richards (1987), for instance, state that "learners pass through fundamentally the same stages acquiring grammatical constructions no matter what teachers and textbook writers may do" (p. 27).

Another hypothesis relevant to the teaching of grammar is Krashen's (1981) *Acquisition/Learning Hypothesis.* For Krashen, there are two different and independent ways of developing ability in second language learning. "We can *acquire* and we can *learn. Acquisition* is defined as the process children use to acquire first language" (p. 35). In contrast, *learning* is "conscious, explicit knowledge about the language. Learning is developed, it is thought, by explicit, or formal instruction, and is thought to be aided by the practice of error correction" (p. 35).

Related to this is Krashen's *Monitor Hypothesis,* which states that second language students can use *learned* (rather than *acquired*) grammatical rules to correct their grammar. Krashen states, "conscious learning does not contribute to fluency, but has only one function: it can be used as an editor, or Monitor" (1987, p. 37). His model is depicted in Figure 3–4.

For Krashen, students use conscious learning to make corrections which improve the form of their English. Krashen also points to the growing literature which suggests that the use of conscious learning is very limited. He posits three conditions which need to be met in order to use the Monitor:

1. *Time* (The learner has to have time to use the Monitor; in ordinary conversation, there is not enough time to recall grammar rules and apply them.)
2. *Focus on Form* (The student has to be concerned with correctness.)
3. *Knowledge of Rule* (The student must know accurate rules that work.)

All this means is that it is difficult to use the Monitor and, as a result, it is used infrequently, mostly on compositions and discrete-point tests, tests in which one linguistic structure is tested at a time. It also suggests that adults, more than children, benefit from grammatical

The Monitor
↓

Input → Language Processing Mechanism → Output

Figure 3–4   The Role of the Monitor in Improving ESL Learner Output

(Adapted from Krashen 1981)

explanations, since adults are more capable of using the complex mental gymnastics often needed to use the Monitor effectively. As Krashen suggests, most children are far less competent than adults in learning and applying grammatical rules.

The question arises whether students of some cultures might Monitor their English to a greater extent than students of other cultures. While there is little research available to support this hypothesis, the possibility seems likely (refer to Chapter 7).

A hypothesis relevant to the successful teaching of grammar is Pienemann's (1984) *Learnability/Teachability Hypothesis.* According to Pienemann (1984), students can benefit from classroom instruction of grammatical structures if they are psychologically *ready* to learn the structures and if the structures are *teachable.* As Long (1988) puts it, the *learnability* of a structure constrains its *teachability.* Like Pienemann and Long, Rutherford and Sharwood Smith (1988) also argue that pedagogical grammar may facilitate language development. Long (1988) cites a number of studies which demonstrate that students of all ages may benefit from classroom instruction and that such instruction may increase the rate of English grammatical structure acquisition.

Implications

Taken together, the research findings have the following applications. The Natural Order Hypothesis suggests that grammar errors are a natural part of second language development. Grammatical errors which occur repeatedly and consistently may simply indicate that a student is not quite ready to be using specific structures. Grammatical structures which are used inconsistently, sometimes correctly and sometimes incorrectly, may indicate that the student is in the process of acquiring these structures. Grammar instruction may be particularly useful for students who are capable of using grammar rules to correct their English via the Monitor. Error correction may be helpful if: (1) it does not embarrass students, thus raising their *Socio-Affective Filter*, and (2) they are psychologically *ready* to use the corrections.

Although some grammatical instruction may be helpful, at this time we do not know which. For example, we do not know whether underlining or highlighting grammatical features is more helpful to students than providing explicit grammatical explanations. Moreover, we do not know which grammatical features are most *teachable/learnable* to which students at which particular stages of second language development. What we do know is that if students are not psychologically *ready* to acquire a grammatical structure, it will be impossible to teach them the structure. All this means is that it is probably best to keep comprehensive grammar explanations to a minimum, and to avoid over-emphasis of form and error. Grammar explanations may help adolescent and adult students when presented by teachers who are sensitive to the particular needs of their students. Such explanations may also help teachers maintain their professional stature. After all, many students request these explanations and consider teachers who do not provide them inept. Optimally, such explanations can serve to motivate students who desire grammar rules, improve their ability to monitor their output, and expedite the acquisition of certain grammatical structures. Yet, perhaps even more important than giving such grammar explanations, it is critical that teachers emphasize the importance of good grammar. The psychological impact of stressing the importance of grammatical accuracy may be of critical importance in acquiring a second language.

Reduced Instruction in Mechanical Grammatical Exercises and Related Drills Which Emphasize the Component Parts of Language

Investigations of native English-speaking students have demonstrated the futility of teaching the component parts of English. Even when students can be successfully taught these parts, having this knowledge does not necessarily help them to improve their grammar. All available research indicates that students should not be spending a great deal of time working on isolated component parts of language; rather, they need to engage in meaningful, purposeful activities which employ their experiences in reading, writing, speaking and listening.

Although teachers acknowledge the fact that native English-speaking children do not need to be taught the component parts of grammar, many still believe that students who are not fully proficient in English are especially in need of such instruction because of the many mistakes in grammar these students make. They believe that their job is to teach their language minority students by mechanical grammar drills. Yet, teachers will not help their language minority students acquire grammatically correct English by using such drills. Most students are unable to successfully transfer their mechanical control of grammatical patterns to real communicative situations. Moreover, language proficiency cannot be compartmentalized in this way. It is difficult, if not impossible to separate different aspects of language competence without referring to their context of use. Nativelike knowledge of English includes more than knowledge of the grammatical rules of the language. Among other things, it includes knowledge of vocabulary, pronunciation, conversation rules (for example, how to open and close a conversation), and register (knowing how to speak in specific situations such as at the doctor's office). (This is further discussed in Chapter 8.)

Implications

There is no longer any reason to utilize mechanical grammar drills which isolate language components in the teaching of ESL.

Reduced Instruction Relying Solely on Comparisons of the First and Second Language (That Is, Contrastive Analysis)

In the 1960s, many ESL pedagogues believed that most of the difficulties facing language minority students came from differences between the first and second languages. It was assumed that where the first and second languages differed, the first language would somehow interfere with the second language, resulting in *negative transfer*, and where the first language and the second language were similar, the first language would help second language learning (resulting in *positive transfer*). Brooks (1960) and Lado (1964) advanced this position. A procedure called *Contrastive Analysis* was developed to establish differences between the first and second languages. Many language pedagogues in the 1960s advocated using contrastive analysis in language teaching. It was thought that showing students the differences between the first and second languages would help the students acquire their second language.

In the 1970's, however, researchers learned that language transfer does not play a central role in second language acquisition. The findings of such researchers as Dulay and Burt (1973), for example, indicated that a large proportion of grammatical errors could not be explained by first language interference.

More recently, researchers have provided richer, more accurate contrastive analyses of learner languages. Research reported in the edited volume of Gass and Selinker (1983), for instance, has demonstrated some of the factors which affect transfer. We now know, for instance, that students tend to transfer some features from the first language more readily than they transfer others. For example, pronunciation appears to be more affected by first language transfer than many aspects of grammar. Older students also tend to retain those features from their first language which they perceive as serving to maintain their ethnic identity. This explains why adults from Japan who have lived in the United States for more than twenty years (such as Professor Fujisaki) continue to have difficulty producing *l*'s and *r*'s. In addition, learners tend to transfer those features from their first language which are most congruent with their own personalities. For instance, some Latinos continue to greet others with *un abrazo* (a hug) even when they have lived here all their lives, perhaps because they perceive the absence of such hugs as *cold* or *indifferent*. Age also appears to affect transfer. Children appear to transfer to a lesser extent than do adults. It is also interesting to note that students transfer between similar languages to a greater extent than they transfer from dissimilar ones. This has been referred to as the *Language Distance Hypothesis* (Kellerman 1979).[3]

Code-switching (that is, the alternating use of two languages, refer to Chapter 1) should not be confused with language transfer.

When learners code-switch, they switch from one language to the other to communicate their messages effectively. Valdes-Fallis (1981) defines and illustrates some of the typical patterns of code-switching in Table 3–1.

As the examples illustrate, code-switching is a common communicative strategy that may indicate advanced levels of proficiency in both languages. (See also Chapter 1.) In describing code-switching, Valdes (1988) states:

> By alternating between their languages, bilinguals are able to use their total speech repertoire, which includes many levels and styles and modes of speaking in two languages. It is helpful to imagine that when bilinguals code-switch, they are in fact using a twelve-string guitar, rather than limiting themselves to two six-string instruments. (p. 126)

Implications

The research suggests drills which contrast language structures in the first and second languages do not facilitate second language development. Children, in particular, who lack the cognitive abilities to understand language comparisons, are unlikely to benefit from contrastive analyses. Krashen (1983) asserts that transfer is most apparent in acquisition-poor environments where there is little access to peers who speak the second language. With few models available, students must fall back on their still-incomplete knowledge of the second language. Teachers who want their older students to avoid first language transfer might do what Krashen suggests: help them acquire more English.

Table 3–1
Principal Code-Switching Patterns

Patterns	Definitions	Examples
Situational switches	Related to the social role of speakers	Mother uses Spanish to chat with daughters but switches to English to reprimand son
Contextual switches	Situation, topic setting, etc., linked to the other language	Students switch to English to discuss details of a math exam
Identity markers	In-group member-ship stressed	*Ese bato, órale, ándale pues,* used in English conversations regardless of actual Spanish fluency

(continued)

Table 3–1
Continued

Patterns	Definitions	Examples
Quotations and paraphrases	Contextual: related to language used by the original speaker	Y lo (luego) me dijó el Mr. Johnson que *I have to study.* (Remark was actually made in English.)
Random switches of high-frequency items	Unpredictable; do not relate to the topic, situation, setting, or language dominance; occur *only* on word level	Very common words such as days of the week or colors. Function like English synonyms: gal-girl; guy-fellow, etc. Fuimos al *party* ayer y estuvo tan suave la fiesta.
Switches that reflect lexical need	Related to language dominance, memory, and spontaneous versus automatic speech	Include the *tip of the tongue* phenomenon; item may be momentarily forgotten
Triggered switches	Due to preceding or following items	Yo lo ví, you know, *but I didn't speak to him.* (Switch is triggered by preformulation.)
Preformulations	Include linguistic routines and automatic speech	*You know, glad to meet you, thanks for calling, no te molestes, que hay de nuevo,* etc.
Discourse markers	*But, and, of course,* etc.	*Este . . . este . . .* yo sí quería ir.
Quotations and paraphrases	Noncontextual: not related to language used by original speaker	He insisted *que no me fuera.* But I did anyway. (Remark was originally made in English.)
Stylistic switches	Obvious stylistic devices used for emphasis or contrast	Me tomé toda la cafetera, *the whole coffee pot.*
Sequential switches	Involve using the last language used by the preceding speaker	Certain speakers will always follow the language switches of other speakers; others will not.

Source: Valdes-Fallis 1978, p. 16

Continuous and Substantial Exposure to Large Quantities of Written and Spoken English Which Is Comprehensible to ESL Students

Krashen's (1985) *Comprehensible Input Hypothesis* is directly relevant here. Applications of this hypothesis are discussed in Chapter 4. Krashen describes three components of his hypothesis as follows:

1. We acquire by understanding input containing structures that are just a little bit beyond our current competence. In terms of the Natural Order hypothesis, we move from our current level i to the next level $i + 1$ by understanding input containing $i + 1$.

   We acquire, the hypothesis states, by going for meaning, by focusing on what is said rather than how it is said. We are aided in this process by extralinguistic context (for instance, pictures and hand movements), and our knowledge of the world. We do not acquire by first learning about the structure of the language. We try to understand the message, and structure is thereby acquired.

2. *Speaking* emerges. We do not teach speaking but give acquirers comprehensible input. Speech will come on its own, when the acquirer feels ready. Early speech is not grammatically accurate, but accuracy develops as the acquirer obtains more comprehensible input.

3. The best input is not grammatically sequenced. Rather, if the acquirer understands the input presented, and enough of it is made available, $i + 1$, the structures will be automatically sequenced. Not only is it not necessary, but it may be harmful, when the goal is acquisition (this is not the case when the goal is conscious learning). The acquirers will receive comprehensible input containing structures just a little beyond them if they are in situations involving genuine communication, and these structures will be constantly provided and automatically reviewed. They need not worry about missing the past tense forever (or at least until next year). With natural, comprehensible input, the hypothesis predicts that they will hear the past tense again and again. (pp. 38–39)

Much of Krashen's work was based on research on what is variously called *baby-talk* or *motherese* (the conversation between mothers and babies) and *foreigner talk* (the conversation between native and non-native English-speakers). Conversation to babies and non-native English-speakers was classified as *simplified* in that it relied less heavily on complex syntactic structures than did conversations between adult native English-speakers. Adults speaking to second language learners were found to adjust their speech to the linguistic and cognitive levels of the learners. In so doing, they use a slower rate of speaking, containing longer pauses between major constituents, clear articulation, a high pitch, and simple vocabulary items. Perhaps most characteristic of such simplified speech is the focus on the *here and now.* That is, native English-speakers tend to discuss topics which are firmly anchored in the present and are frequently contextualized, as in the following example.

> Native English-Speaker: Do you want the book?
> Non-Native English-Speaker: What?
> Native English-Speaker: Book. Book. Big red book. Do you want this book? (picks up book and hands it to non-native English speaker)

As seen in this example, simple repetitions and restatements are also characteristic (see Hatch 1983 for an excellent review of simplified speech). Such modifications are a natural outcome of communication and may facilitate the student's task of communicating and making sense of the English input she received.

Corder (1967) pointed out that all input does not help second language development. As he explains, just presenting a certain linguistic form does not necessarily qualify it for the status of *intake;* input is *what goes in* not what is *available* for going in. Thus, for Corder, only a small portion of the input serves as intake. This notion is illustrated in Figure 3–5.

When discussing input, it is also important to consider who provides that input. As Romaine (1984) states:

> Even in so-called *mainstream* middle-class white societies which have been so extensively studied, it is the case that in a child's

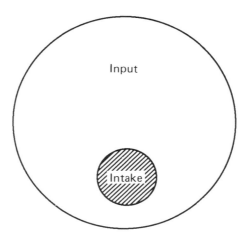

Figure 3–5   Input and Intake

adolescent years other adolescents become more important than adults in providing models. An increasing amount of sociolinguistic research on the structure of intra-group communication has revealed that one of the most important influences in the development of communicative competence is the style of speaking used in peer group interaction and the continuous monitoring from peers to which members are subjected. Studies of peer group language provide us not only with data on the learning of new speech styles but also with important information on how a child may restructure certain aspects of speech in conformity with peer group pressures. (p. 183)

Most school-aged children have some sense of ethnic-identity and are able to identify children of other cultures. However, ethnic identity is most strongly formed during adolescence. (see Labov 1972.) It is especially during this time when peer groups can exert such powerful influences on language minority students that they force these students to conform to group norms which are different from those of their families and schools. Peer group pressure may even extend to school-related areas such as levels of acceptable academic progress and language ability (Labov 1972). Yet, in many situations, language minority students do not learn English from their peers. Wong-Fillmore (1985) states:

> Contrary to the usual assumption that children learn language mainly from peers outside the classroom and not from teachers, it appears that for many LEP (limited English proficient) students, the only place in which they come into regular contact with English speakers is at school. Their language learning, if it is going to take place at all, is going to happen at school. The classroom can be an ideal place to learn English if it allows students to be in close and continuous contact with teachers and classmates who speak the target language (English) well enough to help in its learning. (p. 19)

Related to the question of input is that of the *silent period.* According to Krashen (1982), there is a silent period in which limited English proficient students need to observe others communicating prior to communicating in English themselves. By observing others, Krashen argues, second language students gain both the proficiency and the confidence to participate in conversations with native-English speakers. For Krashen, this period is particularly apparent in child second language learning. He states, ". . . young children in a new country facing a new language may say nothing (except for some memorized sentences and phrases) for several months" (pp. 38–39). According to Krashen, this is a time during which they are building up second language proficiency. When they have acquired enough, they will start to talk.[4]

Vygotsky's notion of the *zone of proximal development* is relevant to this discussion. A zone of proximal development can be considered a map of a student's sphere of readiness to acquire the second language. It is bounded at the lower end by the student's existing level of competence and at the upper end by the competence the student can achieve under favorable circumstances, such as when the student is helped by a friend who is proficient in the second language.

Implications

In brief, we need to create favorable circumstances which allow students to obtain rich sources of comprehensible input.

Regular and Substantial Interaction in English in a Wide Variety of Situations with a Variety of Speakers, Both Inside and Outside of School

Although exposure to input is essential, it does not guarantee mastery. The need for active student participation suggests that interaction is also important. Swain (1986) found that native English-speaking students who were immersed in Canadian French immersion schools and were constantly exposed to comprehensible input did not completely acquire French grammar. She agrees with Long (1983) and others who state that it is not input per se that is important in second language acquisition, but input that occurs in meaningful interaction with others. Since the Canadian immersion students had few chances to use their French in subject-matter classes in which teachers do most of the talking and students do most of the listening, she believes the grammatical development of immersion students suffers because of their relatively limited opportunity to interact. To explain this phenomenon, Swain (1986) proposed the *Comprehensible Output Hypothesis* which suggests that students need tasks which elicit what she terms *comprehensible output*. For Swain, such output consists of talk at the student's i + 1, that is, a level of second language proficiency which is just a bit beyond the current second language proficiency level. She claims that such output provides opportunities for meaningful context-embedded use for the second language which allows students to test out their hypotheses about the language and "move the learner from a purely semantic analysis of the language to a syntactic analysis of it" (p. 252).

Linguists, such as Hatch et al. 1987, Hatch 1983 and Long 1981, have argued that language is acquired by interacting with others. This is consistent with findings "which show that many forms of competence develop through personal interaction in which more skilled individuals guide less skilled, who assist each other through words or actions" (McGroarty 1988, p. 314). Interaction, not only the availability of appropriate comprehensible input, results in second language development.

Implications

Students require experience in using English for a wide range of purposes. Language minority students of all ages need to develop experience in the widest possible array of real, meaningful, contexts. (For more concrete suggestions, see Chapter 5.)

The Opportunity to Communicate for Real, Personally Significant Purposes

Where school programs have stressed using English for a broad range of real purposes, the language minority students' language skills have shown substantial growth. If we are to convince students of the value of mastering English, we need to show them that it is a useful activity. We need to help them find it valuable to use English to accomplish purposes that they themselves desire. They need to use the language about things which matter. This means that teachers need to create speaking and writing tasks that offer genuine opportunities for students to explore, investigate and learn.

There is increasing evidence that active engagement in real communication facilitates second language development. According to Lindfors (1987), when successful language minority students speak, they do not just practice using English for the real thing; communication *is* the real thing. Like Lindfors, Wong-Fillmore (1989) suggests that Latino children benefit from interesting, challenging, relevant tasks in which their teachers provide them opportunities to communicate to accomplish real objectives.

Implications

Unfortunately, communication for real, personally significant purposes is often rare for language minority students in content classes. Limited English proficient students have a particular need for this sort of activity. They need to interact with others whose English is a little better than their own. Tasks which require students to communicate vital information exert a natural pressure on students to edit and revise their writing, and practice and perfect their speech. (This is further discussed in Chapter 6.)

We need to challenge students to take on more and more responsibility for using English to accomplish real goals. We need to demonstrate that they can successfully communicate and develop their confidence in their own abilities to acquire the second language and academic skills.

Conclusion

Principle 2: *Understand language development* implies that language minority students can succeed in content-area classes when their instructors are aware of the factors which affect their language acquisition. This chapter discussed these factors. In the next chapters, these factors will be examined in greater detail. I could not begin to do justice to the research on second language acquisition in one chapter. Readers will want to review the books and journals listed at the end of this chapter.

ACTIVITIES AND DISCUSSION QUESTIONS

1. Some researchers have used the term, *alingualism*, when describing bilinguals who are unable to communicate in either their first or second languages. For Seville-Troike (1979) *alingualism* is non-existent since all students are capable of communicating in specific situations. Do you agree with her opinion? If not, how could you determine whether your students were really *alingual*? Some researchers advance the notion of *semilingualism*, which they use when describing second language students who speak nonstandard varieties of their first and second languages. Does *semi-lingualism* really exist and, if so, how could you test for its existence?

2. Work out what you think would be the advantages and disadvantages of formal grammar instruction with respect to:

   • different age groups (children, preadolescents, adolescents, young adults, older adults, etc.)
   • different educational settings
   • different personalities and learning styles
   • different cultural backgrounds

3. Cummins suggests that two different types of proficiencies are distinct in second language, BICS (basic interpersonal communication skills) and CALP (cognitive academic language proficiency). BICS enables students to participate in everyday communicative exchanges, while CALP enables students to deal in decontextualized language contexts such as academic settings. Cummins' research indicates that BICS is acquired in three to four years and CALP is acquired in seven to eight years. Critically evaluate Cummins' BICS/CALP distinction. What practical application does this distinction have for language instruction?

4. Hatch (1983) provides the following summary of the features of simplified input (the input that mothers give children and native speakers give non-native speakers).

CHARACTERISTICS OF SIMPLIFIED INPUT

Pronunciation

Fewer reduced vowels and contractions
Benefits: Student receives the full word form.
Slow rate
Benefits: Articulation is clearer and easier to understand.

Longer pauses
Benefits: Student can easily hear and attend to language.

Vocabulary

High frequency vocabulary, less slang and fewer idioms
Benefits: Student is more likely to understand words and recognize topic.
Fewer pronoun forms
Benefits: Reference should be clearer.
Definitions are marked. (*This is an X; It's a kinda X.*)
Benefits: Definitions should be salient.
Gestures and pictures accompany lexical items
Benefits: Increases comprehensibility.
Endearment terms
Benefits: May give an affective boost to learning.

Grammar

Short MLU (mean length of utterance; for example, *I see big green ball,* instead of I *see the big ball that is green.*)
Benefits: Should be easier to process and analyze.
Left dislocation of topic (*Friday, Saturday, you have a nice weekend.*)
Benefits: Should be easier to identify topic.
Repetition and restatement
Benefits: Should allow more processing time.
Native speaker fills in the blank
(Non-native speaker: *The car went*
Native speaker: *Over the cliff.*)
Benefits: Provides a model of syntax.

Discourse (Conversation)

More requests for clarification (such as *What? Huh? What do you mean?*)
Benefit: Helps student communicate.
Fewer interruptions
Benefit: Easier to understand.
Conversation components (such as the openings and the ends of conversations)
(*Okay, this is the end of the interview. Good-bye.*)
Benefit: Makes conversation flow more smoothly.
More frames, such as okay (*Okay, this is a green ball, okay?*)
Benefit: Helps student identify utterances.
(Adapted from Hatch 1983, pp. 183–184)
To what extent do you believe teachers can or should simplify their

speech to their language minority students who are at an intermediate stage of English language development and are unable to understand everything their teachers say in English?

USEFUL JOURNALS FOR THOSE INTERESTED IN SECOND LANGUAGE ACQUISITION

Applied Linguistics. Oxford University Press. Walton Street, Oxford, OX2 6DP, England and 200 Madison Avenue, New York, New York, 10016

Canadian Modern Language Review. 237 Hellems Avenue, Welland, Ontario L3B 3B8

English around the World. The English-speaking Union of the United States: 16 East 69th Street, New York, New York 10021

English Language Teaching Journal. Oxford University Press: Walton Street, Oxford OX2 6DP. England and 200 Madison Avenue, New York, New York 10016

Foreign Language Annals. American Council on Teaching Foreign Languages, Inc., 579 Broadway, Hastings-on-Hudson, New York 10706

Language Learning. N4714 University Hospital, University of Michigan, Ann Arbor, Michigan 48109

TESL Canada Journal. TESL Canada Journal, Faculty of Education, McGill University, 3700 McTavish Street, Montreal PQ H3A IY2

TESOL Quarterly. 202 DC Transit Building, Georgetown University, Washington D.C. 20057

International Journal of Applied Linguistics. Julius Groos Verlag, PO Box 102423, Hertzstrasse 6, D-6900 Heidelberg, Germany; back issues may be ordered from Canon House, Folkestone, Ken CT 195EE, England

National Association for Bilingual Education. 1201 16th Street, North West, Rook 407, Washington D.C. 20036.

Studies in Second Language Acquisition. Cambridge University Press, 32, East 57th Street, New York, New York 10022 or outside the United States, to Cambridge University Press, the Edinburgh Building, Shaftesbury Road, Cambridge CB2 2Ru. England

RECOMMENDED READING

BEEBE, L. M. (ed.) 1988. *Issues in Second Language Acquisition.* New York: Harper and Row. This anthology contains recent state-of-the-art overviews of psycholinguistic, sociolinguistic, neurolinguistic, classroom research, and bilingual perspectives on second language acquisition.

KRASHEN, S. D. 1982. *Principles and Practice in Second Language Acquisition.* New York: Pergamon Press. Discusses the research underlying Krashen's theory of second language acquisition; provides practical implications from his theory.

WELLS-LINDFORS, J. 1987. *Children's Language and Learning,* second edition. Englewood-Cliffs, New Jersey: Prentice Hall. Although primarily designed for educators of native English-speaking children, this book also contains information relevant to teachers of non-native English-speaking children; focusing on first language acquisition, language structure, and language learning.

NOTES

1. In critically reviewing the Threshold Hypothesis, McGroarty (1988) states, "The existence of a higher threshold in particular remains highly speculative, as Cummins admits . . . . the evidence adduced in its favor mainly shows that more language skills (in both languages) are better, not that there is a specific cut-off point that triggers other cognitive outcomes" (p. 302).

2. See Gardner and Lambert (1972) for a detailed discussion of the role of motivation in second language acquisition.

3. Thus, Spanish speakers acquiring a similar language such as French would be more likely to transfer than would Chinese speakers who are acquiring a dissimilar language, such as English.

4. It should be noted that Krashen's notion of comprehensible input is frequently criticized. In many cultures, children learn languages without receiving any simplified input at all. Whatever one's view on the facilitating effect of comprehensible input, common sense tells us that it is better to provide our students with input they understand.

CHAPTER FOUR

Providing Comprehensible Lessons

One of our most difficult tasks is providing language minority students with comprehensible English input. Unfortunately, many language minority students do not understand our input. Others, who do understand, fail to respond to our input in meaningful ways which facilitate second language development.

In light of this problem, this chapter suggests strategies for providing language minority students with comprehensible lessons which aid English language development. Strategies which facilitate comprehension should be consistent with several key principles: (1) they should promote English input which is tailored to the students' English proficiency levels; (2) they should involve students in purposeful communication (see also Chapter 3); and (3) they should provide students with *enough* input to facilitate their English language development.

PRINCIPLES FOR PROVIDING LANGUAGE MINORITY STUDENTS WITH INPUT WHICH AIDS SECOND LANGUAGE DEVELOPMENT

Principle 1: Provide Input at the Appropriate Level

Research on children's English language development has shown that children often "unconsciously internalize and then experiment with patterns they hear in the speech going on around them" (Farr and Daniels 1986, p. 60). When students either hear or read English, they may internalize English vocabulary and grammar. Yet, mere exposure to English input may not necessarily facilitate English language development. According to Krashen (1982, 1983, 1985a), optimal input for language minority students approximates their English language proficiency levels. Vygotsky (1978) suggests that it is aimed at the learner's *proximal zone* of English language development. For Vygotsky, input shuld be aimed at the upper limit of a student's sphere of readiness. For Krashen, it is neither too difficult nor too easy. If the input is too easy, the student won't learn anything new about English, but if the input is too hard to understand, it will be beyond the student's grasp.

Principle 2: Get Students to Use the Input for Purposeful Communication

The second principle concerns getting students to respond to English input in meaningful communication. In providing spoken input, we need to ask ourselves what it is we are requiring our students to listen to. As Lindfors (1987) explains: "In the real world, there is usually a reason to listen and when there isn't a reason, we stop listening. We listen to find out something we don't already know, or to establish a caring relationship with someone else." (p. 379) Lindfors laments that many children are coerced to listen. A common remark heard in the elementary school is, *Listen so you'll know where we are when I call on you.* Lindfors asks, "would you or I listen if we were in the child's place?" (p. 379). As she points out, "real listening requires mental activity, the processing of new information, the integrating of new information into one's existing cognitive structure, the encounter with the new idea that triggers a new question one never had before" (p. 380).

Engaging students in meaningful interaction appears to aid the acquisition and retention of input. Like input, assignments requiring output (that is, the English your students actually use) must reflect the proficiency levels for which they are intended, being neither too easy nor too difficult for the students. If students are not challenged by the output tasks you give them, their linguistic abilities are not expanded. If, on the other hand, the output tasks are too difficult they may find means of feigning English proficiency, (for example, by plagiarizing term papers or making oral presentations which have been written by friends and memorized in their entirety). Feigning competence in English probably never facilitates second language acquisition and is, in fact, reported to interfere with second language development (Krashen 1982). English output, like English input, must be tailored to the learner's *proximal zone*. (This is further discussed in Chapter 5.)

Principle 3: Provide *Enough* Input

The third principle suggests that second language development is facilitated when students are exposed to sufficient amounts of English input. Where classrooms have provided input reflecting a broad range of language uses, students' English skills have shown substantial growth. Students should also be exposed to input which represents the language they need to use. For example, within the elementary classroom, students need adequate exposure to others doing *show and tell* so that they, too, can participate in this classroom activity. Within the secondary classroom, they need adequate exposure to the language of discussions, oral presentations and debates so that they can participate in these activities.

Unfortunately, the amount of input required to learn English has probably been grossly underestimated. Cummins (1981), for example, suggests that it takes language minority students approximately six to seven years to acquire native-like competence in what he terms, *Cognitive Academic Language Proficiency* (CALP), and two to three years to become proficient in *Basic Interpersonal Competence* (BICS). For Cummins, CALP enables ESL students to succeed in academic areas, while BICS enables language minority students to communicate with one another in informal situations. Regardless of how long it takes for students to acquire English, our goal is the same: to give all students adequate exposure to English and the occasions to use this input.

> The fact is, it takes time to learn English. No matter what you do with them (your ESL students), whether you put them in a special classroom and teach them English and provide a lot of support, it still takes time. Some put a child in a class for a year or two to learn English and meanwhile forget learning math, forget art, forget social studies. I don't think we can do that. I think we simply have to be more patient and know that it may take one child five years to become proficient, it may take another child ten years. Our goal is the same, though — to educate.
> Vicky Campos, Bilingual Specialist, Orange County
> (reported in Olsen 1988, p. 57)

As discussed in Chapter 3, what may be even more important than sufficient amounts of input may be sufficient opportunity for negotiated meaning. (See Chapter 5.)

STRATEGIES FOR PROVIDING LEARNERS WITH COMPREHENSIBLE INPUT

In the remainder of this chapter I discuss pedagogical strategies which: (1) facilitate the comprehension of spoken and written English; and (2) are consistent with the principles previously discussed. Cultural obstacles to comprehension are discussed in the following.

Tailoring Spoken English to Your Students' Proficiency Levels

As discussed already, it is important to provide English which approximates the proficiency levels of your students. As Krashen (1981) points out, an exact fit is not needed and is probably not possible in natural communication. Simplifying your talk to the students is an important strategy. Redundant, slow speech which is focused on the concrete rather than the abstract is hypothesized to facilitate comprehension by second language learners in much the same way that it is thought to do in the case of many first language learners. Slower, redundant speech gives students more time to process language input. However, it is not necessary to slow down your speech to such an extent as to distort normal intonation. This could appear condescending to students. Here is how an elementary teacher might simplify language for a student who is just beginning to acquire English:

Student:	I throw it - box. (He points to a box on the floor.)
Teacher:	You threw the box.
Student:	No, I threw in the box.
Teacher:	What did you throw in the box?
Student:	My . . . I paint . . .
Teacher:	Your painting?
Student:	Painting?
Teacher:	You know . . . painting. (The teacher makes painting movement on an imaginary paper.)
Student:	Yes, painting.
Teacher:	You threw your painting in the box.
Student:	Yes, I threw my painting in the box.

(Richard-Amato 1988, p. 40)

As illustrated in the example, simplified speech is focused on the immediate environment and contains simple vocabulary, frequent repetitions, explanations, and paraphrases.

Reinforcing key ideas again and again in a variety of situations and activities also aids comprehension. Talking about concepts once or twice is not enough. Students need to be exposed to them several times through a wide range of experiences. If activities are varied, students will not be bored by the repetitive nature of the input. For example, before writing a report, it is helpful for high school students to discuss their report with peers, brainstorm on paper, gather information from books, interview others about their topic, and make oral presentations about their topic.

Relating topics to one another throughout your lesson is an additional way to aid your students' comprehension. For instance, Enright and McCloskey (1988) suggest integrating a series of related topics using speaking, listening, reading and writing activities. In their unit entitled, *Rain Makes Applesauce*, designed for second through fifth graders, students participate in a variety of activities including science, math, literature, art, field trips and cooking "centered on the theme of apples" (p. 281). When topics are related, the syntactic structures and vocabulary words are repeated so that students get additional chances to understand the input (Krashen and Terrell 1983). Homework assignments which are directly related to classroom activities are an excellent way of increasing your students' comprehension of the material. Assignments which are unrelated do not build on your students' existing proficiency.

Your lessons can also be made more comprehensible through contextual support. Audio-visual aids can facilitate the students' understanding of language. Photos/pictures, sketches (overhead transparencies, charts, blackboard), realia (including food), body motions (such as sewing, drinking, hopping), gestures (come here), and facial expressions (such as putting on a sad face) all aid comprehension. Pantomime and puppetry provide additional opportunities for students to hear and use English with rich contextual support. Brown and Palmer (1987) also suggest that teachers of ESL students should have "an almost endless supply of props" (p. 19) and advice ESL teachers to take a lesson from a kindergarten room.

Finding Out/Descubrimiento (originally designed by De Avila and Duncan [1980] to teach science and math), exposes children in second through fifth grades to complex concepts in the areas of mathematics, physics and chemistry. It has been successful in providing language minority students with comprehensible input through intrinsically interesting manipulatives. Students in heterogeneous groups complete the worksheet in each learning center. They take on different roles and help each other in these roles. Students are trained to help one another, to ask questions, offer assistance, explain, and help others without finishing tasks for them.

One particular approach specifically designed to aid comprehension in foreign language and ESL classes is *Total Physical Response* (Asher 1965, 1966, 1969). At first, the technique entails only giving simple commands to students, such as *Stand up* or *Come here*. However, content teachers can incorporate more complex commands for ESL students who are more proficient in English. This approach has already been successfully used in content courses with many different age groups. For example, math teachers ask students to draw squares, right angles, circles, etc.; geography teachers ask students to point to various capitals on maps; and physical education instructors ask students to do a number of exercises.

Preparing students for your lessons further facilitates comprehension. Before your lessons, you can give a brief overview of the content and teach specific study skills for a particular lesson. You can also give your students study guides, frameworks and outlines, which encourage students to look for the main ideas of your lessons. It is useful to explain new or unfamiliar concepts that will cause confusion before instruction begins. Here is how secondary teachers in Canada use charts when teaching about the early sea exploration of the Pacific Northwest Coast. The teachers provide students with charts and, after lecturing to students, ask them to fill in the missing information. Students are then called on to produce an oral or written report using the chart as a basis. Figure 4–1 contains the chart.[1]

Classroom management strategies can aid comprehension in a more global way. Establishing regular predictable classroom events (such as story time, quiz time, and study period) with clearly delineated beginnings and ends also aids comprehension. In investigating good ESL classrooms, Wong-Fillmore (1985) found that "the lessons that appear to work well for language learning were formal, scheduled

Figure 4-1

Early Explorers

Who?	When?	How?	Where?
Russian-Bering		by sea	to Alaska and the Aleutians
Spanish-San José	1774		from Mexico to 55°N.
English-?	1776	by sea	to Nootka Sound

Reproduced from Mohan (1986, p. 27)

lessons with clear boundaries. The beginnings of small group lessons were usualy marked by an actual change in the physical location of the students . . ." (p. 27). She goes on to give some examples of how teachers marked the beginning of their lessons by asking their students to turn their seats around and face one another or move to a specific place in the classroom. They also use formulaic expressions (such as "Tigers and bears over here.") when announcing the beginning of activities. "An impressive consistency in the use of such features was found across lessons in the successful classes. The teachers in these classes tended to follow the same pattern day after day in the way they bracketed their lessons. There was no evidence in these classes of children who appeared not to know where to go, or what to expect at this level, no matter how little English they seem to know." (p. 28) As Wong-Fillmore points out, using the same conversational routines with these activities facilitates the students' comprehension. It also avoids wasting time getting organized since "students knew what to expect and what to do procedurally, because the routine was well established" (p. 28). Students come to expect such conversational routines as "Everyone line up for snack time" or, "Put your books on the floor and take out a sheet of paper." Similarly, it facilitates comprehension when you explain the purpose and procedures of classroom activities.

Wong-Fillmore (1985) also suggests that teachers who successfully teach language minority students are consistent in the lesson format which they use.

In reading lessons, for example, a teacher might follow a format like this: present new vocabulary items used in the text at hand; elicit discussion on the meanings and the uses of the new words and relate them to known words; have the group read the text silently; have individuals take turns reading paragraphs in the text; discuss the meaning of the text with the students; and finally, make an assignment for seatwork to be done individually. While lacking in creativity, such a lesson format soon becomes familiar enough to all students so that they are able to participate easily. (p. 47)

In the list below Wong-Fillmore summarizes structural characteristics that have worked well for language learning.

1. They were formal lessons with clear boundaries:
   - Boundaries marked by changes in location, props
   - Beginnings and ends marked by formulaic cues

2. They were regularly scheduled events:
   - Scheduled time for activity
   - Scheduled place for activity

3. Clear lesson format across groups, from day to day
   - Clear instructions, lesson phases clearly marked

(adapted from Wong-Fillmore 1985, pp. 49-50)

When possible, teachers need to arrange time to communicate individually with language minority students. Talking individually to your students enables you to tailor your speech to their proficiency levels and determine their difficulties in understanding you. A study by Schinke-Llano (1980) suggests that teachers interact very little with their language minority students. Of the language minority student/teacher interactions Schinke-Llano examined, most were brief and managerial (as in "Be quiet.," "Open the book.," and "Come here.)." In Schinke-Llano's words, ". . . the cumulative effect of this pattern over a month's or year's time is staggering" (p. 159) since such impoverished interaction is unlikely to improve the learner's English. Teachers who do not interact with students sometimes oversimplify their speech and over-emphasize the concrete. They end up by enhancing their students' "inability" to deal with abstract thought.

Lectures are appropriate in many classroom situations. Yet, they present particular difficulties for language minority students. Due to the absence of direct and continuous verbal and nonverbal feedback from students, teachers are normally unable to tailor their speech to their students' proficiency levels. Teachers also tend to lecture to those students whose English skills and ethnic identity match their own. Skillful teachers do not assume their students understand their lectures. They make a special effort to look at all students when they speak and check to make sure all students understand (see Chapter 6). They also use preview and follow-up activities whenever possible and write important words and phrases on the chalkboard or on the overhead transparency as they talk. Richard-Amato (1988) gives this advice to teachers. "Use pictures and charts, map out ideas, use gestures, act out, use simplifications, expansions or ideas or whatever is necessary to ensure understanding" (p. 234). She also suggests that it is beneficial: (1) to record your lectures or talks on tape (so that students can listen to them as many times as they need to understand); and (2) to encourage native English-speaking students who take effective, comprehensible notes to share these notes with language minority students.

Providing Enough Spoken Input

Although second language students usually receive at least some English input from the environment, they often return to homes in which they only hear their native tongue. Their classroom may be the only place many second language students receive comprehensible English input. This makes it critical for schools to provide language minority students with large quantities of comprehensible English input.

A variety of professionally audio- and video-taped recordings provide excellent sources of additional input for language minority students. The teacher can make these recordings available at listening and video centers where students can use them as often as they like. The advantage of audio- and video-tapes is that students can use them again and again so that they have additional opportunities to hear and understand the input.

Television and radio programs provide yet another potentially rich source of input. These provide models of a wide range of language uses. Programs such as *Sesame Street* are appropriate means of teaching young children vocabulary, reading skills, and cultural information. Cartoons, which are appropriate for older children, often contain a wealth of vocabulary. Game shows and situation comedies, appropriate for students in the upper grades and beyond, provide students with occasions to hear English lexical, grammatical and conversational features.

Field trips offer a rich source of input for language minority students. A trip to the local library, museum, or movie theatre can enlarge your students' exposure to English. In addition to visits to interesting places, visits to (and by) interesting people (such as government officials, physicians, and chemists) can also provide valuable input.

Other excellent sources of input include conversation groups where language minority students converse with native English-speaking peers, *buddy* systems in which native English-speaking students are paired with language minority students, and school clubs and athletic groups. These sources allow students to continue acquiring comprehensible input even after your class has ended.

The cooperative learning activities proposed by Kagan (1989) involve various group activities which aid the language minority student's understanding of the lesson. In these groups, members are encouraged to check to make sure everyone understands by giving explanations whenever necessary and frequently paraphrasing what others say.

For language minority students who have low English proficiency, peer teaching/tutoring can also provide valuable input. The more proficient learners can help the less proficient learners. Such tutoring is especially valued by Latino, Asian, and native American students who are accustomed to more cooperative learning approaches and are used to peer teaching/tutoring. (See Chapter 7.)

Over the last ten years, a number of practical activities have been designed to aid the language minority student's listening comprehension. I have discussed just a few major ones here. For additional activities, see Krashen and Terrell (1983), Brown and Palmer (1987), and Richard-Amato (1988).

Using Spoken English Purposefully

You can make the content of your lessons even more comprehensible by involving the students in purposeful communication. At the elementary level, students can visit museums, parks, and stores; make puppets; draw maps, etc. At the secondary level, students can participate in demonstrations, experiments and projects.

Engaging students in a project *immediately* after its explanation can be very effective. Here is how one kindergarten teacher describes how she does this:

> Part of my (learning) center requires the children to make a Color Blob Animal by putting paint in the center of the paper, folding, seeing new animals and then drawing new parts to the blob . . . . I had a chart that had words plus the pictures of the steps. I demonstrated and had individual children use words to tell what I was doing — GREAT. Then I had a child show the steps and had many others tell the rest of the class the instructions.
>
> (reported in Enright 1986, p. 144)

Group activities can also provide students with multiple opportunities to communicate purposefully. Those students who have already acquired the English skills necessary to participate verbally in class activities successfully can serve as language models for less proficient speakers. These activities increase your students' opportunities to use the language. Group activities also provide language minority students with more comprehensible input since, in interaction, speakers shape their speech to the needs of their listeners. Keep in mind, however, that the social risks involved in face-to-face interaction may intimidate those students from less verbal backgrounds. Students may be unwilling to risk interaction that might subject them to ridicule in peer sessions or cause them to receive low evaluations from their teachers. The verbal traditions of language play, debate, show and tell and bed-time story-telling prevalent in the United States are entirely absent in many Asian, Latin American and native American cultures.

Interviews, role-plays, simulations, problem-solving activities and games are other activities which can be used to encourage purposeful communication. It is important to bear in mind, however, that speaking tasks vary in terms of their difficulty. Face-to-face interaction (in pair or group work) is far easier for students than oral reports and debates. Also, keep in mind that students from some countries (such as Iran, Turkey, and some Latin American countries) value spoken interaction to a greater extent than students from other countries (such as Korea, Taiwan, Vietnam, and Cambodia). (This does not imply that we should expect less from our Asian students; rather we need to carefully structure our speaking activities to include their participation; refer to Chapter 5.)

Gearing Written English to Your Students' Proficiency Levels

Just as language minority students need extensive listening experiences, they also need rich and continuous reading experiences, "including published literature of acknowledged merit and the work of peers and instructors" (Farr and Daniels 1986, p. 60). Yet to facilitate second language development, readings must be interesting and relevant, comprehensible, with some language elements a little beyond the students' present English proficiency level (Krashen 1985b). Choosing readings at an appropriate level for your students, (neither too easy nor too difficult) presents a challenge. Many content books are far beyond the students' proficiency levels.[2]

One consideration in choosing appropriate material for your students is cultural relevance. The more language minority readers know about the content of the material, the better they comprehend the material. In discussing the selection of culturally relevant materials, K. Goodman (1976) asserts that the more closely the background knowledge of the reader resembles that of the author, the easier it is for the reader to comprehend the author's ideas. The more familiar the content, the easier to recall. Thus, skilled teachers become as informed as possible about the various cultures represented by their students and acknowledge and incorporate their students' cultures whenever possible.

As previously suggested, your language minority students may find a text difficult because it is based on unfamiliar, culturally determined assumptions. In this case, you need to discuss the material with the students and explain those passages which they do not understand. English courses generally place considerable emphasis on literature, but students who have not yet mastered English may find language genres such as poems difficult. Literature becomes more comprehensible when you carefully select texts at an appropriate level for your students. Be aware that the very conciseness of short stories requires considerable inference ability on the part of readers; poems are extremely difficult because the images the authors use are incomprehensible to many language minority students; and the details and complicated subplots frequently contained in novels cannot be understood by many language minority students (Harvey-Cantoni 1987).

Bilingual dictionaries can further help language minority students understand their reading material. Students should be encouraged to use their bilingual dictionaries, but not grow dependent upon them. If they are looking up more than three or four words per page, the reading material is probably too difficult for them. You might also order appropriate content-area books in the students' native languages. These books can be particularly helpful to students who are trying to comprehend concepts at a time when they have not yet acquired English. As discussed in Chapter 3, when students can understand the concepts in their first language, it is easier for them to make sense out of the second.

A number of reading materials provide easier sources of input for your students. You can order readings professionally written for language minority students of diverse proficiency levels, use student-produced materials, choose native-English easy readings: *Reader's Digest* for adults; romance novels for adolescents; *Sesame Street* for children, have native English-speaking students simplify the materials for the ESL students by rewriting them, engage students in pen-pal activities with native English speakers or have the students write their own reading materials.

Providing Enough Written Input

One way for students to obtain sufficient amounts of written English input is through pleasure reading. Krashen (1985) claims that sustained reading of self-selected material changes students into "good readers, pretty good writers, and better spellers" (p. 176). A book cart or book corner with materials which are written at an appropriate level for students can be very beneficial. When students read *narrowly* (reading books by the same author or several texts about the same topic), grammatical and discoursal structures repeat themselves so that the students get many chances to understand the meanings of the texts they read. Your book cart or corner might also contain content materials in both the students' first and second languages. Since students vary widely in their likes and dislikes and there is considerable cross-cultural variation here, you will need to survey your students on their interests. If appropriate, depending on the ages of your students, you might even require a certain amount of pleasure reading each week. At UCI, for example, we require university ESL students to read about 50 pages of pleasure reading each week. Students actually receive credit for doing enjoyable reading.

In line with this suggestion, students should be encouraged to take advantage of the library materials available in most schools in the United States. Many students do not have books in their homes. (This is particularly the case for some Latino and Southeast Asian children who have no tradition of bedtime story reading [Heath 1986].) Students who are unaccustomed to such resources may at first be confused by the amount of materials found in our schools and may be reluctant to use them. You will need to show students where materials are located and how to check them out. You will also need to assure students that they are welcome to use these materials.

One valuable source of reading input is models or samples of the specific sorts of writing that you may assign (Heath and Branscombe 1985).

Students are routinely asked to write book reports, dialogues, position papers, lab reports, literary criticism, term papers and other highly conventionalized genres of writing without ever having seen an example of such discourse done well, either by a peer or a professional. Thus students spend much time groping in the dark, trying to imagine or invent the conventions of an assigned genre, when the opportunity to absorb the characteristics of the form have been withheld.

Farr and Daniels 1966, p. 62

Another source of input is student and teacher produced. In Graves' (1983) approach, the classroom becomes a writing workshop where everyone, including the teacher, is engaged in reading each other's writing. In this approach, the students read each others' writing and their instructor's writing aloud so that both the teacher and the students demonstrate their own writing and writing processes, sharing draft after draft with one another. Bear in mind, however, that students from some cultures are not accustomed to the middle-American concept of writing, in which writers compose several drafts before completing their final product. (Asian students from Japan, Taiwan, Korea, and the People's Republic of China, for example, may be accustomed to writing a finished product the first time around.)[3]

Using Written Input Purposefully

Just as students need opportunities to use what they have heard, so too they need opportunities to use what they have read. Retelling is one such means. Ashton-Warner, in her autobiographical books, *Teacher* (1963) and *I Passed this Way* (1979) describes her experiences in a two-room school for Maori children in rural New Zealand. She used her children's own words as beginning reading texts. Instead of basal readers,

"See Janet, Mother. Janet can run.
Janet can jump."

Ashton-Warner wrote down her children's *key words:* canoe, knife, kiss, etc. Students then retold the stories. When the children arrived at school they told their teacher which words they wanted to learn. The words were written on two cards, one to keep at school and the other to carry around all day, take home, and learn. The next morning, the words kept at school were dumped onto the floor and the students scrambled around searching for their own word. The children then paired off to teach each other words. Eventually the words became sentences and the sentences each other's stories.

A number of other excellent suggestions are given by Heald-Taylor (1989) in her handbook, *Whole Language Strategies for ESL Students.* She suggests that in elementary school, language minority students who have little proficiency in English can dictate stories of personal experiences in the presence of the teacher. Specific dictation strategies outlined in her handbook include, teacher- and student-composed charts, group charts, and published dictation (which is shared with all class members). An example of a teacher-composed chart appears below:

Weekly News

This week we visited all the workers in the school.
Mrs. Hansen is the principal.
Mr. Foster teaches grade one.

(Heald-Taylor 1989, p. 10)

One type of group chart can be composed after students have shared an experience or heard a story. The experience or story can be written down in the form of a group chart.

In dictated stories, the teacher, a more proficient language minority student, or native English-speaking peer writes down the language minority student's story. The person doing the writing may initiate the sentences for the language minority student, but gradually the language minority student should begin to create his or her own stories. Heald-Taylor (1989) suggests that the writer of the story should print exactly what each student desires and after printing the phrase should ask such questions as, *Is this what you wanted to say? Did I get it right?*

Letter writing also fosters purposeful communication. Heath and Branscombe (1985) found a letter writing project involving 9th grade Basic English students and 11th and 12th grade students highly successful in developing English skills of less proficient writers. In this activity, students (of diverse proficiency levels) are paired with one another and asked to correspond on a regular basis. Another kind of letter writing between students and their teacher called dialogue journals has also been successful with language minority students (Kreeft, Shuy, Staton, Reed and Morroy 1984). In dialogue journals, students correspond with their teacher on a regular basis about their personal interests. Instead of correcting their students' grammar, the teacher responds to the content of the students' letters.

There are many other ways to get students to use what they have read. The students can act out a story or, after reading and explaining a story with pictures, the students can participate by pantomining or performing the actions in the story as the book is reread another time. Students can summarize or analyze their reading; discuss it with a partner or group, paint pictures about it, or use it in a project.

Cultural Obstacles to Understanding

This chapter has primarily discussed strategies which make the English language more comprehensible. Yet, cultural obstacles can also prevent students from understanding lessons. If lessons involve cultural references students don't understand, cultural gaps will interfere with their comprehension. For example, Harvey-Cantoni

(1987) tells of an elementary classroom teacher who was reading a story to her class. In the story, two children brought their sick grandmother some beautiful chrysanthemums. When the teacher interrupted the reading to ask what would happen next, she was amazed that her French pupils answered that the grandmother was going to die. When the teacher suggested that the chrysanthemums might help the grandmother feel better, the children looked confused. They had been taught that chrysanthemums, a symbol of death used to decorate graves, should never be given as presents, especially to the elderly. Had the teacher been acquainted with traditional French culture, she would have explained that in the United States chrysanthemums are not considered an omen of death. As Harvey-Cantoni's story illustrates, students who come from different backgrounds attach somewhat different meanings to words and these differences can result in misunderstandings.

Students who do not understand the ways in which language is used in our schools are handicapped academically. Heath (1986) tells of the story of Jesús, a Mexican child who comes to the United States: "In Mexico he had been a reader; he knew what stories were and he could tell them. In his new school setting, differences of reader and storyteller do not include his ways of recognizing or telling stories." (p. 174) In Mexico, Jesús had been an excellent student, but in his school in the United States, Jesús was in the lowest reading group.

We cannot assume that our language minority students know how to tell stories, participate in show and tell, or give oral presentations. These students may never use these *genres* at home, or may use them differently. To help language minority students acquire these genres, we must provide them with appropriate models and, when appropriate, explain how they are used. "If explicit information is not given, newcomers may spend years learning the significance of gestures, distances, or cultural allusions" (Bailey 1987, p. 75).

Conclusion

The fourth principle proposed to prevent language minority students from failing in our classrooms is that the pedagogy should provide students with comprehensible lessons. Although this chapter has illustrated strategies which help language minority students understand your lessons (and, in the process, acquire more English), I have in fact scarcely grazed the surface. Those who wish more information are referred to the suggested readings contained in the references.

ACTIVITIES AND DISCUSSION QUESTIONS

1. Imagine you are using Sesame Street to teach a group of five-year olds who are acquiring English in the United States. What are the advantages of using Sesame Street with young children?
2. What are three sources of English input with which you can provide

your students after school has ended? (If you are not presently teaching, imagine you are teaching a specific group of students at the elementary, secondary or adult education level.)

3. What strategies could you teach adult language minority students which would allow them to control the input they receive?

4. Who would provide optimal input for second language development to these language minority learners who live in the United States:

- a Mexican-American high school student who has intermediate-level English skills;
- a Japanese seven-year-old who has just arrived in the United States and does not speak any English;
- a Puerto Rican university student who is a nearly fluent English speaker;
- A Hmong high school aide who is illiterate in Hmong, but who has acquired advanced English skills.

5. In many schools in the United States, language minority students greatly outnumber native English-speaking students. When the language minority students interact with each other, they sometimes pick up each other's partially acquired, frequently incorrect, English grammar. What are some ways to provide these students with sufficient quantities of comprehensible input and opportunities to use this input? Would it be better to put these students in a classroom taught by a teacher who encouraged group work and cooperative learning, or a tightly controlled classroom in which the teacher directed most of the activities?

RECOMMENDED READING

BLAIR, R. W. 1983. *Innovative Approaches to Language Teaching.* Rowley, Massachusetts: Newbury House Publishers. Well-known pedagogues present innovative approaches to language instruction with which to enhance learner's comprehension of their second language.

KRASHEN, S. D. 1985. *The Input Hypothesis: Issues and Implications.* New York: Longman. Discusses the input hypothesis and its implications for second language instruction.

WINITZ, H. (ed.) 1981. *The Comprehension Approach to Foreign Language Instruction.* Rowley, Massachusetts: Newbury House Publishers. Thirteen articles by proponents of the comprehension approach to foreign language learning, an approach in which learners are not required to speak the foreign language; covers the theory underlying the comprehension approach, empirical reports concerning the success of the approach, and practical classroom applications.

NOTES

1. Mohan (1986) suggests that it makes it more challenging when you leave more parts of the chart blank.

2. When considering the appropriateness of the reading for language minority students, it is probably best to avoid readability formulas. The presidents of the National Council for Teachers of English and of the International Reading Association issued a joint statement on readability (Cullinan and Fitzgerald 1985) in which they warned against using readability formulas to select children's books (especially in the widely used basals). Teachers need to help students guess at meanings first by using context. Assure students that they do not have to understand every word to understand the main idea. Many ESL students pay attention to the literal meaning of the words rather than try to understand the gist.

3. Students who are overly concerned with correctness and performance need to read silently. Silent reading makes students increase their reading speed and embarasses students less than oral reading (Rigg 1986).

CHAPTER FIVE

Encouraging Interaction in the Multicultural Classroom

Teachers in multicultural classrooms frequently complain that their students are unable to communicate effectively because of limited English proficiency. Unfortunately, these teachers often avoid speaking activities in their classrooms. This chapter discusses strategies and activities that are consistent with Principle 4, which states that successful multicultural education for language minority students involves providing these students with opportunities to speak English in a variety of academic contexts.

As discussed in Chapter 3, language minority students need multiple opportunities to practice English. A key factor in second language development is the opportunity to negotiate meaning with interlocutors who have more linguistic resources than the students. The classroom can be especially conducive to providing opportunities to interact. In the outside world, it is sometimes difficult for second language students to practice speaking English. Outside of class, the students may have the chance to interact with the clerk in the market or the bus driver, but as seen in the following example, sustained communication is often only available from friends from the same native language background.

> All the kids hang around with their own country people. I don't have any friends who were born here. Our thinking is different from native students. We respect our parents, and we are not so open. We do not laugh at each other. If the native kids wouldn't attack us with their hatred it would be easier.
> 9th grade Mexican girl, immigrated at age 11
> (reported in Olsen 1988, p. 37)

Even in the classroom, language minority students may have difficulty finding opportunities to interact with native English-speaking peers. The most common activities in public schools in the United States are teacher explaining, lecturing, and reading aloud, closely followed by writing assignments, instructions, and cleanup (Sirotnik

1983). Students participate passively and rarely talk. This type of student participation often fails to develop English speaking proficiency.

There are several problems teachers need to overcome if they are to increase their students' spoken participation in classroom activities. These include: (1) bridging the gap between the language minority students' home cultures and the schools; (2) structuring speaking activities which develop the limited-English-proficient students' speaking proficiency; and (3) helping students overcome communication breakdowns. Solutions to these problems are discussed in the following. (For descriptions of home culture/school discontinuities and communication breakdowns, refer to Chapter 1.)

Bridging the Gap Between the Language Minority Student's Home Culture and School

Beginning second language students often lack the skills they need to participate in classroom activities successfully. As discussed in Chapter 1, a major problem concerns the discontinuity between the students' home culture and school. For example, children who are not taught in their homes to value spoken interaction in public situations often have difficulty communicating in middle-American public schools. Macias (1987) reports on the minimal verbal skills of native American children in the school setting. Papago parents primarily enculturate their children through nonverbal rather than verbal behaviors. Not surprisingly, Papago children are often minimally verbal in middle-American schools. They are shy or restrained not only because of the new surroundings; they also feel confused and unsure of how to act because Papagos rarely speak in public.

In many cultures (including the Korean, Japanese and Chinese), the students accept the teachers' viewpoint and never challenge it. The following letter from a book entitled *Dear Diane: Questions and Answers for Asian-American Women* (Yen-Mei Wong 1983) is illustrative.

> Dear Diane: At school, teachers tell us to ask questions and to challenge what they say. At home, it's just the opposite. Whenever I offer an opinion that is different than what my folks think, they say I'm rude and disobedient. I suppose that I can remain silent in front of them, but isn't there a way that I can express my opinions without them raising the roof?
>
> Korean student (p. 8)

Like Korean children, Punjabi children are said to have difficulties giving their own opinions in the classroom because they have not been enculturated to participate in discussions with adults (Gibson 1987). In Punjabi culture, children are taught to defer to adult authority. Such training, it is argued, "does not prepare Punjabi students to participate in classroom discussions where they have to express ideas different from those of their teachers" (Ogbu and Matute-Bianchi 1986, p. 77). Levine (1983) also points out that teachers experience difficulty when trying to get Saudi students to state their opinions:

> Asked by teachers, *What do you think?* or *What is your opinion?* a Saudi student may offer a rote response. This reaction is not indicative of an inability to articulate an original or creative thought, but rather reflects educational training that discourages independent thinking. Some Saudi students have reported that a teacher who elicits opinions in class or allows a student to challenge ideas is incompetent and therefore unqualified to teach. (pp. 102–103)

Most puzzling and problematic for many language minority students is the relationship between teachers and students (Olsen 1988). In the United States, teachers interact more freely with students, expecting students to interrupt them if they do not understand. "Here teachers do not physically discipline the students and do not usually apply the same types of pressures often used with immigrant children in their native lands" (Olsen 1988, p. 72). This relationship confuses students. Numerous other home/school discontinuities have been reported in the literature. (See Au and Jordan 1980, Mohatt and Erikson 1981, Jordan 1985 and Heath 1986.)

To overcome the problem of home/school discontinuity, the following strategies are suggested:

> Eliminate those aspects of speaking activities that create discomfort and stress for students;
>
> Integrate similar cultural activities with unfamiliar ones; and
>
> Intentionally present students with discontinuous experiences designed to help them acquire the interactional skills necessary for school success.

These strategies are discussed below.

- Perhaps most important, we need to eliminate those aspects of our speaking activities that create discomfort and stress for students. This can be done by:

  1. creating a supportive, nonthreatening classroom environment;
  2. providing the students with models they can relate to;
  3. preparing students for speaking activities;
  4. giving students strategies which enable them to control talk;
  5. using low risk activities;
  6. having the students approach activities in stages; and
  7. creating speaking activities at the students' approximate level of second language proficiency (see Chapter 3).

The first order of business is creating a supportive, nonthreatening environment where students feel free to express themselves and to experiment with English. Such an environment can be a haven in which errors and mistakes can be forgiven. "It can be the place where the skills needed to make the most of natural input are acquired" (Damen 1986, p. 311). To create such an environment, Moskowitz (1978) suggests that students be given the right to pass and never be forced to contribute. Thus, she suggests inviting rather than requiring students to participate in speaking activities. If students become disinterested and withdraw from speaking activities, coercion or punishment should always be avoided. As Trueba (1989) points out, when some beginning second language students are forced to communicate, they may try to *pass* for competent English speakers by pretending "to understand, comply, write, read or compute when in fact they are painfully aware of their inability to function in the classroom" (p. 25). Other beginning ESL students may fear attempting any communication and may wind up by completely withdrawing from classroom activities. Still others may develop discipline problems. After all, they may gain more peer approval as classroom clowns than they do as classroom dummies.

In line with the suggestion of not forcing students to communicate, students who do not wish to participate should not be singled out (see Chapter 7). Ann Landers' response to a *quiet* person illustrates that it is unhelpful to draw attention to those who prefer not to participate in our oral activities.

> DEAR ONE:
> Quiet people are frequently shy, so drawing attention to them because they are *quiet* only amplifies their embarrassment. One wouldn't presume to ask a non-stop talker why he talks so much, so why ask a quiet person why he's so quiet?
> From Ann Landers, *Los Angeles Times,* June 28, 1988

Moskowitz (1978) also suggests that students be given the right to be heard and the right to see their own opinions respected (no *put-downs* allowed). The following examples illustrate the importance of these basic ground rules.

> There is lots of teasing me when I don't pronounce right. Whenever I open my mouth I wonder, I shake and worry, will they laugh? 10th grade Filipino boy, immigrated at age 15 (reported in Olsen 1988, p. 38)

> At first I was shy, but I didn't have problems making friends because in my ESL class were kids from all over the world. I saw the Chinese people, the Vietnamese people, and I felt like we were all together. I was like one of them, and I wanted to be able to talk to them. That's what made me try so hard to learn English. *But in other classes, when I was laughed at because of my poor Eng-*

lish, I didn't want to talk. Cesar Menjivar, Salvadoran immigrant student, Public Testimony-San Francisco (reported in Olsen 1988, p. 38)

Another way we can make students less apprehensive about communicating is by giving them sufficient positive reinforcement. Complimenting the students' conversation abilities goes a long way toward making them feel successful and encouraging them to communicate. (Refer to Chapter 7.) People's beliefs about their abilities affect their subsequent efforts (Robinson 1985). If students believe that their efforts to communicate have been successful, they will feel good about participating in future speaking interactions. Each experience speaking is influenced by previous experiences, which in turn influence subsequent ones. Thus, the students' participation increases if their previous interactions are successful.

Models the students relate to (who can interact successfully) also increase their belief that they can succeed (Bandura 1977). If we see models in a similar situation who have succeeded, we come to believe that we too can succeed. Seeing models perform feared activities (such as making oral reports) with beneficial consequences (such as peer approval or good grades) is likely to motivate students to try out these activities.

In line with this suggestion, it is also beneficial to assign helpful peers or *buddies* to all language minority students — if possible from the students' first culture. Students who lack English proficiency need mentors from their own culture. The experience of working with others who have gone through much of what they are encountering can be a tremendous source of support.

Yet another way to lower student anxiety is to prepare students for speaking activities. One way to do this is by giving students lots to talk about through group and class discussions, videotapes, films, field trips, and reading material. Once students feel knowledgeable about a topic, it may not seem so difficult for them to express their own opinions about it. Also, students need time to prepare and practice. Handouts containing useful vocabulary words and expressions are also beneficial preparation aids.

Strategies for controlling the course of the conversation may also serve to lower student anxiety. "When people believe that the origin of control is within themselves, they are less anxious than when control is mediated externally" (Robinson 1985, p. 89). (Strategies for controlling conversation follow.)

Another way to lower our students' anxieties about speaking is to use low-risk activities so that no one feels threatened. Moskowitz (1978) suggests that all speaking activities should move from low-risk, non-personal content, such as information gathering, reporting, and problem-solving to activities which ask for the sharing of personal values, beliefs and feelings. Too often we give students topics that are *too hot to handle* — topics that require a great deal of personal disclosure (Bassano and Christison 1987). In some cultures, personal disclosure is not permitted, while in others it is. Students should be encouraged to share what *they* want to share — not what their teacher demands.

As Saville-Troike (1977) points out, teachers need to develop sensitivity to what should *not* be discussed in school, what questions should *not* be asked, and what student behaviors should *not* be required. . . . "Even unintentional or well-meaning violations can result at best in student embarrassment or confusion, and at worst in causing the student to reject the traditions of his home" (p.110). The following is a sad illustration.

> The students we are working with now are quite different from the students we had in the 1970's. Some have been displaced because of war, famine, revolution or natural disasters. The issues they come with are difficult. Our teaching methods, no matter how innovative, have had to go through tremendous change. We're dealing with cross-cultural issues as well as individual differences. I remember teaching a spelling lesson to mostly Cambodian youngsters, and I was using a hangman game. One youngster said to me, *You know, that is how my parents died.* That was my coming of age as a teacher of newcomer students.
>
> Judy Levy-Sender, Teacher-Newcomer School, San Francisco (reported in Olsen 1988, p. 66)

Sink or swim approaches to public speaking can be psychologically devastating for beginning second language students. For example, making students who are afraid to speak before an audience give oral reports without any preparation can only raise their anxieties. Social learning theory suggests that students should not perform a feared behavior directly, but approach it in stages (Bandura 1977). They should first observe and then jointly participate with models and eventually perform the task on their own. For example, before students participate in *show and tell*, they should first have many opportunities to watch their classmates participate in this activity. Next, the teacher should provide them with explicit instructions concerning the activity. For example, the teacher might say, "Begin with *Today, boys and girls I am going to share (then say what you are sharing).* Tell us all about what you are sharing and why it is important to you." Next, the teacher might invite beginning second language students to share special objects with their buddies or peer mentors and help the students communicate when they have difficulty, always providing positive feedback. Finally, the teacher might invite the beginning second language students to share special objects by themselves.

As discussed in Chapter 3, asking students to participate in activities far beyond their current level of English language development can cause them considerable distress.

• It is important to integrate familiar interactional activities with unfamiliar ones.

Another way to bridge home culture/school discontinuities is to integrate familiar activities with unfamiliar ones. It is always easier for students to understand new information if it is embedded in old. Two examples of ways in which culturally familiar elements can be incorporated into the instruction of minority children are reported by Heath (1982, 1983) and Au (1980).

Heath (1982) worked cooperatively with parents and educators to modify the learning environment of *Trackton* (North Carolina) students. These students were unfamiliar with many verbal skills their teachers expected them to use. In order to increase the students' verbal skills in naming objects, identifying their characteristics, and providing descriptions out of context, Heath instructed the Trackton teachers on ways to adapt to the Trackton community's ways of asking questions. For example, teachers began social studies lessons with questions that asked for personal experiences and analogic responses, such as, "What's happening there?" "Have you ever been there?" and "What's this like?" These questions resemble those that Trackton parents ask their children at home. The use of these questions was productive, generating active responses from previously passive and *nonverbal* students. Once the teachers increased the participation of the students in lessons using home questioning styles, they were able to begin using the types of questions commonly used by middle-American teachers.

It is also helpful to use culturally familiar content as a point of departure for introducing culturally unfamiliar content. "Jumping right into the content and context which is foreign to the learner is less effective" (Robinson 1985, p. 17). The incorporation of the *talk story* in KEEP reading lessons is the most widely known example of teachers changing classroom practice to accommodate relevant cultural elements. The KEEP reading program includes the children's experiences as part of the lesson's reading discussions to make the reading more relevant (Au 1980, Au and Jordan 1981).

Most of our curriculum is so narrow that language minority students rarely find their own experiences reflected anywhere in the classrooms. When they do, their understanding of the subject matter and motivation increases. Consider the example:

> I was so excited when my history teacher talked about the Vietnam War. Now at last, I thought, we will study about my country. We only studied it one day. Just for that day, I had something to say.
>
> 11th grade Vietnamese girl, immigrated at age 15

• Although it is important to incorporate culturally familiar elements into our instruction, it is also necessary to intentionally present students with discontinuous experiences designed to help them acquire the interactional skills necessary for school success.

It may even be necessary to present new information and experiences which conflict with the students' past learning experiences.

One way in which this is being done successfully with Papago children is by explicitly teaching these children to conform to classroom rules, follow instructions, raise their hands, stand in line, and so forth. Papago socialization gives children little experience or preparation for adapting quickly to these unfamiliar activities (Macias 1987).

Students need information about the types of interaction called for at school. They need to know how they are expected to behave in activities. This is why before inviting them to participate in a speaking activity, it is useful to take them step-by-step through the activity and present them with models and verbal instructions when necessary.

Structuring Speaking Activities Which Develop the Language Minority Student's Speaking Proficiency

Another problem is providing students with multiple opportunities to interact at an appropriate level. In a class in which students have many different levels of English proficiency, it is difficult to tailor speaking activities to each individual. Teachers also encounter difficulties getting language minority students to engage in conversation. As Bassano and Christison (1987) point out,

> Teachers often put students in a circle, give them a topic for discussion that they think is particularly stimulating and then watch the students just sit and look at one another in an embarrassing silence, constrained, nervous and tense. Then the teachers end up doing all the talking! Often there is one aggressive student who seems to feel a need to be the center of attention at all times. Other times students are either too shy to participate or have such low self-esteem that they feel they have nothing of interest to offer the group. (What do I have to contribute? Who could possibly be interested in what I have to say?) (p. 201)

The problem, then, is twofold: (1) to structure activities which elicit interaction at an appropriate level; and (2) to get students to talk enough in a wide range of contexts. (See Chapter 2 for further discussion of this problem.) The following strategies are suggested:

Vary activities according to student ability and preferences;
Provide multiple opportunities for students to interact;
Provide students with repeated exposure to talk within an integrated context; and
Teach conversation and group skills.

These strategies are discussed in the following.

- It is important to vary activities according to student ability and preferences so that everyone can participate (Enright and McCloskey 1980).

One way to do this is by varying the kind of verbal tasks that you ask your students to perform when you call on them. As Wong-Fillmore (1985) suggests, the best way to call for student participation is not to ask questions only of your most proficient English speakers or to ask only low-level questions of everyone or to skip asking questions altogether. The best way is to match your request for student participation to the current English proficiency levels of your students. An excellent example of how this can be accomplished comes from Enright and McCloskey (1988).

> Let's say you are reading a children's novel to your group each day (we'll use *Charlotte's Web*) and you want to start off a particular day's reading with an update of what has happened so far. Using your knowledge of your students' abilities and their social styles, you might start off by asking the entire group to remind you (chorally) of the identity of the heroine (*What was the name of that old spider again?*) Then you might hand the book to Rafael — an outgoing and confident beginning second language student — and ask him to find a picture of Charlotte and show it to the class. (*Rafael, help me find Charlotte in here. Can you show a picture of her to the class?*) This requires that Rafael comprehend your request and demonstrate his comprehension through a public act, but it does not require that he say anything at all! As Rafael holds the book up for the class to see, you might have Moon Hee, a beginning second language student who is not yet ready for public displays, confirm whether the animal Rafael has found is indeed Charlotte by nodding her head yes or no. (*Is Rafael right, Moon Hee? Is that Charlotte?*) Then you might do a quick review of the other items that Rafael has found in the picture — asking some students for one-word answers (Raise your hand if you know what the thing hanging above Charlotte is called.) asking other students to simply point (*Wilbur? Is Wilbur the pig in this picture? Bui, come show me where Wilbur is.*), and asking still other students to provide full utterances about the picture (*Lucretia, where are all those cows and sheep going?*) After you finally let poor Rafael sit down, you might have the students review what happened the day before (*What was Wilbur's boast? What did the rat tie on Wilbur? Where did he tie it? Where did Wilbur get that idea that he could spin a web?*) and speculate on what might happen today. (p. 143)

At the same time teachers are providing the linguistic and emotional support that students need, they should also be encouraging their students to use their abilities to the utmost. As Swain (1986) suggests, students can communicate quite effectively with grammatically deviant forms and inappropriate language. "Negotiating meaning needs to incorporate the notion of being pushed toward the delivery of a message that is not only conveyed, but that is conveyed precisely, coherently and appropriately" (pp. 248–249). (Chapter 3 discusses Swain's *Comprehensible Output Hypothesis* in greater detail.)

On the other hand, students who lack English proficiency should not be pushed to communicate beyond their current level of English speaking proficiency. Too often the demands made on beginning second language students to communicate are too harsh. If students have to use too many new vocabulary words and/or grammatical structures in an activity, they may spend too much time translating or consciously trying to string sentences together. It is the teacher's job to make sure that the language the students need to use to converse is not too far beyond their current English proficiency level.

Both the content and the genre contribute to task difficulty. Wallerstein (1988) suggests that the easiest content for language minority students to handle is related to their everyday activities — their families and their neighborhoods. Topics which are culturally familiar to the students are also easier to discuss than topics which are not. In addition, they generally have less difficulty participating in informal dyadic and small group conversations than they do giving oral reports in front of a large audience, since they can control their input and output in face-to-face interaction by using such conversational devices as questions. *Props* such as photos, slides, handouts, and objects help language minority students who are not quite ready to make an oral presentation successfully on their own.

- Teachers need to provide multiple opportunities for students to interact.

Students need multiple opportunities to interact. Although they may feel more comfortable in a quiet environment, Enright and McCloskey (1988) point out that keeping students quiet is not a sign of good teaching. They state, "*No talking* is a rule of many classrooms. It won't suffice to simply permit talking; we need to encourage it" (p. 72). They also suggest a new rule: *Yes, talking.* Teachers need to help students get used to noise and activity. To do this, teachers will need to create new management and discipline activities which create a supportive social environment where students who lack language proficiency can talk. As suggested by Enright and McCloskey, *Do your own work* needs to be changed to: *Rely on your friends for help.*

Teachers also need to show students that they expect them to participate in oral activities by constantly inviting every member of the class to participate. They can show through their words and actions that they both expect the students to accept the invitation and care whether the students accept the invitation to speak.[1]

As shown in Chapter 3, students need to participate in the widest possible range of oral language contexts with a variety of speakers. Teachers may introduce students to a variety of models through films, visitors, team teaching, peer teaching, and teaching by students who have successfully completed the course or who are in the next course. Peer teachers can invite students to movies, sports events and other activities. Clubs and organizations can involve them in parties and retreats. "Participation in voluntary associations, such as sports teams, Scout groups, church groups and music lessons give added practice in uses of language similar to those in school" (Heath 1986, p. 176). A variety of models the student can relate to also motivates students, who may reason, *If a variety of people like me can interact successfully, why can't I?*

Cooperative activities provide rich additional sources of interaction for language minority students. Paired and small group activities increase the amount of meaningful and interesting interaction and greatly multiply the number of opportunities available to practice and use English.

Students also need opportunities to interact in other academic situations — reporting information, summarizing, synthesizing, and debating. Cummins (1981) points out that language minority students frequently acquire conversational skills in their first few years in the United States, but lack the ability to communicate in academic, *decontextualized* situations, in which they cannot guess the meaning of the language they read or hear from the context. He maintains that communicative demands of schooling and the acquisition of literacy and academic skills require more than daily face-to-face, one-to-one interaction.[2]

- Students need to be provided with repeated exposure to talk within an integrated context.

Many schools fail to take advantage of the natural reinforcement provided by integrating topics of study. For example, most public schools offer field trips, guest lectures, writing assignments and library work. Yet these activities are seldom related to one another (Robinson 1985).

Also, students often participate in speaking activities on a one-time basis. Yet, making an oral report once a year is probably not enough to give students confidence in public speaking, let alone develop their English proficiency.

- Students need to be taught conversation and group skills.

Students need experience taking turns talking, interrupting and listening actively. They need to know how to hold back the more vocal members and draw out the more timid or self-conscious ones. They need to know how to ask for clarification (*what?*) and how to ask others to repeat (*huh? excuse me*), to slow down, and to explain; they need to know how to gain time to think (by using hesitation markers such as *uhm* and *let's see*) and how to change the topic; they also need to know how to look interested to keep the conversation going (by using such back channel cues as *right, uhuh* and *that's interesting*). Such tools of conversation enable students to manage their own input and output. Krashen and Terrell (1981) point out that "an added advantage of being able to use these aspects of conversational competence is that they help make it possible to converse with speakers of the target language outside the classroom" (p. 99). Many of the cooperative learning activities suggested by Kagan (1989) are designed to help students acquire conversational skills.

Students also need group management strategies. Instructors can teach these strategies by asking their students to evaluate the group by raising such questions as: "Did everyone have a chance to participate?"; "Did everyone listen to one another?" and "Did everyone take responsibility for completing the task?"

Class meetings offer an excellent opportunity for teachers to model effective group interaction skills. Enright and McCloskey (1988) suggest that during these meetings the teachers demonstrate those skills they want students to use in later group work. They also give this advice to teachers:

> . . . be explicit. Label actions that you are performing. *I'm trying to make sure everyone has a chance to talk. I'm summarizing what has been said.* Explain that students should use these same actions when they have their own small group meetings.
>
> (pp. 245–246)

Enright and McCloskey suggest that teachers see that everyone talks in turn and listens while others talk and that all students understand the issues being discussed as much as possible. They also suggest that teachers make sure that everyone has an opportunity to participate, that students' ideas are restated, and that all contributions are respected even when others disagree.

Helping Students Overcome Communication Breakdowns

Communication breakdowns can constitute a different obstacle in multicultural classrooms. A lengthy literature documents the difficulties non-native speakers have communicating with native-English speakers. (See for example, Gumperz, Jupp and Roberts 1979.) As discussed in Chapter 1, communication difficulties often arise because of mismatches in communication styles. Robinson (1985) gives this example of the type of communication breakdowns which occur when native and non-native speakers interact.

> In the crosscultural training film *Take Two* (IRI 1982) non-reciprocity of speech initiation and content is illustrated between an American student and a Vietnamese student. In an attempt to keep the conversation going, the American continually asks questions; the Vietnamese responds, often with a *yes* or a *no*, or with a very short answer, without elaboration or extension. After this conversation filmed in *Take One*, each student is interviewed as to their feelings. The American comments that it was difficult to converse with the Vietnamese student; the American felt the Vietnamese student was not interested in her, because she never

asked the American any questions in return. The Vietnamese student on the other hand felt that the American kept *firing* questions at her, without giving her enough time to respond. (For the American, any pauses after the student's response was uncomfortable.) She was also not accustomed to the American style of elaborating and then asking back. After intervention training, the American pauses after each question and does not jump in with another question until the Vietnamese student has had ample chance to reply. The Vietnamese student has also learned to ask questions back to the American. (pp. 59–60)

Teachers may use the following strategies to help students overcome communication breakdowns.

Encourage the development of friendship;
Emphasize commonalities;
Create a place in which the experiences, capacities, interests and goals of every classroom member are simultaneously utilized for the benefit of all;
Teach all students how their communication styles can be misinterpreted.

Each of these strategies is discussed in the following.

• Students need help in getting to know one another.

Often our expectations are unrealistic. As discussed earlier, teachers sometimes put a room full of strangers from different cultural backgrounds together in group activities, and expect them to act as close friends before they are even acquainted with one another. A number of conversation starters and activities can be used to help students establish friendships. (See Bassano and Christison 1987, Krashen and Terrell 1981, and Littlewood 1981.)

• Commonalities should be emphasized.

We can create commonalities by structuring events in which participants share experiences (such as field trips and collaborative tasks). Such activities can bring individuals and groups closer so that students can continue interacting even after the class has ended.

• We need to work to create a place in which the experiences, capacities, interests and goals of every classroom member are simultaneously utilized for the benefit of all.

Rarely do language minority students and native-English speakers have the opportunity to learn about one another. We need to provide many opportunities for collaboration so that students can share their interests. Negative evaluations can be countered by making each student's skills/participation necessary for others.

- Native and non-native English-speaking students can learn how their communication styles can be misinterpreted.

Clearly, both native and non-native students would benefit from instruction about how their own cultural conventions may be misinterpreted. As Robinson (1983) puts it, "learning about cultural differences in speech conventions, ways of structuring arguments, cultural assumptions and interaction patterns has an important role to play in programs aimed at developing positive crosscultural communication" (p. 63).

Reducing Prejudice

Unfortunately, communication breakdowns often give rise to prejudice. By *prejudice,* I mean "a unified, stable, and consistent tendency to respond in a negative way toward members of a particular ethnic group" (Aboud 1988, p. 6). Despite the teacher's best efforts to help native and non-native students interact, prejudice can lead to the non-native students' segregation. Powerless individuals are easy targets of prejudice because they cannot retaliate easily. Yet prejudice is not only a middle-American phenomenon. Language minority students often are prejudiced toward other minority groups. To combat prejudice, several educators, recognizing that prejudice seldom goes away on its own, have created school activities which foster cross-cultural understanding. The ultimate goal of these activities is to establish a positive climate among diverse cultural groups. Before discussing these activities, it is useful to consider some of the theories which have been proposed to explain prejudice and some strategies which have been suggested to reduce prejudice. Garcia (1982) suggests isolating the causes of prejudice and then implementing strategies for reducing it. Causes and strategies, summarized by Garcia (1982), are given in Table 5–1.

In addition to understanding the possible causes of prejudice, we must also consider those developmental factors which affect prejudice. Aboud (1988) states:

> People often blame a child's prejudice on the parents. They assume that the parents are prejudiced and teach these attitudes to their child. This is unjustified. Pre-7 children do not adopt their parents' attitudes and are often more prejudiced than their parents. Post-7 children are influenced by their parents but not solely by them. Other factors shape attitudes too. (p. 128)

As suggested by the discussion above, the problem of dealing with prejudice is thorny. There are a number of types of prejudice that are simply beyond the teacher's control. Nonetheless, as indicated in Table 5–1, the teacher can take a number of positive steps to reduce prejudice.

Table 5–1
Theories and Strategies for Reducing Racism

Theory	Cause of Racism	Change Strategy
Ignorance	Ethnic/racial illiteracy; poor under-understanding of culturally different populations	Provide new data; new information about cultura different populations
Unpleasant Experience	Bad experience with cultural/ racial groups.	Create positive experiences with cultura racial groups, preferably on a one-to-one basis.
Negative Trait	Same as ignorance, but stress stereotypes about cultural/racial groups.	Same as Ignorance, but stress frontal attack on stereotypes. Do not replace stereotypes with positive stereotypes; rather, study racial/cultu groups from the groups' perspective.
Scapegoat	Racism and prejudice with a purpose. Racism represents something more basic, such as desire to maintain class/caste system in which minority groups remain second class citizens. Frustrations ostensibly caused by racial/cultural group; thus, racist hostile toward members of the group.	Reason with students about how democracy cannot function with tyranny of the majority, which is self-defeating, or with a second class citizenship class/caste system. Appeal to universal human rights.
Anti-Minority Liberation	Economic and political change provokes fears and insecurities in racist, who benefits from the status quo; thus racist attempts to block progress of cultural/racial group.	Make fundamental changes in government and financial system.
Pathological	A pathological syndrome of deeply repressed fears, anxieties and other emotional disorders causes racism.	Give competent psycho analysis or therapy.
Ethnic Purity	This extreme form of ethnocentrism uses racist attitudes and actions to prevent contact with certain racial/ cultural groups.	Encourage planned, an controlled contact with hated group. Unplanne arbitrary contact can d more harm than good.
Internal Colony	Racism is a functional myth used to sustain a color/caste system within the United States.	Fundamental economi and political rearrange-ments are needed to dismantle the internal colonial structure.

(adapted from Garcia 1982, p. 84)

One way to reduce prejudice is through school-wide activities which include an international day (which focuses on having fun and a feeling of togetherness), school-wide celebration of holidays (such as Cinco de Mayo, Lunar New Year), international variety shows and pot luck dinners. However, these alone are not enough to create an environment which fosters cultural diversity. In fact, they may create a *we/they* atmosphere if the students' cultures are not thoroughly integrated into the curriculum (refer to Chapter 11).

The most common way to combat prejudice is to increase one cultural group's knowledge about another group — on the assumption that if we have accurate information we will not hold misconceptions and false stereotypes. After all, "the less that is known about a group, the easier it is to assign it negative attributes" (Aboud 1988, p. 21). Yet research shows that giving out information about cultural groups is an ineffective approach. Knowledge may aid the reduction of prejudice, but it alone will not reduce it. Teachers need to reach their students at both the cognitive and affective levels.

One way to reach both cognitive and affective levels is to create a multicultural advisory committee, composed of students, interested faculty members, counselors, interested parents and community members. This committee meets regularly to discuss cross-cultural issues and to view presentations designed to meet its needs. On one high school campus described by Baron (1987), students made presentations on the separatism of cultural groups on campus, attitudes towards hearing languages other than English spoken on campus, and the necessity of confronting racism.

Most teachers are familiar with the power of audiovisual techniques and the application of these techniques in modifying student attitudes. Several video-tapes and films have been designed to increase cross-cultural understanding (refer to the appendix). A number of games have also been produced (see, for instance, *Ba-fa, Ba-fa*).

Teachers can also help reduce prejudice within the classroom by encouraging students to work together harmoniously on classroom assignments (such as those described by Kagan 1989). Criteria for grouping can be based on cultural differences as well as linguistic ability or academic attainment. (Kagan [1989] provides a variety of practical suggestions for grouping students.) It is worth noting, however, that the social contacts teachers establish may reduce prejudice only under certain conditions: when there is an opportunity for students to get to know one another as individuals; the contact is positive; the students have equal status in the assignments; the students have some common interests and characteristics (such as age); the social norms favor an association between the cultural groups; the circumstances favor cooperation; and the activities of the group help individuals achieve meaningful goals (Pedersen 1988; see also Banks 1988). As Garcia (1982) points out:

> Mere contact alone may exacerbate the prevalent group's hostilities. What is done with the contact — how school officials and teachers create a school climate conducive to equal-status contact

— will determine the contact's efficacy . . . . It is naive to believe that unplanned or uncontrolled contact between minority and majority group students will make a positive difference in their interpersonal relationships. In fact, this type of contact may do more damage than no contact at all. Since the history of racial minorities and whites in our society has consistently placed minorities in a subordinate role and status, there is no reason to believe that mere in-school contact will change the attitudes and beliefs of white or minority students.

(p. 88)

Teachers can serve as models by becoming advocates of their language minority students and by fostering a sense of acceptance of all cultures within the class through the curriculum they teach, the visitors they invite to class, and the multicultural activities in which they themselves participate.

Perhaps most important, teachers can acknowledge the existing power relations which result in prejudice against minority students and help empower these students to recognize, critically analyze, and actively address injustices. This will be further discussed in Chapter 11.[3]

Conclusion

It is not always easy to encourage non-native students to interact with native English-speaking peers. Contact alone will not do it. Hanvey (1979) suggests that "there must be a readiness to respect and accept, and a capacity to participate" (p. 18). This chapter has discussed some strategies for helping students to develop this readiness and capacity.

ACTIVITIES AND DISCUSSION QUESTIONS

1. Although researchers such as Krashen claim that students do not need to talk in order to acquire the second language, others, most notably Swain (1986) and Long (1988), argue that talking helps second language development. Consider the advantages and disadvantages of encouraging language minority students of limited English proficiency to interact with native-English speakers in small group problem-solving. Then explain your own stand on this issue. What are some additional advantages and disadvantages of encouraging language minority students who lack English proficiency to interact with native-English speakers?

Advantages of Interaction

- may encourage others to provide more input
- may personalize the input

- may provide *charged* input which strikes deeply (Stevick 1979)

- may provide native speakers with better feedback so that they can adjust their speech to the ESL student's English proficiency level
- may provide a meaningful context for the input

- may provide more interesting, relevant input

Disadvantages

- may raise the students' anxieties
- may place early communicative demands on the student, forcing communication before the student is ready
- may encourage the student to *fake* competence in the second language; this in turn may encourage *difficult* input
- may encourage the student to fall back on the first language when communicating in the second

- may result in cross-cultural communication breakdowns which could lead to negative stereotyping and negative attitudes towards the target culture

2. Observe a language minority student participate in classroom activities. How often does the student interact with the teacher and classmates? What is the nature of the interaction? What could the student's teacher do to increase the student's oral participation?

3. Consider the following letter to Dear Diane. How would you respond to *LOOKING FOR ASIAN FRIENDS*? What specific activities can you suggest for high school students who want to interact with different cultural groups?

> Dear Diane:
> The Asians in my school never seem to spend time with people outside of their own ethnic groups. The Chinese stay with the Chinese; the Vietnamese with the Vietnamese; It's the same for the Koreans, Filipinos, and Japanese, too. I'm Filipino, born in America, and I had hoped I could make friends with all different kinds of Asians. Am I too naive? What can I do?
> LOOKING FOR ASIAN FRIENDS

4. When compared to children, adolescents have superior conversational skills. In what specific ways do adolescents' superior conversational skills allow them to manage conversations in such a way that they receive *optimal* input for second language acquisition. What English conversational skills should be explicitly taught to children, adolescents and adults? Why?

5. It is sometimes hypothesized that the use of specific conversational features is closely related to cultural identity. According to this hypothesis, giving up the conversational features of the first language (such as interruption patterns) to acquire those of the second entails giving up one's own culture. If this is the case, how can

students avoid giving up their cultural identity when acquiring English conversational features?

RECOMMENDED READING

Practical Teaching Volumes Pertaining to Interaction

BRUMFIT, C. J., and JOHNSON, K. (eds.) 1979. *The Communicative Approach to Language Teaching.* Oxford: Oxford University Press. Contains articles which discuss various ways to encourage language minority students to communicate purposefully.

CHRISTISON, M. A., and BASSANO, S. 1981. *Look Who's Talking.* San Francisco: Alemany Press. Guides teachers in the development of successful conversation groups in intermediate and advanced ESL classrooms; provides junior high school, high school, and adult education teachers with a practical set of classroom activities and strategies for fostering interaction in the ESL classroom.

ENRIGHT, D. S., and McCLOSKEY, M. L. 1988. *Integrating English: Developing English and Language Literacy in the Multilingual Classroom.* Reading, Massachusetts: Addison-Wesley. Discusses many innovative activities for fostering interaction. Elementary school teachers will find it particularly helpful.

JOHNSON, K., and MORROW, K. (eds.) 1981. *Communication in the Classroom.* London: Longman. Focuses on implications and problems associated with being communicative. An introductory chapter sketches some of the background to communicative language teaching while the first part deals primarily with syllabus and course design. The second part is concerned mainly with communicative methodology.

RICHARDS, J. C., and SCHMIDT, R. W. (eds.) 1983. *Language and Communication.* London: Longman. This collection of papers offers a comprehensive account of research on the components of communication and of the application of this research to ESL teaching methodology.

SAVIGNON, S. J. 1983. *Communicative Competence: Theory and Classroom Practice: Texts and Contexts in Second Language Learning.* Reading, Massachusetts: Addison-Wesley. Intended for classroom teachers and teachers in training, this book contains worthwhile suggestions for ways in which programs can be made more responsive to the communicative goals of both students and teachers.

Theoretical Aspects of Interaction in a Second Language

COULTHARD, M. 1985. *An Introduction to Discourse Analysis*, second edition. London: Longman. Brings up-to-date the influential work of the author and his colleagues at the University of Birmingham and represents the Birmingham approach to conversational analysis. An important reference for many teachers and students, it has applications in the areas of language teaching and acquisition, sylistics, reading and writing studies, pathology and testing. Coulthard brings together work from a range of disciplines, including linguistics, social anthropology, philosophy, and psychology. The book deals with the characterization of speaker/writing meaning and its explanation in the context of use. It also portrays the structure of social interaction. The chapters range from speech acts and conversational maxims, the ethnography of speaking, and conversational analysis to intonation, linguistics, discourse analysis, language teaching, the acquisition of discourse and the analysis of literary discourse.

DAY, R. (ed.) 1986. *Talking to Learn*. Rowley, Massachusetts: Newbury House Publishers. This anthology makes available a range of empirical reports of second language acquisition relating to conversation among native and non-native speakers, and non-native speakers with other non-native speakers, both in the classroom and outside the classroom. While Section One presents theoretical concerns, Section Two contains chapters that focus on the nature of conversational interaction in the classroom, both content classes and ESL classes, where language minority students are studying English. The focus on language in the classroom is continued in Section Three, but looks more closely at small-group or task activities. The papers in the final section examine the more socially oriented conversations that language minority students have with each other as well as with native-English speakers outside the classroom.

FAERCH, C., and KASPAR, K. (eds.) 1983. *Strategies in Interlanguage Communication*. London: Longman. The editors refer to strategies in inter-language communication as potential conscious plans set up by the student in order to solve problems in communication. Exclusively focused on speaking, the volume highlights ways learners use their inter-language in interaction as well as the variables which influence the use of communication strategies. The three parts are: definitions of communication strategies, empirical studies, and problems in analyzing communication strategies. It contains a comprehensive bibliography.

FINE, J. (ed.) 1988. *Second Language Discourse: A Textbook of Current Research*. In the series, *Advanced in Discourse Processes*. Norwood, New Jersey: Ablex Publishing Co. Attempts to relate some of the diverse theoretical approaches, methods and findings of discourse analysis to second language teaching and learning. Chapters include both oral and written language, theoretical and applied perspectives, experimental and descriptive studies, sociolinguistic and psycholinguistic considerations, classroom and real life discourse, teaching and evaluation.

LARSEN-FREEMAN, D. 1980. *Discourse Analysis in Second Language Research*. Rowley, Massachusetts: Newbury House Publishers. The contributors are pioneers in the application of discourse analysis to the second language field. With the exception of the first chapter, an extensive literature survey by Hatch and Long, each of the articles is a research report which though preliminary, tackles interesting questions in the field of second language acquisition from the perspective of discourse analysis. The contributors address these questions:

1. What is the effect of context on the form and meaning of linguistic structures?

2. What is the nature of pragmatic knowledge that a student must acquire when studying a second language?

3. What discourse rules do second language students violate?
4. What is the nature of the second language input to the student?
5. What is the structure of the conversations in which language minority students engage?
6. What can conversational analysis contribute to the optimal age issue?
7. What is the nature of the discourse which transpires between teacher and students and among students?

LOVEDAY, L. 1982. *The Sociolinguistics of Learning and Using a Non-Native Language.* Oxford: Pergamon Press. Aims to provide insights into the social dimensions of assimilating, employing and imparting a linguistics system different from that acquired natively; includes a comprehensive, critical review of the research in sociolinguistics related to interaction in a second language. Loveday also considers the dynamics of bilingualism and the cultural dimension of non-native language development.

SCARCELLA, R., ANDERSEN, E. S., and KRASHEN, S. 1990. *Developing Communicative Competence in a Second Language.* New York: Harper and Row. Focuses on various aspects of communicative competence in first and second language development. While the first section provides background information concerning communicative competence, three following sections examine discourse competence, sociolinguistic competence and strategic competence and the final sections discuss communicative competence in the workplace and in the school.

WOLFSON, N. 1989. *Perspectives: Sociolinguistics and TESOL.* Cambridge: Harper and Row. Designed to give classroom language teachers in the United States a thorough understanding of sociolinguistics and its application in ESL teaching; includes current overviews of the literature on conversation, bilingual education, standard and nonstandard dialects, miscommunication and speech acts. Heavy emphasis is placed on the ethnography of education.

APPENDIX

Still Burning: Confronting Ethnoviolence on Campus is a two-part videotape that examines acts of college campus violence. The tapes, which were shown at the recent National Association of Higher Education Conference, offer preventative measures and response strategies.

Contact: Marketing Coordinator, Instructional Technology, University of Maryland at Baltimore, Maryland 21228-5398.

Irvine High School in Irvine Unified School District has developed a series of videotapes presenting the experiences and conflicts facing immigrant and ethnic minority students. The topics include: introduction of a new immigrant student to class, immigrant students speaking their native language in an English class, and general discussion of students of different cultural backgrounds.

Contact: Bruce Barron, Irvine Unified School District, 5050 Barranca Parkway, Irvine, California 92714

NOTES

1. Enright and McCloskey (1988) also suggest that it is helpful for teachers to vary their requests for student participation — the ways in which they call on students for contributions. Calling on language minority students with weak English skills is likely to lead to their embarassment. Several other types of requests for student participation can be used in teacher-led classroom activities. Teachers can ask for students to volunteer answers to their questions, respond to questions chorally with the entire class, and follow a pattern in which students take turns in responding to questions. Teachers can encourage students to answer questions on a volunteer basis by asking them to raise their hands when they want to be called upon. Enright and McCloskey (1988) give an example of what teachers might *say* to get students to volunteer answers: "A rainbow is hard to explain. Anyone want to give it a try?" In choral elicitations, the entire class responds. Enright and McCloskey suggest a teacher might say the following to elicit a choral response: "We practiced the names of all the planets in our solar system yesterday. Let's do them again today as I point to the chart. Everyone." Patterned elicitations set up a specific pattern in which the students take turns responding to their teachers' questions. The pattern is usually explicitly described in advance. This could be done by explaining the pattern, as this teacher does: "I'd like to go around the class and have each of you tell what your favorite sport is and why."

2. Native-English speakers also have difficulty using academic, decontextualized, speech. Wells (1984) gives one reason for this:

> Some children have little difficulty in participating in such *decontextualized* talk, but others clearly find it bewildering. For although the objects or events that the teacher asks about may be well known to them as part of their out-of-school experience, that experience is not easily accessible to them when the familiar context in which it is normally embedded is absent and has to be recalled or manipulated through the medium of language alone. (pp. 232–233)

3. For descriptions of other activities designed to reduce prejudice, refer to Aboud 1988. For examples of cross-cultural training volumes which focus on strategies for increasing multicultural awareness and sensitivity, see Albert 1983; Brislin, Cusher, Cherrie and Yang 1986; and Pedersen 1988.

CHAPTER SIX

Appealing to a
Variety of Learning Styles

Students are entitled to educational experiences tailored to their unique cultural needs. We fail to provide these experiences when we create classroom environments which are incompatible with our students' learning styles. Educators use the term *learning style* to refer to cognitive and interactional patterns which affect the ways in which students perceive, remember, and think.

If the learning styles used by your students are incompatible with those which you foster through your teaching, you may find that your students suffer the consequences. Anthropologists have provided several critical examples of cultural groups responding with failure to school settings that are culturally inappropriate. In one study, Hawaiian children performing poorly when a phonics-based method of reading instruction was used reacted successfully to a more culturally appropriate comprehension-based reading program (Au 1980). According to Au and Jordan (1981), the comprehension-based method was culturally appropriate because it includes small-group discussions of the reading stories that matched the *talk story* language experiences of the Hawaiian children.

Research suggests that when we capitalize on our students' learning style preferences, the students learn more with less effort and remember better (Carbo, Dunn, and Dunn 1986). This chapter discusses strategies which complement a variety of learning styles. The goals of this chapter are: 1) to develop an awareness of the types of learning our schools tend to foster—more analytic, field-independent and discovery-oriented than reflective, field-sensitive and demonstration-oriented or mixed-in approaches (Cox and Ramirez 1981); 2) to appreciate our students' preferred learning styles; 3) to help our students become more comfortable with learning styles which they have not previously experienced, which means, encouraging learning style flexibility. In the sections which follow, I briefly discuss the following types of learning styles: sensory strength modality; global/analytical; field sensitive/field independent; and cooperative/individualistic. These learning styles have been reported to vary across cultures.

Before turning to this discussion, however, it is important to emphasize that there are grave dangers in stereotyping. Clearly, there is no particular cognitive style adhered to by any particular cultural group. There is great diversity even within cultures, and the task, the subject, and the teaching materials influence which learning styles students use. A student may be demonstration-oriented in one situation and discovery-oriented in another. Also, there are dangers in *mis*identifying learning styles and then developing instructional practices which build on learning styles which students do not use. Therefore, I do not advocate assessing student learning styles, labeling them, and employing specific instructional practices with specific students. Rather, I advocate deliberately varying teaching approaches to appeal to a wide variety of learning styles and encouraging students to try out new behaviors.

Sensory Modality Strength

One learning style which has been reported to vary across cultures is *sensory modality strength* (Cazden and Leggett 1981). Those who categorize students according to modality believe that students can be identified according to the sensory input which they seem to depend on most for information. Visual students remember well through the things that they see or read. Auditory students remember best what is heard. Tactile-kinesthetic learners must write or use their hands in some manipulative way to remember. Most students rely more heavily on one sense than the others. Yet, to say a student prefers one sense does not mean that he or she cannot function effectively using other senses (Carbo, Dunn and Dunn 1981). The student simply indicates a preference. One child may find it easy to sit still and attend to visual stimuli for forty minutes while a more active student may use so much energy sitting still that there is nothing left for the learning task. The volume of sound that pleases some children may be painful or distracting to others. The level of light may be perfect for some, but too bright or dim for others. Some students work well at the back of the classroom while others are so distracted by the other children that they can only concentrate on what the teacher is saying when they are sitting in front.

To treat every student exactly the same way is to favor some and penalize others. A classroom can have areas that are quiet in an auditory sense—a *no talking* table; seating can be arranged to fit individual needs. For a student who has always had trouble remembering spoken instructions but who can follow written directions, it can be an exciting revelation to discover that for a particular task his visual system works better than his auditory one. (Williams 1983, p. 51)

Visual Learners

Many teachers observe informally that some children seem to learn more through their eyes while other children learn more through their ears. Cazden and John (1971) report extensive observations on the visual strengths of native American children from many tribes, and Philips (1974) adds observations from the Warm Spring Reservation in Oregon. John-Steiner and Osterreich (1975) also report visual strengths in a study of learning styles among Pueblo children. In a similar vein, Cheng (1987) reports that many Asian students learn through observation and modelling.

Similarly, Laosa (1982) claims that some Mexican-Americans prefer a modelling approach which relies heavily on the visual modality. In some ways, Laosa's work echoes the work of Ramirez and Castaneda (1974), who suggest that demonstrating tasks to some groups of Mexican-Americans is particularly important because it capitalizes on the Mexican-Americans' strengths in visual memory.

Middle-American schools in general rely too heavily on verbal presentations by teachers. But this over-reliance on the auditory channel is especially unfortunate in classrooms where students are not auditory students. For those students who do not find it easy to remember a great deal of what they hear, teachers who are lecturing or discussing important information with their classes should always write the key words that are being discussed on the chalkboard or on acetate on an overhead projector. Pictures, slides, drawings and photos also help visual students. (Chapter 4 provides additional suggestions.) Visual students who learn easily by viewing, watching and observing may also benefit from reading about a new concept the night before it is taught in class. They may also benefit from demonstrations and field trips.

Many students can benefit from the wide variety of multi-sensory materials now available.[1] For instance, Pellowski (1984) has collected stories that use many visual devices and has included directions for using them. Enright and McCloskey (1988) suggest additional ways to make lessons meaningful for visually oriented elementary school children. They state:

> You can create sketch or picture stories. During key points in the story, you can add an element to the drawing. You can use the felt board and simple felt pieces and figures to add a similar cumulative visual dimension and focus to your story. You can also use string stories, finger-play stories, and figurine stories to provide a visual component. (pp. 24–25)

Auditory Learners

Auditory learners recall much of what is discussed or heard in their lessons. They can recreate what they hear by concentrating on previous lessons. Students who learn easily and well by listening should be introduced to new information by hearing it (Carbo, Dunn, and Dunn 1981). Teachers working with auditory learners should audio-tape record class lessons so that their students can play the recorded lessons back for review.

Tactile-Kinesthetic Learners

While the majority of students prefer the visual or auditory channel, there are some who are primarily tactile-kinesthetic. These students are less able to learn by hearing and seeing than by touching (tactile) and moving (kinesthetic). "For them, information is most easily taken in through their hands and through movement. They like to handle things, to move them around and to move themselves around" (Williams 1983, p. 151). They remember more easily when they write, doodle, draw, or move their fingers. In many cultures, storytelling involves a tactile or kinesthetic accompaniment. Two examples are making marks in the sand (for example, the Walbiri of Australia, as reported in Pellowski 1984) and using story knives to carve in the snow (for instance, the Eskimos as reported by Enright and McCloskey 1988). Middle-American schools rarely complement the styles of tactually or kinesthetically oriented students. This is a sense which has been historically overlooked. Teachers can accommodate young tactile-kinesthetic students by working with students with sandpaper letters and substances of different textures and shapes. They can also have students learn math or spelling facts while clapping. Taking trips, baking, building, making art projects and objects, interviewing, and acting are just a few kinesthetic activities. Talking or reading about a subject may not capture the interest of tactile-kinesthetic students. They are more likely to succeed by participating in laboratory experiments and field trips, and by manipulating materials (puzzles, models, collections of objects). Kinesthetic experiences can also be created in a classroom through simulation and role playing.

Research supports what many teachers have intuitively known, which is that students learn through their senses and prefer some senses over others in specific situations. When lessons are presented visually as well as verbally, and when all the senses are engaged in the learning process, students are able not only to learn in the way best suited to their style, but also to develop a full and varied repertoire of learning styles. The best strategy presently is, then, a deliberately multisensory one. As Bissell, White and Zivin (1971) point out:

> By teaching the concept of a [math] set or any other concept with a multisensory approach, one is not only more likely to reach all the children in a class but also more likely to make each child's learning experience a richer thing. (p. 150)

Global/Analytic

Related to the learning style dimension of sensory strength is that of global/analytic thinking. Research on the hemispheres of the brain suggests that we possess two different ways of processing information, *global* (spatial, relational), in the right hemisphere, and *analytic* (linear, step-by-step) in the left hemisphere. This still speculative research suggests that global learners require an overall picture first. Analytic learners, by contrast, piece the details together to form an understanding. The analytic learner moves from one point to another in a step-by-step manner, while the global learner separates parts. Pulling the pieces back together through synthesis, the global learner constructs patterns and recognizes relationships efficiently through visual and spatial processing. Global styles rest on experience, impressions and sensing. (Table 6-1 summarizes the proposed characteristics of the two learner types.)

To say that students are either global or analytic is clearly a simplification. Students merely prefer one style to another in specific situations. Some students are flexible and use one strategy or the other to fit the requirement of the situation or problem. Others limit themselves to just one—regardless of the learning situation. These students are less likely to be effective problem solvers.

Middle-Americans are often considered *analytic*. According to Stewart (1972), for many middle-Americans, the world is composed of facts, not patterns. Mainstream American schools are particularly suited to analytical persons, but analysis is not always the most efficient way to approach problems. Many problems are better understood through pictures, maps, diagrams, charts and mind maps. The Chinese pattern of thinking is said to provide an accentuated example of the global style; it is sometimes suggested that Chinese thinking strives for unity between events or objects. Similarly, some propose

Table 6-1
Characteristics of Global and Analytical Learners

Global	Analytical
(right hemisphere, spatial relational)	*(left hemisphere, linear, step by step)*
• likes the whole picture	• pieces together the separate pieces
• is impulsive	• is critical
• processes simultaneously	• processes sequentially
• is spatial	• is temporal
• seeks patterns	• seeks parts

that the Chinese are more likely to think by means of analogies and to make greater use of metaphors and similes in drawing conclusions.

One way to appeal to global learners is through fantasy, the ability to generate and manipulate mental imagery. For example, Williams (1983) suggests that:

> . . .a textbook analysis of osmosis is too abstract and technical for some students to master. A fantasy in which students imagine themselves either as a membrane or a molecule passing through a membrane creates inner imagery which is useful to visual thinkers and provides a concrete experience that has the power to stimulate and involve many thinkers who are less responsive to a textbook [analytical] approach. (p. 32)

It is helpful to identify your own predisposition towards analytic and global thinking and intentionally vary your teaching styles for your students. For example, you can build topics both analytically and globally. If you are used to introducing a topic with a story and then zeroing in on its substantive facts midway through the lesson, you can begin with the important facts first and then overview the topic. Building the topic both globally and analytically will reach both types of students.

Reflectivity/impulsivity is another learning style contrast which is closely related to the global/analytic dichotomy. Reflective learners search slowly for answers and impulsive learners make quick guesses (Damen 1988). Most middle-American teachers are *impulsive* in that they value quick answers to questions and sometimes even judge students who respond slowly as *reticent* or *stupid*. However, as Damen (1988) points out, some cultures emphasize reflectivity.

> A case in point can be found among students from Asia, especially Japan. To make a mistake is painful; to guess is to admit not having spent enough time in finding the right answer. Being only partially *right*, which may be acceptable to the impulsive learners, is often seen as totally *wrong* by those whose reflective learning styles are culturally sanctioned. Such styles are often accompanied by a relativistic approach to *truth* in which several choices or answers on True/False tests may represent *correct* answers. Silent periods of reflection before responding are observed in many cultures, particularly in the Far East. Such pauses are often interpreted incorrectly by teachers as an inability, or even a refusal, to respond. Lowered eyes and bowed heads, rather than silence, are more likely to be the nonverbal signals indicating no response is forthcoming. (pp. 301–302)

Field Sensitivity/Field Independence

Research on the learning style dimension called field sensitivity/field independence began when Witkin conducted a series of studies investigating individuals' learning preferences. He examined the extent to which an individual's perception is influenced by the surrounding environment.[2] According to Ramirez and Castañeda (1974),

> In a *field dependent* mode of perception, the organization of the *field as a whole dominates perception* of its parts; an item within a field is experienced as fused with the organized ground. In a *field independent* mode of perception, the person is able to perceive *items as discrete* from the organized field. (p. 65)

Witkin and others found that in many situations, field-sensitive students exhibit some of the following behaviors: they like to work with others to achieve a common goal, enjoy assisting others, are sensitive to feelings and opinions of others, seek guidance and demonstration from the teacher, deal well with concepts in humanized story format, and function well when curriculum content is made relevant to personal interests and experiences. In contrast, field-independent students prefer to work independently, like to compete and gain individual recognition, are task oriented and inattentive to the social environment, restrict interactions with the teacher to tasks at hand, like to try new tasks without the teacher's help, focus on details and parts of things, and like discovery or trial and error learning. (Refer to Table 6–2.) Both styles are used by individuals, but all individuals may prefer one style in specific situations.

Table 6–2
Characteristics of Field-Sensitive and Field-Independent Learners

Field-Sensitive	Field-Independent
• like to work with others to achieve a common goal	• like to work independently
• enjoy assisting others	• like to compete
• are sensitive to the feelings and opinions of others	• are inattentive to the social environment
• seek guidance and demonstration from the teacher	• restrict interaction with teacher to the task at hand
• deal well with concepts in humanized story format	• focus on details and parts of things
• function well when curriculum is relevant to personal interests and experiences	• like discovery or trial-and-error learning

Cox and Ramirez 1981

Few families encourage only one learning style, even though *on the average* they may use one type of strategy more than the other in some situations. Cox and Ramirez (1981) state:

> One family may emphasize the importance of people—how people relate to each other, who does what in the family. Children in this family may learn about motivation—why people do things. They may learn many things by modelling what they see older people or siblings doing. Another family may encourage their children to find out things for themselves at an early age. Children from such families learn to work things out for themselves by trial and error and may not enjoy learning concepts which require careful observation and imitating. They may not learn to feel themselves to be a part of a group as early as will the children from the family that encourages more social interaction. (p. 63)

Currently, the organization of most classrooms tends to reflect the style which is characteristic of mainstream schooling: namely field independence. In mainstream American schools, instruction is organized "to promote individual achievement, ability to analyze individual components and to detach oneself from the object of study" (Robinson 1985, p. 21).

Research reported by Ramirez and Castañeda (1974), Kagan and Buriel (1977), Keogh, Welles and Weiss (1972) and others indicates that, on the average, some groups of young Mexican and Black students are more field-sensitive than field-independent. For example, the particular minority groups they researched were more group-oriented, more sensitive to and distracted by the social environment, and more positively responsive to adult modelling than non-minority students. Furthermore, the students they investigated were, on the average, less competitive, less sensitive to spatial incursions by others; less comfortable in trial-and error situations; and less interested in the fine details of concepts, materials, or tasks that are non-social. These behaviors often appear together and describe field sensitive individuals.[3]

It should be noted that ways to test field sensitivity and field independence, such as the Embedded Figures Test (EFT) and the Portable Rod and Frame Test (PRFT), assume there is a unidimensional construct underlying field sensitivity/field independence. This is questionable. The presence of one behavior does not mean that other behaviors will also be present. For instance, just because a student likes to work alone does not mean that he or she is discovery-oriented. Also, the EFT and PRFT do not use actual classroom observations; to assess field sensitivity and field independence accurately, it is important to observe your students directly and examine their functioning in the classroom. (Cox and Ramirez, 1981, give guidelines for observing students; refer to the appendix.)

Robinson (1985) points out the difficulty of labeling students on the basis of preferred or dominant learning style. She states:

First, there are problems with the instruments used to measure field independence and field sensitivity as learning styles. Second, even if we could accurately identify cultural tendencies in preferred perceptual or learning style, it would not mean that all members of that culture perceive, organize or interpret information as culturally anticipated. While experiences within a particular culture, as defined by ethnicity, may contribute to the dominance of one style over the other, a given individual usually is a member of various groups (such as those defined by gender, socio-economic status, nationality), which also affects perception. (pp. 21-22)

Middle-American classrooms tend to be more suitable for field-independent students. Yet, field sensitivity is a valuable learning style which should be fostered. Tasks which allow for more interpersonal interaction can be used to develop and complement field-sensitive learning styles. Such tasks can be created through the cooperative approaches discussed in Chapter 5. If teachers want to provide learning experiences which complement field sensitive styles, they need to model behaviors and solutions, express warmth, elicit synthesis, draw attention to global characteristics and generalizations, devise cooperative tasks and group projects, adapt materials to student experiences (in other words, *personalize* their lessons, use student-developed materials, give social rather than nonsocial rewards; Robinson 1985). Robinson (1985) suggests that rather than labeling students, educators can structure tasks to develop the *cultural versatility* of all students.

Cooperation versus Individualism

Closely related to the dimension of field sensitivity/field independence is the cooperation/individualism dimension. Middle-American students are generally individualistic rather than cooperative. Maller (1929) states:

The frequent staging of contests, the constant emphasis upon making and breaking of records, and the glorification of the heroic individual achievement and championship in our present educational system lead toward the acquisition of the habit of competitiveness. The child is trained to look at the members of his group as constant competitors and urged to put forth a maximum effort to excel them. The lack of practice in group activities and community projects in which the child works with his fellows for a common goal precludes the formation of habits of cooperativeness and group loyalty. (p. 163)

Goodlad's (1984) recent survey of over 1,000 classrooms echoes Maller's lament. Goodlad states, "For the most part, the teachers in our sample of schools controlled rather firmly the central role of deciding what, where, when and how the students were to learn. When students played a role, it was somewhat peripheral, such as deciding where they sat" (p. 109). Researchers agree that in most classrooms, students are expected to sit quietly and work independently most of the day. Children are generally asked to suppress their help-giving, rewards are administered individually, and authority is vested in a single adult, the teacher.

People from some cultures value cooperativeness to a greater extent than do middle-Americans. For example, in their detailed analysis of the cooperativeness of a South Pacific Island population, Graves and Graves (1983) found that children from more traditional homes were more cooperative during social interaction games. Children from traditional homes had difficulty adjusting to their teachers' interactional styles which normally reflected Western values.

Similarly, extensive research documents the cooperativeness of some groups of Mexican-American students. For instance, in one set of experiments, it was established that compared to mainstream American students, Mexican-American students and other minority students have lower achievement if the achievement is for themselves, but have higher achievement if the achievement is for their family (Kagan 1986). Delgado-Gaitán (1987) examined Mexican children in Los Portales, California. She found that the children's abilities to cooperate were not usually recognized in the classroom, noting:

> Collectivity and competitiveness was one area of continuity-discontinuity observed in Los Portales home and classroom activities. Home data show a stronger cooperative ethic in their work and play, including sharing of work load, turn-taking, collective group games, and frequent negotiation tasks. Children in Los Portales do have experience in competitive skills in home tasks that require children to work alone or in play where only one winner is possible in a game. However, such occasions are infrequent in the home life of the children observed. Their transition to a highly competitive emphasis in school does not permit the expression of their familiar collective practices at home in a way that would assist them in sharing ideas or developing language skills. Children attempt to work together whenever they are assigned independent seatwork, but usually such sharing of information is against classroom rules as it is considered disruptive and a form of cheating. (p. 357)

There is evidence that black, Asian, and native American students are also relatively more cooperative than middle-American students. Kagan (1989) summarizes the negative consequences of a mismatch between home/culture and school/classroom values related to cooperation. In his words:

> If a culture places a strong value on cooperative work and the school communicates through the relatively exclusive choice of competitive and individualistic structures that it places little or no

value on cooperative work, there is a mismatch between home/culture values on one side and school/culture values on the other. The likely consequence of this mismatch is alienation of minority students. Tragically, these students may be caught between the two value systems, and end up alienated to some extent from both home and school values. When there is alienation from the school value system, there is consequent alienation from the language of the school. In the struggle to form an identity which expresses the mismatch between home and school values, some minority students may avoid acquisition of speech patterns provided by the school; part of the formation of a counter culture is the formation of speech patterns which distinguish it from the mainstream culture. (3.6–3.7)

In most middle-American classrooms, the teacher is *in control.* Classroom seating arrangements provide an excellent example of expectations of *authority* and *control.* A common arrangement in middle-American classrooms involves individuals seated row-by-row, with the teacher standing at the front of the room. *Classroom control* may include such behaviors as strong projection of voice, sustained eye contact from a standing position, obvious displays of enthusiasm or displeasure, and public comments (questions, praise, challenge, reprimand) directed to individuals.

Some cultural groups expect the teacher to exert even more control than that exerted by most middle-American teachers. Cheng (1987), for example, states that most Asian students expect their teachers to run the class in a highly controlled manner. Asian students are accustomed to working in a quiet environment and never roam freely around the classroom as do some of their mainstream American peers. They expect to listen to adults, not interrupt, sit quietly and listen attentively, never challenging the teacher.

Yet, other cultural groups, such as Mexican-American and native American children may do better (at least initially) given more autonomy than that usually allowed in middle-American classrooms. Delgado-Gaitán (1987) noted that Mexican-American children in Los Portales, California, follow the authority of their parents; however, parents at home allow children to negotiate with them and make decisions for themselves about the manner in which they will accomplish tasks.

> The adults in the school usually organize the entire task and exclude children from the decision-making process so that alternative ways of accomplishing tasks are not an option. Furthermore, parents in the home often leave children an opportunity to feel confident about their abilities. Teachers are often unaware that this is a form of leadership potential that children can teach one another. The manifestation of authority in the [traditional] classroom conceivably limits children's language expression with peers and inhibits their ability to demonstrate independent leadership skills. (p. 357)

Along similar lines, Macias (1987) found that Papago native American children value autonomy and are not restricted or directed by adults in their play while on the reservation. They are raised with very few limitations on their freedom and children are not accustomed to being controlled. Respect in the form of a deep appreciation of each child's distinctiveness is an important characteristic of Papago childrearing (William 1958). But this type of respect depends upon noninterference with children's autonomy. In other words, Papagos place an emphasis on individual rights and choice.

Competition is the primary method among middle-Americans of motivating members of a group and some have seen it as a basic characteristic of mainstream American society.

> Americans with their individualism and ideas of achieving, respond well to this technique but where the same approach is applied to members of another culture who do not hold the same values, the effort is ineffective at best and may produce undesirable consequences. People for whom saving face is important or for whom dependency on others is desirable will not accept competition among members of the group with the same enthusiasm as Americans. Thus, attempts to instill a competitive spirit in Laotian and Cambodian children have met with failure. The communal feeling toward each group excludes the incentive to excel over others either as a member of a group or individually.
>
> (Stewart 1972, p. 42)

Research indicates that cooperatively oriented students perform better in cooperatively structured classrooms and competitively-oriented students perform better in competitively structured classes. (see Klein and Eshel 1980 and Kagan 1986.)

One way to appeal to the cooperative learning styles of your students is to incorporate cooperative learning activities. Enright and McCloskey (1988) suggest that rules and procedures be created that promote cooperation, collaboration and multicultural understanding. For example, at the beginning of the year, they suggest that teachers "establish a supportive, cooperative, collaborative environment which helps students learn about one another and about the cultures represented in the classroom" and that teachers build "cooperation into the learning tasks students perform by creating *must* cooperate tasks." These tasks could include "cooperative projects, peer conferences, cooperative games, learning-centers where students can work independently without teacher supervision" (Enright and McCloskey 1988, p. 242; see also Chapter 11).

The cooperative learning activities suggested by Kagan (1986, 1989) can also be incorporated effectively in your classroom.[4] In these activities, students help other students within groups of four to five persons in an effort to reach goals. Teammates support rather than put down or dismiss the achievements of others.

In cooperative structures students are active, self-directing and communicative. Student behaviors, norms and relationships change: students engage in peer tutoring, evolve norms and sanctions supporting achievement and have relationships that are more often characterized by equal status. (Kagan 1986, p. 261)

Adaptations of cooperative learning can be effective at many different age levels from the late elementary grades through the high school and adult levels. They can be used in second and foreign language teaching situations as well as content classes in almost any subject. They are especially useful when native or near-native English-speaking students are able to provide *comprehensible* input to language minority students in a comfortable environment (Richard-Amato 1988).

Group seating allows a teacher to instruct some groups of children (such as native American) in a manner which is culturally familiar to them. In this way, the teacher can take the opportunity to sit with the children at their own eye level, speak softly, maintain a calm demeanor, demonstrate skills, and support the children as they practice.

Unfortunately, educators sometimes marginalize those students whose learning styles do not match their own. As Hartnett (1985) puts it, "teachers tend to value students whose cognitive style is like theirs, reinforcing a positive self-image in their students. When mismatching occurs, the student is likely to feel frustrated and hostile to the subject matter, and learning in general." (p. 28)

Conclusion

Teachers need to learn about their students' learning styles and understand how to acknowledge and utilize them. Some researchers have suggested that the school curriculum be changed and teachers be trained explicitly to teach ways to accommodate to the children's stylistic differences (Ramirez and Castañeda 1974), but this strategy is questionable, and it is difficult to assess the effectiveness of this approach (Diaz 1983, Diaz, Moll and Mehan 1986). We can, however, acknowledge and respect our students' preferences and attempt to build upon them. This means genuinely appreciating differences in learning styles. If we do not appreciate these preferences, we do not serve our students adequately. As Hymes (1981) states: "One can honor cultural pride on the walls of a room yet inhibit learning within them." (p. 59)

ACTIVITIES AND DISCUSSION QUESTIONS

1. Do you personally have difficulty labelling students as *field independent* and *field dependent*? Is it really possible to identify such

students accurately? What problems might arise if students are inaccurately identified?

2. Use the Cox and Ramirez' (1981) Observable Student Behaviors form (contained in the appendix) with a small group of language minority students. To what extent do you think it is possible to use forms such as this to identify student learning styles? If possible, observe this same group of students in a classroom setting. Based on your own observations, how accurately do you think the Cox and Ramirez form identifies field independent and dependent learners?

3. Briefly describe the various means of appealing to students of diverse learning styles discussed here. Which ones do you personally prefer? (For example, do you consider yourself an analytical learner or a global one?) Explain your rationale for your choice. Next, consider whether you vary your learning style according to the situation in which you find yourself. If you do, give examples.

4. Examine a textbook you are currently using. Which learning styles does it most appeal to? How can you supplement your textbook to appeal to other learning styles?

5. What specific activities can you use to encourage students to be tolerant of others' learning styles?

6. Design at least one classroom activity which would employ teaching strategies which appeal to a variety of learning styles.

RECOMMENDED READING

CARBO, M., DUNN, R., and DUNN, R. 1986. *Teaching Students to Read through their Individual Learning Styles.* Englewood Cliffs, New Jersey: Prentice Hall. Includes a variety of useful suggestions for increasing the reading ability of children in primary grades by matching methods and materials to individual strengths.

OXFORD, R. 1989. *Language Learning Strategies: What Every Teacher Should Know.* New York: Harper and Row. Based on current research; provides practical recommendations for developing students' second language learning strategies. Among the strategies Oxford suggests are memory strategies for remembering new information and compensatory strategies for using new language despite limitations. Detailed suggestions for strategy use in each of the four language skills are included.

RAMIREZ, M., and CASTAÑEDA, A. 1974. *Cultural Democracy, Bicognitive Development, and Education.* New York: Academic Press. For teachers interested in reading about the classical research on field dependence and field independence.

WILLIAMS, L. V. 1983. *Teaching for the Two-Sided Mind: A Guide to Right Brain/Left Brain Education.* Englewood Cliffs, New Jersey: Prentice-Hall. Suggests strategies for appealing to both global and analytical learners in school settings.

Appendix

OBSERVABLE STUDENT BEHAVIORS

Date of Observation_____

Field Sensitive   **Field-Independent**

Relationship to Peers

1. Likes to work with others to achieve a common goal.
2. Likes to assist others.
3. Is sensitive to feelings and opinions of others.

1. Prefers to work independently.
2. Likes to compete and gain individual recognition.
3. Task-oriented; is inattentive to social environment when working.

Personal Relationship to Teacher

1. Openly expresses positive feelings for teacher.
2. Asks questions about teacher's tastes and personal experiences; seeks to become like teacher.

1. Avoids physical contact with teacher.
2. Formal; interactions with teacher are restricted to tasks at hand.

Instructional Relationship to Teacher

1. Seeks guidance and demonstration from teacher.
2. Seeks rewards which strengthen relationship with teacher.
3. Is highly motivated when working individually with teacher.

1. Likes to try new tasks without teacher's help.
2. Impatient to begin tasks; likes to finish first.
3. Seeks nonsocial rewards.

Thinking Style

1. Functions well when objectives are carefully explained or things modeled prior to activity.
2. Deals well with concepts in humanized or story format.
3. Functions well when curriculum is made relevant to personal interests and experiences.

1. Focuses on details and parts of lesson.
2. Deals well with math and science concepts.
3. Likes discovery or trial-and-error learning.

CODE: Never   Seldom   Sometimes   Usually

Cox and Ramirez (1981, p. 67)

NOTES

1. Considerable research suggests that middle-American children are more visual than auditory and that adults are more adept than children varying the sensory modality they rely upon when problem-solving.

2. Several tests were used for this purpose, including *The Embedded Figures Test* (which requires subjects to find a simple design within a more complex one) and *The Rod and Frame Test* (which requires subjects to adjust a rod to a position perceived as vertical within a square frame that is tilted). See, for example, Witkin and Goodenough 1976 and Witkin et al. 1974.

3. *Field sensitivity* has replaced the term, *field dependence*, because of negative connotations often associated with *dependence* in the United States.

4. For information regarding cooperative learning, educators should contact D. Spencer Kagan, Resources for Teachers, 27134 Paseo Espada, #202, San Juan Capistrano, California 92675 (714) 248–7757.

CHAPTER SEVEN

Providing Effective Feedback

As teachers of multicultural classes, we must provide effective feedback to language minority students of diverse cultural backgrounds. This means accurately interpreting our language minority students' reactions to our lessons and understanding our own methods of giving feedback. By maintaining certain expectations about communication, teachers may unwittingly ask language minority students to violate deeply ingrained cultural patterns. For example, middle-American teachers usually expect students to look them in the eye when answering their questions. If the students fail to maintain eye contact when addressing a teacher, the teacher may become annoyed and view the students as insolent. When their teacher's use and interpretation of feedback is inconsistent with their own, language minority students may become victims of the miscommunication.

How can information about cross-cultural differences help us provide our students with more effective feedback? Children learn feedback patterns in their homes, but once they reach the age of five or six, their days are spent at schools where their teachers usually do not share their use and interpretation of feedback.[1] Students who are unable to acquire middle-American feedback behaviors are handicapped in our schools. (Refer to the home/school discontinuities explanation for academic failure discussed in Chapter 1.)

This chapter provides teachers with ideas for providing language minority students with feedback which is sensitive to the needs of diverse cultural groups. Although a compendium of feedback with respect to all cultural groups is not given, the cultural patterns discussed here are shared by many and suggest areas in which possible cultural misunderstandings might occur. The following aspects of feedback are considered:

1. Interpreting student feedback: how teachers interpret the feedback students use to let them know they are following and understanding their lessons; what constitutes *paying attention* and *understanding* from the teacher's point of view;

2. Complimenting and criticizing: what constitutes *compliments* and *criticism* from the teachers' and students' perspectives;

3. Correcting student errors: how students value error correction;

4. Requesting clarification: how students make requests for clarification and help; how teachers interpret these requests;

5. Spotlighting: how teachers call attention to an individual student's behavior in front of others; the teacher's use of *singling out;*

6. Questioning and answering: how questions are used by teachers to check student comprehension and how students answer these questions;

7. Pausing: how much time students need to respond to their teacher's questions; how fast the teacher and students interact.

Each of these aspects of feedback is discussed below. However, before turning to this discussion, it is important to consider the serious problems involved in generalizing research about cross-cultural differences to specific students. Cultural groups are not homogeneous. Such factors as age, gender, personality, motivation, and acculturation affect the students' use and interpretation of feedback. For instance, Native Americans come from many tribes with distinct languages, values, and rituals of their own. Latinos speak different dialects of Spanish, come from diverse social and economic classes, and follow different cultural norms and traditions. The Asian and Latino students in your classes may be immigrants who recently arrived in the United States, but they may also be sixth- or seventh-generation Americans. All this means that you will need to consider whether your students actually use the feedback patterns discussed. With this reservation in mind, I would like to turn to a discussion of those patterns said to lead to cultural misunderstandings in multicultural classrooms.

CROSS-CULTURAL DIFFERENCES

Interpreting Student Feedback

One possible misunderstanding may result from misinterpreting your students' feedback. How do you interpret the feedback your students give you when talking to them? You may be used to seeing considerable enthusiasm on the part of mainstream American students. Your students' eye gaze, nods, and smiles let you know that they are paying attention and understanding you. But, attention and interest are displayed differently across cultures. Choctaw (Native American) students don't display as much excitement as middle-

American students, but that doesn't mean that they are not interested or that they dislike you (Richmond 1987). Latino students may avoid looking at you when you speak, but their lack of eye contact may indicate respect and is not intended to display dislike, defiance or disinterest. Head nods may signal that Asian students are politely listening, not necessarily *understanding* what you are saying. The Asian student's smile may simply mean that the student is politely attending to your speech, not that he agrees with you, finds your lessons amusing, or comprehends what you are saying (Tran 1984). Many Asian children are taught to mask their emotions. Displays of emotion are not encouraged by many Asian adults; when these displays occur, parents may punish children for not controlling their feelings (Stover 1962).

Cross-cultural differences in this area can lead to serious misunderstandings. When Mohatt and Erickson (1981) observed a middle-American teacher instructing Odawa Indian children, they noted that the mainstream American teacher called on those children who seemed most interested in their lessons and seemed likely to know the answers to their questions; Mohatt and Erickson point out that, for middle-Americans, the most salient cue that a student is following you is that he or she is *looking up at you.* Yet, Odawa Indian children do not use the same nonverbal behavior to signal their interest. They look down when addressed. Eye contact, as practiced in the United States, is not a universal signal that a student is listening. This explains the *silent Indian* phenomenon so frequently discussed in the literature. (see Philips 1972, 1974, 1983)

Complimenting and Criticizing Students

Just as you may misinterpret the feedback your students give you, your students may misinterpret the feedback you give them. For example, some Japanese students may be confused when they find check marks on their papers. Damen (1988) comments, "the Japanese system of marking answers correct or incorrect includes the following: correct-O or X; incorrect-V. Can you imagine how confusing this might be for a Japanese student who receives all checkmarks from an uninitiated teacher?" (p. 234)

How do you praise your students? Most middle-American teachers give their students frequent compliments. In fact, many middle-American children have come to expect happy faces on their papers and frequent compliments. When students do not receive such praise from their teachers, they may feel as though they have done something wrong, that they are incompetent in some way.

Students from some cultures do not value compliments to the same extent as mainstream Americans. For example, Asian students may view frequent verbal praise as insincere (Condon 1986). One university student from Japan specifically asked me to give him poor grades on his essays and only an occasional high grade. "This way," he said, "I will believe you when you say my essay is good." Some

Asian children may be surprised to find happy faces drawn on their papers on a daily basis and may be unaccustomed to stickers and stamps. Praise might even cause some students shame since humility is considered a virtue in many Asian cultures. Iwatake (1978) states: "Asians, with their strong sense of humbleness, feel uncomfortable accepting compliments. They tend to reject compliments sincerely feeling unworthy." (p. 80)

In contrast to some Asian groups, other ethnic groups may expect more praise than is usually given by mainstream American teachers. Some groups of Latinos, for instance, give and expect more positive comments (such as *right, good, yes*) than middle-Americans and prefer praise to be given in more personal, face-to-face encounters (Scarcella 1983). This is not surprising since personal attention is a vital ingredient in Latino communication (Damen 1987).

Some children are accustomed to more body contact than is usually given by middle-American educators. Middle-American teachers apparently have less tactile involvement with students than Latino teachers. A young Brazilian teacher who taught mainstream American children in the United States told of her students' surprise when she patted them on their shoulders and backs (Harrison 1983). Cross-cultural differences in tactile behavior could be difficult for Mediterranean and Latino children who may be more accustomed to embraces and pats than mainstream Americans. (Byers and Byers 1972, Dumont 1972, Collier 1973, Mehan 1973)

In line with this, the body gestures middle-American teachers use to convey positive feedback may be misunderstood by students or may be perceived as offensive. For instance, some Arabs may perceive touching a student of the opposite sex and winking to be offensive, some East Asians may perceive touching a student on the head and hugging as offensive, and some Latinos may perceive the *okay* sign as taboo, since it means *Screw you!* (Damen 1987).

The distance from which praise is delivered might affect teacher/student communication in more subtle ways. The observation that Latinos and Middle Easterners appreciate interpersonal communication at closer distances than mainstream Americans do is frequently discussed in the literature. Mainstream Americans talking to one another stand at least one foot further back than some groups of Latinos (Harrison 1983). Praise delivered in front of others instead of face-to-face in close proximity may seem impersonal to some students and embarrassing to others (refer to discussion of *spotlighting* below).

In sum, language minority students may find middle-American praise effusive, insufficient, or inappropriate. They may also fail to recognize their middle-American teacher's efforts to give them positive feedback. As Saville-Troike (1977) puts it, "direct eye contact with a student may be positive, but it may be interpreted as aggressive or humiliating; smiling may be positive, but it may be derisive; touching may be positive, but it may be embarassing or repugnant" (p. 107).

Like positive feedback, there are wide disparities in the use and interpretation of negative feedback. For this reason, teachers should particularly avoid reprimanding students in front of others. In Mexico, for instance, any public action or remark that may be interpreted as a slight to the person's dignity may be regarded as a grave offense (Condon 1986). Most Saudis, like most Latinos, are easily affected by public criticism and normally do not respond positively. Middle Easterners regard the mainstream American's willingness to openly criticize as immoral; for the Middle Easterner, one should not go on record describing other's faults (Parker 1986, Frechette 1987). Most Asian groups seem to view direct confrontation as rude and inappropriate (Iwatake 1978, Condon 1986). Tran (1984) states, "The Vietnamese avoid confrontation at all costs. A Vietnamese may say *yes* when he means *no* in order to avoid confrontation." (p. 23) In many cultures, reprimands are heightened when teachers raise their voices. A raised voice may represent authority and strength to many middle-Americans, but it represents loss of control to many Asian, Native American and Latino students.

Psychological difficulties undoubtedly affect the perception of criticism. Immigrant students from Afghanistan, Central America, Cambodia, Vietnam, Laos, and Lebanon have suffered trauma from war and political violence. Many have lost close friends or relatives and have themselves been threatened by excessive violence, starvation, and war atrocities. Along with differences in feedback patterns, these students often bring to the classroom their psychological problems. One student writes:

> The tragedy during the war hurts inside when I remember what happened in the past. I try not to think about it, but at night I dream and see my brother who they killed. I dream about him trying to find us. I dream they keep shooting him and shooting him until I wake up. 10th grade Cambodian boy, immigrated at age 12. (reported in Olsen 1988, p. 22)

Latinos who come to the United States illegally and are separated from family members, lost, or deserted also suffer from emotional turmoil. A Mexican student states, in describing his trip to the United States:

> It was scary to me. We went separate across. I was caught the first time and sent back to my aunt's house. This time she paid a lot of money to a coyote [who smuggles people across the border] to get me across. He put me in a sack in the back of a truck with potatoes and told me to be totally quiet until he came to get me. I was hot and couldn't breathe and so scared. I cried with no sound until he came to get me. I had gotten across. But where was my mother? 9th grade Mexican boy, immigrated at age 7. (reported in Olsen 1988, p. 26)

Students who are emotionally troubled may be particularly vulnerable to criticism. Since teachers really cannot know the traumas individual students may have experienced, treating them gently in general is a better guideline. Less criticism as a rule is better than more. (Pedagogical suggestions for providing these students with feedback are given in the next section. See also Chapter 1.)

Correcting Student Errors

Just as the perception of compliments and criticism varies widely across cultures, so too does the perception of error correction. Many cultures place great value on explicit correction. In the United States, many teachers explicitly correct their students (making such explicit statements as: "That's an incomplete sentence," "You got the wrong answer," and "Try harder." "You've forgotten the right answer.") Other cultures may, however, place an even greater emphasis on error correction. For instance, in examining classroom practices by French teachers, Dannequin (1977) observes that pupils do not have the *right* to make mistakes, but must instead conform to teachers' standards. One important aspect of Japanese life is learning the proper form. Great value is placed on doing things *right*. According to Thompson (1987): "the traditional Japanese regard for authority and formality is in tune with teacher-dominated lessons where much heed is paid to the *correct* answer, learning of grammar rules and item-by-item (rather than contextualized) vocabulary" (p. 223). A salient feature of Chinese education is obsessive concern with correctness (Maley 1986). Lewis (1974) observes the stress in Soviet pedagogy on the value of error correction. It is not surprising then that students from these cultures experience frustration when participating in a class in which there is no error correction.

However, not all cultures believe that error correction is important. For instance, Chipeweyan adults assume that good grammatical performance is only expected of older people. It is generally believed that Chipeweyan takes a lifetime to learn because it is so difficult. Similarly, Blount (1977) notes that in Luo and Koya society, care-givers are not responsive to the language mistakes made by children. Schieffelin (1983) reports that the major strategy for teaching young Kaluli children to talk involves telling the child what to say to someone in ongoing interactions. The mother provides the model utterance, followed by the imperative, *Say like that.* This approach to language development does not entail any error correction at all.

Requesting Clarification

The ways in which students ask their teachers to clarify their lessons may also lead to misunderstandings. Middle-American students are often eager to ask questions when they don't understand their teachers. Yet, some Latino students may be unaccustomed to asking their teacher to clarify and feel that it is impolite to take the teacher's time in this way. Many Asian students are also reluctant to request clarification (Sato 1981). Like some Latino students, they may be afraid that such admissions on their part will seem aggressive and disrespectful. Some Native Americans may make silent requests, looking up from seatwork to ask for help silently. Students who expect more formal, structured classroom environments (such as those in many Asian countries, India, Saudi Arabia, and the Soviet Union) may be surprised that middle-American teachers expect students to make requests for clarification in the middle of such activities as lectures, story-time, and reading sessions.

Spotlighting

Students from many cultures are unaccustomed to the mainstream American technique of spotlighting, singling out a student and asking this student to perform correctly before others. Directives (such as "Joe, stand up.") can put the spotlight of public attention on children in front of an audience. Mohatt and Erickson (1981) note:

> Part of the *spotlighting* effect comes from using the name of an individual student. Another part can come from what Hall (1966) terms a proxemic relationship—interpersonal distance that carries social meaning. If the teacher calls out a directive to a single individual from all the way across the room, the spotlight effect is heightened, giving the directive the force of a command or rebuke rather than a suggestion. (p. 223)

Loudly referring to the names of the students you are not teaching also heightens the negative effect of spotlighting. (For instance, reprimanding a student who is in a math group when you are working with the reading group accentuates the spotlighting effect.) The effect is further heightened when you give a direct command (such as "Come here.") instead of an indirect one (such as "Would you mind coming here?" or, yet less direct, "I need to talk to you for a minute").

Richmond (1987) found that Choctaws (Native Americans) find being put on the spot in front of peers may directly conflict with home training. She states, "At home, they [Choctaws] quietly observe the skills they are to learn, practice them by doing as much with an adult there to watch and help, and then demonstrate them when they are reasonably certain of success" (p. 234).

Similarly, Philips (1972,1974, 1983) found that Warm Spring Indian children participated more enthusiastically and performed more effectively in classroom activities which minimized the obligation on the part of the students to perform *publicly* as individuals and in settings where the teacher did not control performance of the students and correct their errors.

Like many Native Americans, many Asians do not like spotlighting (Sato 1981). Condon (1984) writes, "The Japanese do not care to be put on the spot in public; getting it wrong can be a cause of real shame, especially in front of classmates who are younger or socially inferior ..." (p. 58).

Questioning and Answering

Questions allow teachers to assess their students' comprehension of their lessons and are frequently used by middle-American teachers. Unfortunately, they present a number of difficulties for our language minority students. The questions you use may be entirely misconstrued by your students. For example, Heath (1982, 1983), who examined questioning strategies in black and white working-class communities, found that the questions middle-American teachers used at school were misunderstood by their black students. The most frequent type of question these teachers used was a question to elicit an answer which the teacher already knew, as in "What is this?" (said while pointing to a calendar). Questions of this type accounted for nearly half the data. In the homes of blacks, children were asked questions of a different type. They were generally asked, "What's that like?" or "What's happening?" Heath (1982) cites classroom incidents in which a teacher persisted in asking questions about a story the children had just read. When the teacher asked, "Who is it the story is talking about?", one child replied, "Ain't nobody can talk about things being about themselves." The boy could not understand why the teacher so often asked questions when she already had the answers to these questions. Heath notes that when the teacher asked the children question types with which they were familiar, the children responded and became involved in the lessons because they knew how to answer.

Another type of question which might present a stumbling block for some groups of students is the personal opinion question, ("What do you think of X?"). Middle-Americans have been given extensive training in stating their own opinions — at bedtime, story time, in show and tell, in question/answer sessions with parents. In many cultures, however, children are taught *not* to give their own opinions. Levine (1982), points out:

> Asked by teachers, *What do you think?* or *What is your opinion?* a Saudi student may simply offer a rote response. This response is not indicative of an inability to articulate an original or creative thought, but rather reflects educational training that discourages independent thinking. Some Saudi students have reported that a teacher who elicits opinions in class or allows a student to challenge ideas is incompetent and therefore unqualified to teach. (pp. 101–102)

Like the Saudi student discussed by Levine, many Asian students may also have difficulty stating their own opinion. These students have not been taught to give personal opinions and may be reluctant to give an opinion different from the teacher's out of fear of receiving a negative evaluation.

A further area of potential misunderstanding concerns the middle-American teacher's expectation that students will volunteer to answer questions. Middle-American students usually feel free to answer questions when they know the answers. However, when you ask language minority students questions to check their comprehension, they may or may not volunteer to answer. For example, Asians may not volunteer to answer because volunteering answers displays their knowledge, and they have been taught to be humble. Iwatake (1978) notes, "The traditional classroom in Asia places the teacher at the front of the room, lecturing. When the teacher asks a question, he usually calls on a student to answer." (p. 80; see also Sato 1981). Asian students may also feel that if they give the wrong answer, it not only humiliates them but also brings shame on their families (Sue 1983). Phap (1980) writes, "The Vietnamese child will not participate in class activities unless specifically called on. This emphasis on modesty has made it difficult for Vietnamese to demonstrate their capabilities or voice their knowledge or skills" (p. 23). Cole (1987) reports that Haitians may also be shy, reticent, and reluctant to volunteer answers.

In cultures which place great value on spoken interaction, (such as Iran, Turkey, and Saudi Arabia), students may be eager to answer teacher questions when they have the English proficiency to do so. If these students take up too much class time, this too can lead to difficulties. Thompson (1987b), for example, states that "Turks tend to voice their opinions openly and attach little importance to compromises" (p. 168).

Another serious problem affecting the language minority students' difficulty answering questions concerns the school setting. Language minority students may feel so uncomfortable with an unfamiliar school setting that the very situation may make them reluctant to answer teacher questions. For example, Philips' (1972, 1974, 1983) careful observation of the Warm Spring Indians suggests that Warm Spring Indian children were so uncomfortable with the structure of the classroom that they failed to answer questions, giggled nervously, and remained silent. Boggs (1972) reports that Hawaiian children participate in choral responses and individually volunteer information to teachers when they can sense receptivity but become silent if called on by name. Dumont (1972) contrasts two Cherokee classrooms—one in which children are silent and one in which children talk excitedly and productively about all their learning tasks. In the silent classroom, teacher-dominated recitations fail. In the other classroom, children have choices of when and how to participate, and small group projects not directed by the teacher are encouraged. These observations suggest that children from several minority groups are more likely to perform in situations which are more congruent with their expectations of schooling. Teachers of these students might find it helpful to give longer periods of individual attention to students, and to arrange for more group work.

Perhaps the most serious problem related to questions is that middle-American teachers tend to question students of their own ethnic backgrounds to a greater extent than they question students of other ethnic backgrounds. Unfortunately, teachers often *pass over* students whose ethnic identity is different from their own. Jackson and Cosca's (1974) report found that mainstream American teachers directed 21% more questions to middle-Americans than to Chicanos. They conclude that, "Chicanos in the Southwest receive substantially less of those types of teacher behavior presently known to be most strongly related to gains in student achievement" (p. 227).

Pausing

Wait time, that is the amount of time students take before answering teacher questions, seems to constitute another source of potential misunderstanding between the teacher and student. In the United States, questions tend to be answered fairly quickly (Richards 1980). Teachers often feel uncomfortable with silence and tend to interpret silence as an indicator of the student's inability to answer a question. Mainstream Americans usually associate silence with something negative—tension, hostility, awkwardness, or shyness. Yet, in some cultures, students take considerable time to answer questions. For instance, in many Asian and Native American Indian cultures it is courteous and respectful to pause and weigh one's words before responding to a question or comment. Mohatt and Erickson (1981) point out that Odawa Indians frequently speak slowly, pause often, and respond to teacher questions after reflecting on the question for some time. Among many East Asian students, silent periods of reflection are appropriate responses to teacher questions and "lowered eyes and bowed heads, rather than silence, are more likely to be the nonverbal signals indicating no response is coming" (Condon, 1984, p. 302). On the other hand, some Iranian and Saudi students may appear to *jump* to answer questions, even answering them before the teacher has had a chance to finish. It is not unusual for a Saudi student to rush to a teacher's side to loudly answer a question (Damen 1987). Damen suggests that Arab loudness means strength. In their culture, responses to questions are given quickly and indicate interest and active involvement, not aggression. In this culture, interruptions are permitted at times. In fact, speakers in this culture often overlap one another when talking, trying to display friendliness and interest.

Thus far, we have examined cultural differences with respect to specific behaviors which may result in potential misunderstandings in the multicultural classroom. Yet, three other factors affect these behaviors: peers, age, and gender. These factors are discussed in the following.

Peer Feedback

In most middle-American classrooms, it is the teacher who provides feedback to students in the classroom. Yet, in classrooms across the world, this is not always the case. In many Korean elementary classrooms, for example, students help one another. The students work in small groups and each student is responsible for his or her own work as well as the work of his or her entire group. In all Mexican elementary schools, children work together on group projects. This cooperative work makes the better students responsible for giving feedback to the weaker students. While adults are primarily responsible for teaching young children in the United States, in other cultures, peers as well as adults are responsible for teaching small children. This is the case in Samoa (Ochs 1983), in Hawaii with Hawaiian children (Boggs, 1972, Au and Jordan 1981), in Papua New Guinea with Kaluli children (Schieffelin 1983), and in Mexico (Laosa 1984), as well as in many Native American groups (Philips 1972, 1974, 1983, Weeks 1983). For these groups, it may be useful to form peer teaching/learning interactions. Bear in mind, however, that the feedback immigrant students receive from mainstream American peers is not always supportive. One student reports:

> Before I came to America I had a beautiful dream about this country. At that time, I didn't know that the first word I learned in this country would be a dirty word. American students always picked on us, made fun of us, laughed at our English. They broke our lockers, threw food on us in the cafeteria, said dirty words to us, pushed us on the campus. Many times they shouted at me, *Get out of here, you chink, go back to your country.* Many times they pushed me and yell on me. I've been pushed, I had gum thrown on my hair. I've been hit by stones, I've been shot by air-gun. I've been insulted by all the dirty words in English. All this really made me frustrated and sad. I often asked myself, *Why do they pick on me?*
> Christina Tien, Chinese Immigrant Student, Public Testimony, Los Angeles (reported in Olsen 1988, p. 34)

Another student comments:

> There is lots of teasing me when I don't pronounce right. Whenever I open my mouth, I wonder, I shake and worry, will they laugh? They think if we speak Tagalog that we are saying something bad about them, and sometimes they fight us for speaking our language. I am afraid to even try. And I find myself with fear about speaking Tagalog.
> 10th grade Filipino boy, immigrated at age 14 (reported in Olsen 1988, p. 38)

This means that, to provide optimal feedback group work, teachers need to be sensitive to patterns of prejudice and conflict. (Refer to Chapter 5.)

Age and Gender

In many cultures feedback patterns vary as a function of age and gender. In hierarchical cultures such as Thai in which seniority in years is respected, it is critical in classes of mixed ages, to make sure "that older learners are not in any way made to lose face (for example, by leaving a long pause after a question which the learner cannot answer, brushing aside pedantic questions as irrelevant, etc.)" (Smyth 1987, p. 262). In addition, the casual mixing of genders in the classroom can cause emotional havoc for many cultural groups. Shackle (1987) points out that teachers may find it hard to elicit responses from some female Indian students unless they are in all–female classes. In group work, males from some cultures may prefer receiving feedback from males, and females from females. (Refer to Chapter 4 for further discussion.) Also, Smith (1987) advises that female teachers remember that in many Arab countries, "men are not allowed to speak to any women outside their own immediate circle" (p. 154). This might make it difficult for female instructors to provide some Arab students with constructive criticism.

PRACTICAL STRATEGIES

I asked earlier how information about cross-cultural differences can help teachers provide students of diverse cultural backgrounds with more effective feedback. My purpose here has been to highlight potential areas of cultural misunderstanding rather than specific between-group or within-group differences. I reiterate here the danger of over-generalization of information concerning cross-cultural differences. Although it is impossible to provide teachers with a definitive list of do's and don'ts (*do give this type of feedback, don't give this type ...*), there are some general strategies which are helpful in providing feedback to language minority students of all cultural backgrounds. A list follows:

1. Develop cross-cultural tolerance; given the tremendous possibility for cultural misunderstandings in the area of feedback, be tolerant of your students' feedback behaviors and avoid stereotyping (refer to Chapter 1).

2. Join forces with your students, community leaders and others who speak your students' first languages to gather information about the types of feedback which your students prefer. Find out about feedback strategies which work for others from successful teachers. Watch native speaker volunteers interact with your students and observe successful feedback behaviors (Richmond 1987).

3. If appropriate, show students the types of feedback you use and how you interpret student feedback. When people from diverse cultures are aware of areas in which cultural behaviors differ, they are not as likely to misunderstand one another. Explain, for example, your system of marking papers. Also, to the extent that strategies of questioning are different at home than they are at school, teachers need to openly

discuss with students the different kinds of questions and answers which they expect to be used in the classroom (Heath 1982, 1983).

4. Try to adapt your feedback to make some provision for the different feedback patterns of your students. For example, you might use some of the questioning strategies which your students are familiar with. Heath (1982) suggests that the middle-American teachers she observed might use some questions like "What's this like?" and "What's happening here?" with the black students she studied; if appropriate, you might also want to allow for group work and informal peer feedback. (Refer to Chapter 5.)

5. Do not assume students will volunteer to answer your questions. Develop a plan which will allow *all* students opportunities to answer your questions. Students may feel more comfortable answering your questions in face-to-face encounters or small groups.

6. Organize classroom seating arrangements to maximize student opportunities to participate and to minimize discrimination. Many teachers tend to communicate more with those students who share their own ethnic identity and literally *pass over* students who do not share their ethnic identity. For this reason, you need to consciously form a plan which will call for interaction with all students.

7. Be aware of your means of complimenting students. Students from all cultures are likely to appreciate praise which is delivered sincerely, and is specific. Compliments as, "I like the way you write your name so clearly." (said to a kindergartener), seem more sincere than general, all-purpose compliments such as "very good."

8. Encourage students to ask questions when they do not understand and make it clear to them that demands for clarification, simplification and repetition are welcome, expected and even desired. You might lower your language minority students' anxieties by reminding them that they have not mastered English yet and are not expected to understand everything they hear or read. Modelling appropriate interruption behavior can help some students. You can also tell students that they are welcome to interrupt with such expressions as "What?" and "Excuse me. I'm not sure I understand."

9. Do not assume students will ask you questions when they do not understand something. Also, when you ask students if they understand you, and the entire class nods *yes*, do not assume that the students understand. Frequently check your students' understanding (when apppropriate, by questioning them, using true-false quizzes, or asking students to participate in a follow-up activity such as group work).

10. Question your students in a non-threatening manner. When you use questions, you may want to avoid relying upon the verbally demanding open-ended questions "Why?" and "How?" and use the following question types which are verbally less demanding:

yes/no questions: "Did John ride his bike to school?"

or - choice questions: "Did John ride his bike or skateboard to school?"

what questions (with one word response): "What did John ride home?"

You might want to accept written, non-verbal answers or short answers. Also, when you are speaking individually with students, there is no reason why they should not answer your questions in their native language when their proficiency in English is insufficient to allow communication to take place and you know their first language.[2]

11. Give students plenty of *wait* time. Your language minority students may need more time than native speakers to respond to your questions. (Some teachers like to count to five silently.) It is probably best to discuss differences in wait time with your students and then provide students with plenty of time to answer your questions. All students (including middle-Americans) might appreciate this procedure.

12. Avoid strategies which embarrass or frustrate students such as the mainstream American technique of *spotlighting*, putting one student *on the spot.* One way to avoid *spotlighting* is to have your students participate in small group activities; another is to arrange to give students feedback individually in face-to-face situations.

13. Establish good rapport. Good rapport with your students can help them overlook misunderstandings. Be patient in establishing relationships.

14. As Moskowitz (1978) suggests, set ground rules. Do not allow *put downs.* Encourage students to help one another and ask questions when they do not understand your lessons. (See also Chapter 4.) Do not force students to participate before others; students are entitled to the right to *pass.*

15. Be consistent with your feedback. Wong-Fillmore (1985) suggests that the most successful teachers of language minority students are those who provide consistent feedback and employ systematic turn-allocation at least some of the time. Students will be able to interpret your feedback better if you use it consistently.

Conclusion

Many mainstream American strategies used to interpret and to provide feedback in our classes may be ineffective with students in multicultural classrooms.[3] Culturally-sensitive feedback, tailored to your students' individual backgrounds (taking into account their ages, proficiency levels, goals, etc.) seems most effective. After all, feedback should instill a sense of success in students from all cultural backgrounds.

ACTIVITIES AND DISCUSSION QUESTIONS

1. Imagine you teach social science to junior high school students. You have just given a lecture. Describe three specific ways you can determine whether your students understood your lecture.

2. At UCLA, Harold Garfinkel asked his students to consciously insert specific pause fillers such as *uhm, er* and *ya know* into their speech. His students failed miserably. To what extent do you think it is possible to consciously change your own feedback behaviors? Do you think it would help your students acquire middle-American feedback patterns if you taught explicit rules? Why?

3. What difficulties do you think adult language minority students would have using and interpreting middle-American feedback patterns that young language minority students would not have?

4. How can a teacher with five different cultural groups provide effective feedback for all students?

5. At Stanford University, Charles Ferguson conducted an experiment in which he did not provide the types of feedback others expected. For example, if others greeted him, he said nothing. Try not to give feedback to others. For example, avoid giving back channel cues such as *uhum* and *right* and look down when your addressee speaks to you. Then, make observations about what happened. Was this a positive or a negative experience?

6. If you are a teacher, try not to correct your students' mistakes publicly for one whole class period. Then, make observations about what happened.

RECOMMENDED READINGS

HEATH, S. B. 1983. *Ways with Words.* Cambridge: Cambridge University Press. Classic ethnographic study of children living in two neighboring working-class communities — one white and one black. On the basis of her research, Heath demonstrates that the style of school language for the black children conflicts with the style of language used in the children's homes.

PHILIPS, S. 1983. *The Invisible Culture: Communication in Classroom and Community on the Warm Spring Indian Reservation.* New York: Longman. Philips describes her research in the Warm Spring Indian community and schools. Because Warm Spring Indian children do not share the verbal styles of their middle-American teachers, Philips argues that they are at an immediate disadvantage when they enter schools taught by mainstream Americans.

SWAN, M., and SMITH, B. 1987. (eds.) *Learner English.* Cambridge: Cambridge University Press. This book provides descriptions of the first languages and, in many cases, communication styles of language minority learners of diverse cultures.

TRUEBA, H., GUTHRIE, P., and AU, K. (eds.) 1981. *Culture and Bilingual Classrooms: Studies in Classroom Ethnography.* Rowley, Massachusetts: Newbury House Publishers. Includes research papers related to home/school discontinuities which prevent language minority students from achieving success in our schools.

NOTES

1. In general, teachers begin instructing students in the use of these norms (raising hands, taking speaking turns, talking when called on, etc.) in the early grades, but in the more advanced grades, teachers usually expect students to know how to give and interpret middle-American forms of feedback appropriately. As students advance in school, they find themselves giving and receiving more complex forms of feedback, such as that given in extended question/answer periods. (See Heath 1986)

2. This only implies that you might use your student's first language when speaking individually with him or her. In a multicultural classroom, if you speak Spanish and English, your Korean, Chinese and Tagalog speakers may feel less valued and important.

3. Research done in the Kamehameha Early Education Program (KEEP) in Honolulu (Jordan et al., 1978, Au 1980, Au and Jordan 1981) suggests that successful educational programs for culturally diverse students are sensitive to the feedback patterns of the students. These programs accept some of the patterns of the students, but not all. For example, children in the KEEP Program are allowed to overlap one another's answers and to receive help from peers rather than the teacher. On the other hand, the teacher in the KEEP Program does not use the *Creolized* forms of feedback used in the children's homes. These programs also attempt to reverse some of the children's feedback patterns so that children reared in peer-affiliation milieu "become attentive to the adult teacher." (Cazden and Legett 1981, p. 82)

CHAPTER EIGHT

Testing in Culturally Responsive Ways

Principle 8 states that successful education for language minority students entails testing in culturally-responsive ways. In order to achieve any degree of consistency and validity in the assessment of language minority students, it is imperative that we assess our students fairly; if we fail, then our test results are likely to be ethnocentrically skewed. To help teachers prevent such failure, the present chapter examines potential areas of cultural bias in specific tests: placement exams (which determine when language minority students are ready to be *mainstreamed* into content-area classes that assume full English proficiency); standardized tests (which distinguish student *language* difficulties from student *learning* difficulties); and teacher-constructed tests (which test the language minority students' knowledge of various content areas).

Placement Decisions

Far too often, language minority students students are placed in the wrong grade level or required to do academic course work which they find either too difficult or too easy. Frequently, age and English proficiency are the sole considerations for a student's placement. For example, in Olsen's (1988) study of 360 school-aged immigrant students in California, 40% of the students believed that they were placed in the wrong grade level. They had to repeat course material they already knew or were placed in classes based on their chronological age regardless of their skills and proficiencies.[1] Olsen's report contains numerous quotations from *misplaced* immigrant students. One student laments:

> It was too hard for me. I didn't know anything. I didn't know the ABCs or the arithmetic and I felt so stupid. I should have been in 1st or 2nd grade, not in 5th. I told my parents I want to change, but the teacher said no because it depends on your age. I cried because I didn't understand.

Ninth grade Lao child, immigrated at age 10; (reported in Olsen 1988, p. 50)

Another student complains:

For me, they shouldn't have put me in Basic Math. I should have been in Algebra. But there is more English vocabulary in Algebra so they said I couldn't take it until I learned more English. I felt I was spending time with things I already knew, but then that's required of Latin immigrants. We waste our time because we don't know English yet.

Eleventh grade Mexican student, immigrated at age 14, (reported in Olsen 1988, p. 50)

Perhaps one reason language minority students are frequently *misplaced* is that, as discussed in Chapter 3, they require, on the average, five to seven years to approach grade norms in English academic skills, yet show peer-appropriate second language conversational skills within about two years of arrival (see Cummins 1984). Their teachers may advance them on the basis of their interactional skills in English rather than their ability to handle specific academic coursework successfully.

Team approaches to assessment can provide a successful means of placing language minority students into appropriate grade levels and determining when these students are ready to be *mainstreamed* into classes which assume nativelike English proficiency. Cheng's (1987) team approach to assessing Asian students involves bilingual teachers, aides, parents, community representatives, and others. She suggests that monolingual teachers use observation, consultation and tests to evaluate the *communicative competence* of children in their first and second languages.

Hymes (1961), refers to *communicative competence* as "the ability to say the right thing in the right way at the right time in the right place" (p. 125). According to Canale and Swain (1980), communicative competence minimally involves four areas of knowledge and skills. These include: grammatical competence (which reflects knowledge of the linguistic code itself and includes knowledge of vocabulary and word formation); sociolinguistic competence (which addresses the extent to which sentences are produced and understood appropriately and includes knowledge of speech acts such as apologies, compliments, and refusals), discourse competence (which involves knowing how to start a conversation and keep it going); and strategic competence (which refers to the mastery of the communication strategies needed to enhance the effectiveness of communication or to compensate for breakdowns in communication due to limiting factors in actual communication or to insufficient competence in one or more of the other components of communicative competence). Language minority students can achieve varying degrees of proficiency in the different components of communicative competence. This means that grammar tests can no longer be the sole means of testing the competence of language minority students. Instead, other tests are needed which examine all aspects of the students' communicative performance — especially those aspects students need to succeed academically. Although it is beyond the scope of this volume to discuss these communicative tests, examples are given in the appendix.

Yet, we cannot rely on communicative tests exclusively to place students accurately. Cheng (1987) suggests the following guidelines:

1. Students should be tested in multiple settings since they often behave differently in different settings with different partners. They can be observed in many places: in the classroom, at home or on the playground.

2. With the help of a trained interpreter/translator if necessary, teachers may obtain thorough histories — including medical, family, previous education, immigration history (refugee, illegal alien), time of arrival, intervening experiences, the number of years in the US, home languages, psychological or adjustment history.

3. Classroom teachers can provide valuable information about a student's rate of learning and learning style, personal relational style, cognitive style, and classroom behavior; the teacher has had the opportunity to observe the student in multiple contexts, such as reading, show and tell, sharing, group assignments, group projects and individual desk work. Those who teach language minority students can provide information concerning second language development and rate of acquisition compared to other students (or siblings) who entered the United States at the same time in similar circumstances.

4. School personnel can also be helpful, especially if they are capable of assessing the student's home language, home culture and cognitive/linguistic skills.

5. The student's parents can provide information about the child's language and performance skills since they can judge the student at home and in the community. Other family members may also serve as informants and interactants in the assessment process. A student's interactions with care-givers and siblings reveal the student's communication skills.

What should we do about students who lack sufficient English communication skills to take our placement tests? For students with limited knowledge of English, it is important to administer an individual test in the students' first language. If trained professionals are not proficient in the student's first language, there is a need to rely on interpreters or translators to administer this test.[2]

Performance, nonverbal, and numeracy tests needing a minimum of verbal skills may reflect the limited-English proficiency students' academic status more faithfully than verbal tests. Yet these tests are also limited. They tell us very little about students' verbal abilities which are highly relevant to their academic progress. Additional information on English and native language proficiency — listening, speaking, reading and writing — is needed before counselors and curriculum specialists can make informed judgements about placing limited-English proficiency students.

6. Another important part of placement procedures is successfully communicating with the parents of our students. Under law, parents must be informed about placement decisions and given the right to formally challenge such decisions (e.g. Arreola vs. Board of Education 1968). Although we may normally communicate quite well with middle-American parents, we often fail miserably when attempting to communicate with the parents of our language minority students. Why is such communication essential? Cheng's (1987) examples clearly demonstrate the reasons.

> In one instance, for example, a Laotian father attended a meeting to discuss an individualized education program (IEP) for his son. Throughout the meeting, the father nodded and said, *Yes*, when the different participants in the meeting talked about their impression of the child and their recommendations. Finally the father was asked whether he agreed with the placement and the recommendations. To everyone's surprise, he said *No*. Frustrated, the IEP team members did not understand why the father had continued to indicate *yes* when he did not agree with what was said. The father had nodded merely to indicate that he understood, however, not to indicate that he agreed. This behavior, however, caused a communication breakdown and resulted in misinterpretation.
>
> In another case, bilateral neurosensory hearing loss was diagnosed in a 5-year-old Hmong boy with fluid in the middle ears. The school audiologist informed the father of the diagnosis and explained that the child needed to wear hearing aids and to take medication for otitis media. The father said, *Yes*, when the audiologist asked him if he understood her. The audiologist felt uneasy about the session, however, and sought the help of a Hmong interpreter in the community. When the Hmong interpreter asked the father questions about the child's hearing problem, the father replied, I *don't know because I couldn't understand the lady [audiologist].* The Hmong interpreter then explained to the father about the child's hearing loss, the importance of the hearing aid, and the need for medication. (Cheng 1987, p. 121)

Cheng's (1987) study suggests that it is important that we convey placement decisions to our language minority students' parents in their first languages.

How can we determine whether language minority students have learning problems or English problems? School districts throughout the United States have long been placing disproportionately large numbers of minority children into special education classes for the mentally retarded. Many studies have shown that approximately twice as many Mexican-American students are enrolled in classes for the educable mentally retarded (EMR) than white, middle-American students. (See Gaarder 1977; Mercer 1973, 1983; Williams 1968.) This over-representation of Mexican-Americans in classes for the mentally retarded has been attributed to culturally-biased tests (Mercer 1973). Because most schools reflect middle-class, monolingual, monocultural values, students' academic potential or *IQ* is assessed in relation to these norms. (For a fascinating discussion, refer to Gould 1981.) The IQ test has thus traditionally legitimized the labelling of many minority students as *retarded* or *slow* and their consequent placement in special classes. The Coleman report *On Equality of Educational Opportunity* (1966) showed that twelfth grade Hispanic students were about three and a half years behind national norms in academic achievement, while similar trends have been reported in more recent National Assessment of Educational Progress surveys (1977, 1983a, 1983b).[3]

As Cummins (1984) points out, many teachers assume that students are capable of taking IQ tests after one year of being in the United States. They want to know if students have language learning problems, learning disabilities or both. Unfortunately, language minority students who have recently arrived in the United States often lack the English proficiency necessary to take IQ tests. Acquisition of fluent English speaking and listening skills does not necessarily imply commensurate academic development. Many teachers underestimate their students' academic potential by assessing their performance before they have had sufficient time to attain age appropriate levels of English proficiency.[4]

The review of the literature on *learning disabilities* reveals that the usual definitions of this term are almost universally regarded as problematic from a logical point of view (Cummins 1984). As Cummins suggests, no measure or set of measures is capable of revealing the existence of such disabilities; that is, no measure has demonstrated construct validity, and early identification procedures may very well succeed in contributing to the disabilities they are designed to offset. This is because once teachers tell students that they have learning disabilities, these students frequently live up to their teachers' expectations. We cannot assume that students have processing skills deficits simply because they cannot do well with some aspects of our academic programs.

Cole (1975) suggests that it is important to focus on what minority children *do* know, rather than on focusing on the limited and biased sample of their knowledge provided by mainstream American-oriented standardized tests. One obvious means of obtaining more information on our students' academic potential is to consider their adaptive behavior in nonacademic settings. Another way is to give students tests in their first languages, especially if they have been in the United States for fewer than two years or have weak English abilities.

Yet, attempts to assess minority students' intellectual functioning in the first language by means of IQ tests have proved problematic (Cummins 1984). A major factor which limits the usefulness of translated IQ instruments is the loss of children's first language cognitive/academic proficiency in a situation in which there is no strong promotion of first language in the school. Regional and other dialectal differences also make test score interpretation problematic.[5]

Cummins (1984) suggests that alternative cognitive assessment procedures such as the so-called *culture-fair* tests (including Cattell's Culture-Fair Intelligence Tests, Raven's Progressive Matrices, and DeAvila and Havassy's Cartoon Conservation Scales) make some contribution toward either determining students' academic potential and need for special assistance or discovering strengths and weaknesses in student cognitive processing skills and academic knowledge. However, all require sensitive interpretation and even with this sensitivity, there is no guarantee that the interpretation of the test performance is accurate. These tests tell us very little about students' verbal abilities, which are highly relevant to their academic progress.

Cummins (1984) gives this advice for those attempting to distinguish language minority learning difficulties from ESL language difficulties: first, find out as much as possible about the students' background culture, education, and language, and interpret responses sympathetically in light of this knowledge; second, examine how the students behave outside the school — in the home, in the community, and with the peer group. If students use skills to cope intelligently with the nonacademic world, then they may have motivation problems rather than learning problems; and third, never regard an IQ test as meaningful for language minority students.

Cultural Bias in Testing

The need for culturally non-biased testing makes it essential for us to examine our own teacher-constructed tests closely to determine their possible biases. What follows is a brief description of some of these biases.

1. Student perceptions and understanding of tests affects their scores on tests.

   Deyhle (1987) reports an ethnographic study of tests and test-taking among Navajo children in a Bureau of Indian Affairs day school and middle-American children in an urban area. Among her findings were two of particular importance: (1) that not all children recognize the gate-keeping role that tests often play; and (2) test-taking skills need to be taught to *all* children. The Navajo students in her study failed to take tests seriously, and this attitude was reinforced by their teachers who "spoke with pride of the gamelike testing environment they had created" (p. 96). Unfortunately, "observations and interviews indicated that the Navajo students did not share an understanding of the importance of testing as representative of personal progress in school" (p. 97). Unlike the Navajo second grade children, middle-American second grade children associated learning and grades with testing. (See also Rist 1978.)

Language minority students need to become *test wise*. If tests are used in gate-keeping capacities, it is only fair that students understand the significance of these tests.

2. The cultural referents of the test items may be unfamiliar to language minority students.

Vocabulary frequently presents an obstacle to language minority students. Cole (1975) makes this trenchant observation:

> We know that children from different subcultural groups are exposed to different vocabulary. How children (or adults) respond to a problem (even one so simple as saying what comes to mind when we say *peach*) depends in large measure on their familiarity with the content of the problem, and this familiarity varies in unknown ways with children's home culture. (pp. 51–52)

Reibero's (1980) study, [based on his administration of Weschler's Intelligence Test for Children (Revised) to over 350 low income Portuguese-speaking children in Massachusetts], illustrates the types of problems unfamiliar vocabulary words cause our language minority students. In discussing this study, Cummins (1984) points out that one item on the Weschler's Intelligence for Children asks, *from what animal do we get bacon?*. Although most Portuguese families consider sausage a staple, Portuguese children are generally unfamiliar with the term, *bacon*. Reibeiro suggests that very few children would fail this item if it were expressed, *from what animal do we get sausages (chouricos)?*

Cheng (1987) lists a number of vocabulary words Asian minority children might have difficulty understanding. These include items for baking (associated with ovens); vehicles (including trains, cable car, ambulances, and garbage trucks); sports (such as football, hockey, tobogganing, skiing, sky-diving, and surfing); musical instruments (such as drums, guitar, banjo and harmonica). Many newcomers to the United States might have difficulties with historical events and people (Thanksgiving, George Washington, Abraham Lincoln, pioneer, Daniel Boone, astronaut); nursery rhymes (*Twinkle, Twinkle Little Star*; *Little Jack Horner*); and children's stories (*Snow White, Cinderella, The Three Bears*).

What can we do about cultural bias and test items? Be aware of bias and interpret scores sympathetically. In addition, we can encourage students to explain why they choose the answers they do.

3. Picture cues may also be misunderstood by language minority students.

Pictures are another source of bias. For example, in one ESL proficiency test, the students are told, *The boy is happy* and are then shown a picture of a boy smiling. They are then shown another picture cue with a girl smiling; the expected answer is, *A girl is smiling.* According to Cargill (1987), the test is heavily biased. "We know that a smiling face usually means that a person is happy. However, experience in Vietnamese programs shows that a smiling Vietnamese boy may not be happy; he may be embarrassed, confused, or even angry." (p. 1)

Again, to overcome this shortcoming, potentially biased test questions should be noted when results are recorded and analyzed. Results should be interpreted sympathetically in light of student explanations.

4. A culturally insensitive teacher administering the tests may also bias the results.

For instance, teachers who give oral interviews need to be aware that "most Asians nod their heads during an interview, giving the impression that they clearly understand what is being said. Such a gesture is a matter of courtesy, however, and may not actually indicate that they understand the discussion" (Cheng 1987, p. 120).

Interviewers need to frequently check to see that the student understands the questions and provide examples. In addition, they need to encourage feedback from the student, keep the environment relaxed, non-threatening and comfortable, and avoid eye contact if it is too threatening.

5. The familiarity of the person tested with the *type of behavior* which the test taker expects, (for example, a quick response) can also bias the results.

Gay and Abrahams (1983) suggest that direct question/answer pen and paper questions "net little substantive data from blacks because they violate black culturally determined ways of soliciting and giving out information" (p. 336).

> Black children hear hostility in questions. The teacher may see the child's failure to respond as uncooperation or hostility or even mental disabilities of the child. The effect is compounded, of course, when the questions emerge in the con-

text of a test situation. Here the query technique is combined with the cold medium of the instrument being administered.

Testing also violates the learned interactional practices of the Black child in a number of ways. First, he is given a written test when he is accustomed to demonstrating his abilities verbally. Second, he is asked to function individually, isolated from his compatriots, when his culture background sanctions cooperative efforts. Third, the environment is rigidly structured and formalized, while, within the black community, he learns in an informal, social setting. All of these interferences operate on the child before he has opportunity to address himself adequately to the task itself. (p. 337)

Cargill (1987) gives an additional example. She suggests that in most classrooms, students are encouraged to ask questions during a test if they are too puzzled to go on. "Frequently a student will discover that last typographical error which we failed to find before test time. An American student would simply inquire, and the correction would be noted for the benefit of the whole class. . . ." (p. 4) But, the freedom to ask questions during a test is absent in many cultures. Cargill notes that many language minority students would rather leave a section blank, and risk failing the test, than venture to ask a simple question.

Language minority students often need information about the types of behaviors expected during tests. Many students find explicit instruction, models and practice exams helpful.

6. The comfort or discomfort experienced by language minority students constitutes another potential source of bias.

Timing tests may cause students anxiety. Many students have not experienced timed tests. Blacks and Chicanos have reportedly scored poorly on timed essay exams because they sometimes fall apart under the pressure of time. Similarly, specific test formats such as multiple-choice tests or cloze tests may cause some students anxiety. As with timed tests, students who are unfamiliar with specific test formats are at least temporarily confused, even when given a battery of instructions explaining what multiple-choice tests or cloze tests require.

What can be done to avoid these problems? Allow students extra time; familiarize students with the test formats they encounter in our classes and allow them to take *practice exams*. Efforts should also be made to give exams in low-anxiety situations.

7. The motivation which students have to do well on tests may also bias test results; If ESL students feel that tests are unfair and not worth taking, they may score poorly on them.

Gay and Abraham (1983) found that some black children are taught early on to be suspicious of whites and may, as a result, score poorly on exams. They point out:

> The effect of such an attitude on any situation in which the test is being administered by a white is obvious. Blacks learn to test the tester to see where they are coming from. They can draw on a cultural repertoire of manipulative behaviors. The diagnostician can talk himself blue without getting any indication whether he has been understood ... the testee remains silent.

> (p. 333)

Similarly, Labov's (1972) analysis of the verbal performance of black youths from New York City in different testing situations provides one of the clearest examples of how the tester can negatively affect test results. Labov found that the length of black children's speech in testing situations conducted by white adults made them appear extremely dull and linguistically deprived. However, having knowledge of these children and their peers in other situations, Labov surmised that the reasons for the youths' inarticulateness were to be found in the social situation, not personal characteristics or language. His hypothesis was given support when he repeated the testing exercise with a black adult, and the children's verbal production remained much the same, but became quite elaborate when a black interviewer transformed testing situations into more informal conversations. In this social situation, children who had previously responded in monosyllables eagerly entered into conversation. Rather than use language in a minimal, defensive way, they used it productively.

What can teachers do to combat prejudice? For starters, teachers might also assure students that they have a fair chance to do well on our tests.

8. Stereotyping students also results in bias.

For instance, Cheng (1987) points out that many teachers believe their Asian students are math whizzes. While it is true that many Asians excel in math, many do not. We must not overlook the Richard E. Kims, Maxine Hong Kingstons, and Ved Mehtas who will be the prominent Asian writers of the twenty-first century by failing to assess our Asian students' interest and abilities in the areas of speaking and writing.

9. Failure to recognize important physical or emotional characteristics of our students may also reflect bias.

War trauma can lead to emotional difficulties or physical disabilities which affect test performance. Emotional problems and difficulties with vision, hearing, motor coordination and other biological problems should be identified in school. Although teachers usually do not screen for emotional and physical problems, it makes little sense to test language minority students in academic content without first checking to see if they have emotional or physical difficulties which affect their test performance (Mercer 1977).

Having discussed some general sources of cultural bias, I would like to consider cultural bias with respect to three specific types of teacher-constructed tests: criterion-reference exams, oral presentations, and written compositions.

Criterion-referenced tests are gaining popularity because they are said to be closely tied to instructional goals. The student's performance is not compared to others, but is expressed in the form of actual skills or tasks performed. Usually a binary format is used; the student has reached the criterion or has not. Teacher-constructed criterion-referenced tests are used to cover curricular materials, guide the instructional process and elicit information on the students' current skills or knowledge. However, even criterion-referenced tests are biased: Who specifies the criterion to be obtained? Certainly it is not Native Americans, Chicanos or blacks. Most criterion – referenced tests reflect the monocultural, monolingual, middle-American character of the curriculum.

> Because present edumetric (criterion-referenced) tests are an integral part of the present curriculum, they reflect the monocultural, monolingual, Anglo-centric characteristics of that curriculum. Development of multilingual and multicultural curricula will require dramatic extensions of present testing practices to cover new academic areas. In a truly bilingual program, students would take edumetric tests in more than one language. In a truly multilingual school, students would take tests covering the language, values, institutions, and history of numerous cultural streams. The decision concerning the nature of the curriculum is culturally limited.
>
> An edumetric test has content validity to the extent that it accurately mirrors what is being taught. It has pragmatic validity to the extent that it accurately identifies those students who have or have not mastered a particular curriculum. It is racially and culturally nondiscriminatory to the extent that it is equally proficient in measuring the competencies of students from differing racial and cultural backgrounds in a particular curriculum. The fact that students from some groups may be less proficient in a particular curriculum and tests of that curriculum than students from other groups is not evidence that the tests, per se, are at fault. The source of the differences is more fundamental and rests, at least in part, with a limited curriculum that represents the cultural tradition of one group. Students less familiar with that tradition will do less well in the curriculum and less well on criterion-referenced tests based on that curriculum. When the curriculum is changed, the tests will change. The relative proficiency of different groups may also change. (Mercer 1977, p. 97)

Another type of teacher-constructed test frequently used in schools in the United States is the oral presentation. Oral assignments may present particular difficulties for students who are unfamiliar with the behaviors which teachers expect students to use when making oral presentations. Michael's (1981) research, for instance, shows that even young children are expected to use a highly formal routine during *sharing time.* The black students she watched related topics loosely as they did in their own homes, while the white children she observed used explicit discourse markers to link their topics tightly and explicitly.

Students of diverse cultural backgrounds need information about teacher expectations and grading criteria, models of successful oral presentations they are required to make, and experience making such presentations in a non-threatening environment.

Like oral presentations, composition exams are also popularly used across the nation. However, how fair are these exams? Can language minority students understand the reading prompt which is used to elicit the essay? Is the language too difficult? Are cultural referents used which are beyond our students' comprehension? What about the grading of the exams? If the content of the student's essay exam is brilliant, but the grammar is terrible, how should the exam be graded? Obviously, the reading prompt used to elicit the composition must be accessible to all students. If the language contained in the reading prompt is too difficult, the students do not have a fair chance to respond. If the language contains cultural referents beyond the students' grasp, again, the test is biased in favor of middle American students.

What about grammar? Teachers cannot afford to ignore the grammar mistakes their students make. As suggested by Ommagio (1986) and others, grammar is important and we need to let students know that we value it. While the literature suggests that grammar mistakes are a normal part of second language development, if we do not grade our students *down* on grammar, they may even decide that grammar is unimportant or, even worse, that they have already acquired enough English to *get by* in school. One solution is simply to inform students tactfully when their grammar is weak and grade them down for grammar errors in the same way we do native English speakers. A different solution is to give students two grades—one for content and the other for grammar.

Conclusion

Language minority students need teachers who hold high expectations for their success and serve as their advocates. As suggested by Cummins (1989), when we analyze our students' shortcomings, we need to stop blaming the student, and instead consider some of the social, political, and economic variables which affect the student's academic progress. We need to ask what we can do to provide better instruction and support for the student.

ACTIVITIES AND DISCUSSION QUESTIONS

1. Swain (1985) suggests that, when testing ESL proficiency level, it is important to *bias for the best*. By this she means, elicit the best sample of the student's language that we can. What specific suggestions can you make for helping ESL students to write their best during a sit-down composition exam? (Among those factors which might affect student performance on the exam are the amount of time you give the students, the topic of the exam you choose, and the setting of the exam.)

2. Content teachers often complain that it is difficult to grade the written reports of language minority students who lack nativelike proficiency in English. Imagine you are a highschool history teacher. A language minority student turned in a twenty page typed report which was brilliant in terms of content, but dotted with grammatical errors. You know that the language minority student has worked harder on the paper than any other student in your class. How would you grade the paper and what advice would you give the student?

3. It is often difficult to judge the English proficiency level of young children who have not yet learned to write. Imagine that your supervisor has asked you to do an oral interview of a six-year-old Latino child in order to evaluate his or her English proficiency level. What can you do to make the child feel more comfortable?

4. Perhaps the most criticized of all exams are standardized reading tests. Many claim that these tests are biased. What are three possible sources of cultural bias which might affect these tests?

5. How can you determine whether a language minority student who lacks English proficiency is academically gifted?

RECOMMENDED READING

CUMMINS. J. 1984. *Bilingualism and Special Education: Issues in Assessment and Pedagogy.* England: Multilingual Matters Ltd. Discusses central issues in assessing the language and academic abilities of limited English proficient students.

COHEN, A. 1984. *Testing Language Ability in the Classroom.* Rowley, Massachusetts: Newbury House Publishers. Discusses how to administer and score ESL tests, create ESL quizzes and tests, and assess functional language ability.

HENNING. G. 1988. *A Guide to Language Testing: Development, Evaluation, Research.* Cambridge: Harper and Row. Provides a thorough treatment of ESL testing and introduces principles of test and questionnaire development as used in placing ESL students and evaluating their progress in acquiring English.

NOTES

1. The first step in many school districts for identifying who can benefit from ESL courses (that is, who is not ready to participate in classes with native English-speaking peers) is the Home Language Survey — filled out when the child registers. Olsen (1988) points out that there is considerable difficulty with these forms, some stemming from well-meaning secretaries, friends and relatives who inaccurately fill out the forms.

2. These could be members of the student's community, a family member or friend, or if necessary, a student who is proficient in the home language of the student. The interpreter/translator should understand the need for confidentiality, be familiar with the confidentiality procedures and policies of the school, and receive training in collecting information about language minority students through tests, questionnaires, and interviews.

3. Tests which purportedly measure intelligence (the IQ tests) include: the Stanford-Binet; the Weschler Intelligence Scale for Children-Revised; and the Slosson as well as norm-referenced *achievement tests.* These tests measure skills not tied to particular aspects of the curriculum, but sample skills and information generally believed to be available in the *societal curriculum* of the middle-American core-culture child. "Bias against culturally different minority groups is almost inevitably built into the development of IQ tests." (Cummins 1984, p. 4)

4. Banks (1988) makes the poignant observation:

> The assumption that IQ and other tests of mental ability can accurately measure innate mental ability is institutionalized and perpetuated within the schools. Students are assigned to academic tracks based on their performance on tests of mental ability and on other factors such as teacher recommendation and grades. A highly disproportionate number of lower-class and ethnic minority students are assigned to lower-ability tracks. Assignment to lower academic tracks actualizes the self-fulfilling prophecy. Research by Oakes documents how teacher expectations of students vary in different kinds of tracks. Students in higher academic tracks are expected to learn more and are consequently taught more; those in lower tracks are expected to learn less and are consequently taught less. (Banks 1988, p. 105)

5. Cummins (1984) describes New York's exemplary placement procedures.

> In New York, for example, educators who speak the languages and who are knowledgeable of the school systems in the countries of origin carry out initial educational assessment of students (in their own languages), provide advice to staff on placement and programming, and give information to parents about the school system and their child's program. Within three to four months after the initial assessment, a Multicultural Consultant follows up the students' placement and makes further contact with the parents to ask if they have any concerns regarding their children's progress. Each consultant also supervises a number of Trained Assessment Translators who carry out similar assessments for groups whose numbers are too small to warrant a full-time consultant. Many of these Assessment Translators are teachers in the board's heritage language program. The assessment procedures were developed by the Multicultural Consultants who first identified key questions to elicit the required information on

students' previous educational background and progress, and then assembled, field-tested and revised appropriate testing materials. (Cummins 1984, pp. 190–191)

CHAPTER NINE

Interacting with Parents

This chapter discusses specific means of overcoming constraints which bar language minority parent participation in our schools. In so doing, it discusses cultural differences in parental assumptions regarding schooling. Research has repeatedly demonstrated the role of parents in the educational achievement of children in the United States. In *Becoming a Nation of Readers* (1985), the National Academy of Education emphasized, "the single most important activity for building the knowledge required for eventual success in reading is reading aloud to children" (p. 23). As part of the educational excellence movement in California, the State Department of Education has initiated a *Parents are Teachers, Too* campaign focusing on how parents can support their children's education. Parents are advised to supervise homework and *make sure that assignments are completed* and *to read to their children on a daily basis.*

Unfortunately, many language minority parents feel that they have been excluded from participating in our schools. In some cases, teachers have not known how to encourage parents to become involved. In other cases, although lip service is paid to parent participation, in actual fact, language minority parents have not been welcome.

Perhaps as a consequence, many language minority students do not have family members supervising their academic placement and performance. As Vu-Doc Vuong, Executive Director of the Center for Southeast Refugee Resettlement in San Francisco, laments:

> The refugee parents are frustrated. On the one hand they want to push their children academically, to become someone in the society, to work hard and study well. On the other hand, they cannot effectively intervene in the educational process. They cannot attend school functions, PTA meetings, even school conferences because of language and not understanding the process.
> Vu-Doc Vuong, Executive Director
> Center for Southeast Refugee Resettlement
> Public Testimony, San Francisco
> (reported in Olsen 1988, pp. 82–83)

Teachers are often frustrated by what they perceive as a lack of concern on the part of language minority parents (Phenice, Martinez and Grant 1986, Olsen 1988). They complain, "Hispanic families just don't value education" or "Immigrant parents never even come to conferences or Back to School nights, even though we need a chance to talk about their children's progress" (Olsen 1988, p. 80).

There are special difficulties barring language minority parent involvement in the schools, the most obvious being language. Frequently, parents avoid going to schools because they cannot communicate in English, and there is no one at school who speaks their native language. Language minority parents are often unable to read school reports, bulletins, newsletters and notes sent home by the teacher if they are written only in English. Because parents are sometimes unable to read in their native languages, they may also be unable to make sense of the translated materials sent home from schools.

Poverty, difficult work schedules, the absence of adequate child care and split families all prevent many language minority parents from participating in our schools. Belous, Levitan and Gallo (1988) report that the percentage of children living in *poor* families (making an annual income of $8,000 or less each year) has risen in the United States. Working mothers outnumber homemakers. Children living with single parents now account for 24%. Married mothers in the work force account for 64%. These statistics are even higher for language minority families (Phenice, Martinez, and Grant 1986). Single parents with small children have difficulty finding childcare so that they can attend school events. Language minority parents with five or six children may have neither the time nor the energy to volunteer in their children's classrooms. Added to difficulties with time schedules and childcare, immigrant children often come to the United States without their parents. Some come without their families. Who will serve as advocates for these children in our schools?

There are also cultural barriers which prevent parents from participation in our schools. Language minority students come from schools that differ from those in the United States. (See, for example, Spindler and Spindler 1987 for a recent review.)

> Many immigrant parents understand little about the role of homework, the structure of our educational system, or many of the content areas their children are studying. They are often confused by many aspects of Anglo-American education, including the fact that in our school system time is allocated for play, that extracurricular activities are considered an important part of the school programs, that learning takes place and is presented through different people, sources and experiences, that homework is used to supplement regular classroom learning. They are particularly bothered by what they view as the lack of discipline and lack of respect shown for teachers. (Olsen 1988, pp. 81–82)

The degree to which middle-American parents are involved in their children's schools is often surprising to many people of other countries. Mainstream American education is singular in its dependence on parents to advocate their children's schooling, influence school policy, supervise homework, and volunteer in a constellation of school activities (Baker 1983). Most schools have organizations consisting of both parents and teachers that meet together regularly to talk about various concerns pertaining to the school — curriculum, faculty salaries, library facilities, etc. Parents often volunteer to assist with classroom or extra-curricular activities on a weekly basis. Some work regularly with the teacher with small groups of students. Conferences provide parents with opportunities to meet privately with teachers to discuss their child's problems and progress. All these activities may be unfamiliar to language minority parents.

Middle-American patterns of volunteering in schools are not prevalent in many cultures. In some cultures, parents feel they should not volunteer their time to work in schools; for these parents, the job of schools is *schooling* and the job of parents is *parenting*, which includes getting children to school, but does not include volunteering in schools. This is the case in many Latino and Asian cultures. One explanation of why the Vietnamese do not frequently volunteer follows:

> One comes to his life with certain credits and debits from previous lives. These dictate one's position and luck in this life. Since *bad luck* is a necessary payment for past bad actions, Vietnamese do not seem to feel much personal responsibility for others. This suggests a reason for the traditional lack of interest in social services and community affairs
> (*A Guide to Two Cultures* 1975, p. 15)

Another cultural constraint preventing parent participation is student embarrassment. Language minority students sometimes fear that their parents will be ridiculed for their customs (Olsen 1988).

> Our parents don't come [to school events] because they don't know any English. I don't even tell them when they are supposed to come. They dress so different and I don't want our parents to come because the others will laugh at them and tease us. We are ashamed.
> 9th grade Filipino girl, immigrated at age 11 (reported in Olsen 1988, p. 82)

A different reason language minority parents fail to become involved in our schools is that some teachers discourage their involvement (Cummins 1986, 1989). These teachers view parents as the root of their language minority students' inability to speak English. They believe that their interaction with their children in their first language actually prevents the children from acquiring English. Sometimes these teachers even advise the parents of their language minority students, who often have not acquired English themselves, to speak

English at home. This is bad advice. When language minority parents switch to English, they often deprive their children of exposure to valuable input in their first language, eradicate their children's cultural identities, and expose their children to an imperfect variety of English. As Cummins (1989) puts it, the attitudes of these prejudiced teachers, which are communicated "subtly but surely to students, contribute directly to the disabling of minority students within the classroom" (p. 63).

In view of the difficulties previously discussed, innovative, flexible parent involvement programs should be created to encourage wider parent participation. When scheduling various events, teachers need to be flexible, considering before- and after-work hours as well as weekends. Alternative dates give parents greater opportunity to participate in their children's school activities. For example, optional dates could be offered for *Back to School Night* by scheduling the event on both Friday evening and the following Saturday morning. Whenever possible, teachers need to arrange childcare for language minority families, since parents with small children have difficulty attending meetings if childcare is not provided or if small children are not allowed. Parent volunteers can provide childcare to families with young children. In addition, for those language minority children who come from families without parents, teachers can invite guardians, relatives or friends who can serve as these children's advocates. If parents feel intimidated by the schools in which teachers normally hold parent/teacher meetings, teachers need to hold their meetings at other locations (such as the public library).

Parental Assumptions

Parents differ in their assumptions regarding the school's role and their own role in educating their children. Some parents may believe they are responsible not only for nurturing their children, but also for teaching them. In this view, the responsibility for the child's learning rests primarily with the parent. This is the view of some groups of Asian parents (Heath 1986). Another parental view sees the child as having an active role in his or her own learning; the parents expect the child to teach him or herself. Some Mexican parents take this perspective (Phenice, Martinez and Grant 1986). Yet another view emphasizes communal responsibility for the young. Infants belong to their families as well as their communities, and teaching the child is too important to be taken over completely by the parents (Heath 1986). This is the perspective of many Samoan parents (Ochs 1986).

Not all people from the same culture have the same values and beliefs; there are tremendous individual differences. For this reason, it is necessary to be extremely careful when making cultural assumptions. However, an awareness of the general assumptions of major language minority populations makes it possible for the teacher to communicate more effectively with language minority parents, to recognize their difficulties, to avoid potential conflicts, and to establish an atmosphere that encourages parent participation in schooling. A discussion of parental assumptions of specific cultural groups follows.

Asian Parents

Most Asian parents expect discipline in the classroom and may not approve of teachers who allow students to freely choose activities or wander about the classroom without permission. They may also perceive open classrooms and interest centers as chaotic, confusing, and unorganized. Not surprisingly, the differences between the Asian parents' and middle-American teachers' perception of the role of the teacher sometimes confuse Asian students.

> The conflicting messages given by teachers and parents confuse the children, sometimes leading to misbehavior. The children may be perceived as discipline problems, when they are, in fact, simply unfamiliar with the pragmatic and cultural social rules of the school. Compared with Anglo-American children, most Asian children have been raised in a more rigid, disciplined and sheltered environment. They have learned to attend school with a formal attitude and need assistance in adjusting to the relative informality and casual atmosphere of American schools. (Cheng 1987, p. 13.)

Cheng (1987) suggests that although middle-American teachers expect a two-way exchange with the parent, Asian parents generally expect a one-way communication from the teacher, an authority. By and large, Asian parents prefer to leave educational decisions to the educators. They are baffled when teachers request their input on school concerns and often fail to respond to such requests. Thus, many teachers come to view Asian parents as unresponsive and unconcerned about the placement and curriculum of their children. In actuality, however, Asian parents' reluctance to participate is a sign of respect, not apathy; they feel that they are not in a position to challenge the decisions and authority of teachers.

Most Asian children must defer to adults, who determine what they can do and tell them when they should do it. According to Heath (1986), Chinese parents and other family members:

> . . . provide children with special toys and books, expect them to take care of these items, to learn to use them appropriately, and to read to learn. The extent of reinforcement of school norms and the provision at home of books and other items that support school activities vary along class lines. However, families see their role as complementing that of the school; and they tell their children to listen to the teacher, to obey, and to recognize that practicing

habits rewarded by the school will help ensure their future job opportunities. (Heath 1986, p. 159)

Many Asian parents regard teachers highly and expect them to give numerous assignments. In fact, the majority of Asian parents perceive as incompetent a teacher who does not assign a great deal of homework. They appreciate hard *work* and expect it of their children.

As discussed in Chapter 2, most Asian parents value education and generally expect their children to succeed academically. They value factual information and want their children to learn facts. They often emphasize the importance of practical skills and, impressed with *no frills* curricula, are pleased when their children learn the *basics* (reading, writing and arithmetic).

Most Asian parents want their children to obtain as much education as they can. Parents from Taiwan and Korea who come from middle and upper-middle class backgrounds often help their older children pay for both their undergraduate and graduate educations. However, higher education and achievement for a Chinese, Korean, Vietnamese or Japanese daughter is often not considered as important as it is for a son.

Asian parents may view parent/teacher conferences as problematic. The parents often interpret a request for a conference as an indication that their children are being naughty at school. Interpreters are often needed to facilitate communication and to assure Asian parents that their children are not misbehaving, but only need academic support.

Cheng (1987) summarizes Asian parents' and mainstream American teachers' expectations of schooling in Table 9–1.

Vietnamese Parents

While it is beyond the scope of this volume to discuss each Asian group separately, the numbers of Vietnamese in the United States and their special circumstances warrant a closer examination of their assumptions about education. Most Indo-Chinese groups in the United States have little or no hope of returning to their homelands, and they place a high value on education, viewing their children's education as a key to family success in the new land (Hoskins 1971). Pressure on the child can be intense as a result of these expectations.

I'm the only one in my family who can read and write, and they think I'll be something successful. Sometimes I get angry about that, and I fear I won't be able to do well enough. I study and study over and over again, harder than the other kids. If I don't get the best grade, my parents get angry at me and tell me I should do better.
10th grade Vietnamese girl, immigrated at age 13, (reported in Olsen 1988, p. 32)

Table 9-1
Incongruities between Mainstream American Teachers'
Expectations and Asian Parents' Expectations

Mainstream American Teachers' Expectations	Asian Parents' Expectations
Students should participate in classroom activities and discussion.	Students should be quiet and obedient.
Students should be creative.	Students should be told what to do.
Students learn through inquiries and debate.	Students learn through memorization and observation.
Students generally do well on their own.	Teachers should teach; students should be directed to *study*. It is important to deal with the real world.
Critical thinking is important. Analytical thinking is important.	Analysis is the teacher's job; synthesis is the student's.
Creativity and fantasy should be encouraged.	Factual information is important; fantasy is not.
Problem solving is important.	Students should be taught the steps to solve problems.
Students should ask questions.	Students should not ask questions.
Reading is a way of discovering.	Reading is the decoding of information and facts.

(adapted from Cheng 1988, p. 14)

There is a tendency for the Vietnamese to agree. Recalling the traditional Vietnamese respect and awe with which the teacher is regarded, one realizes that the teacher can expect the total support of the parents. Learning is highly valued, and teachers are ranked just below the king and above the father.

When discussing interpersonal relationships outside of the family, Li (1982) makes this observation:

While family relationships provide a basis for immediate and continued trust, close relationships with people outside the circle of relatives develop only gradually over a prolonged period of time. On meeting new people, Vietnamese are polite, somewhat distrustful, expecting a person to look for his/her advantage. (Li 1982, p. 6)

As seen in Chapter 2, the Vietnamese, like other Asians, feel that it is impolite to look in the eyes of people holding a higher status position. In ancient Vietnam, anyone who looked directly in the eye of the emperor was beheaded on the spot. As the reader will correctly guess, traditional Vietnamese parents would never look a teacher in the eyes (Eriksen and Cuceloglu 1987). Traditional Vietnamese teachers, when talking with parents or especially with students, stand or sit at a higher level than that at which the parents or students sit.

Latino Parents

Most Latino parents consider teachers to be authorities on intellectual matters. In general, they do not explicitly instruct their children in the same way as many middle-American parents do. For example, unlike many mainstream Americans, most Latinos do not generally accompany their actions with step-by-step directions, monitor their children's actions by giving sequential orders, or ask children to verbalize what they are doing as they work. Unlike many middle-American parents, some Latino parents seldom ask questions that require children to repeat facts, rehearse the sequence of events, or tell about what they will do in the future (Heath 1986). Most consider teaching children academic tasks, such as reading and writing, the function of schools, not the home.

Because many Latino parents have jobs that do not provide them with the financial resources or security necessary for planning for the future and for supporting their children's prospective college education, these parents often do not concern themselves with high educational expectations for their offspring. Heath (1986) has explained, "Adults expect children to go further in life than they have gone, but they rarely suggest specific future careers for their children or seek out opportunities for their children to observe, talk with or be apprenticed to adults in particular careers. Children probably hear little specific talk of how to envision themselves in diverse work settings" (p. 164). Like Heath, in examining the family lifestyles of Mexican children, Delgado-Gaitan (1987a) found that, for the most part, parents, in spite of their desire to have their children achieve, "do not know the precise steps that they should take to advise their children about a specific career" (p. 155). The parents of many young Latinos who have recently arrived in the United States are unable to offer their children academic counseling because they are usually unacquainted with the school system and unfamiliar with United States laws and requirements concerning the number of years and the nature of schooling required for their children to achieve educational success. As a result, it is the teachers who must provide the parents with specific information concerning higher education, so that they can help those parents envision their children in different and diverse work environments. It is also the teacher who must encourage these parents to acknowledge their children's efforts and to support them in their work at school. Delgado-Gaitan (1987a) also suggests the establishment of parent education classes, in which families are taught "facts about career opportunities" (p. 155).

There are special difficulties encouraging some groups of Latino parents to participate in parent involvement programs. One problem is that many fear being identified as illegal immigrants — although schools are required by law to educate all children and are not responsible for determining who is legal and who is not. Another problem is that many parents have not had a good experience themselves and may feel threatened by the school. Since their own school experiences were sometimes hostile and unrewarding, many Latino migrant parents believe that they will be treated with contempt by the school (Jordan 1980; see also Carter 1980). In line with this problem, many parents worry that their requests or demands may result in reprisals against their children.

Dependence upon extended family members for shared responsibility in child-rearing has been customary among members of recent migrant groups from Mexico, at least in their years before migration. Circumstances after these families migrate to the United States often alter this family pattern. The ideal remains, however, that parents, especially mothers, will have the primary care-giving responsibility while children are young; but the entire extended family accepts the new child as a member of the group immediately at birth, and parents may therefore expect other family members to share some responsibilities for child-rearing (Laosa 1984). Thus, if a parent is unable to come to a parent/teacher conference, for example, it is quite common that an older sibling will take over the responsibility instead.

Although it is not always the parent of the child who may attend a planned parent/teacher conference, this does not mean that the Latino parents lack respect for the authority represented by the teacher. Quite the contrary, the Latino value of respect for authority dictates that the home respect the school. Indeed, Latino parents are often upset by what they see as the lack of discipline in middle-American classrooms. They expect students to respect their teachers and teachers to maintain their authority. Good manners require that children be respectful of their elders, that they answer talk directed to them, and that they not initiate social conversations with elders (refer to Chapter 10 for a discussion of Latino values).

In traditional Latino homes, authority is delegated primarily to males and elders (Alvarez, Bean and Williams 1982). However, females also play an important role in decision-making. Both male and female teachers are respected as authority figures *in loco parentis* to make decisions about the direction of children's schooling and behavioral development.

Middle-Americans often perceive Latino children as exhibiting docile or passive behavior exclusively, but this perception is erroneous. Latinos do not value passive obedience. Children in Latino families are allowed to question adults about the nature of the tasks they are given and are then free to carry out the tasks in the manner they wish. They may choose to involve friends or siblings in the task or choose to do it alone. By and large, they determine their own work style and shape the parameters of their own tasks. "They may request assistance from adults if the task is unfamiliar, but generally children are left to decide independently the course they take in accomplishing work" (Delgado-Gaitan 1987b, p. 349). Latino children are resourceful and independent and parents often assign them tasks which draw upon their many creative abilities.

Latino children are also given responsibilities and are taught and expected to perform them capably at an early age (Levine and Bartz 1979). This is reflected in the behavior of older children, who often share in the responsibility of caring for younger siblings. Not surprisingly, Latino parents sometimes feel that teachers do not give their children enough responsibility at school. Their children are not afforded enough opportunities to demonstrate their capable, responsible behavior in the classroom, and if they are perceived by their middle-American teachers as impassive, they are not encouraged to participate in responsible behaviors, either.

Participation and cooperation are encouraged by Latino adults. Parents usually assign tasks to children and expect them to work together to assist around the house with family chores. Because of this presumption that most activities in life are group efforts, Latino parents are sometimes confused by the emphasis on individual competition in middle-American education. They are puzzled when their children are compared with others, and they usually do not respond by encouraging them to compete to be better than others in their classes.

As Latino children progress though mainstream American schools, they begin to notice the gap between the non-competitive, group-nurturing environment that they enjoy at home and the competitive, active role that they feel their teachers forcing upon them at school. As a result, children's evaluations of teachers and curricula become increasingly less favorable to parents as their children pass through their school years. Indeed, according to Carter and Segura (1979), Latino parents often end up viewing their children's teachers as prejudiced. And, when asked to participate in school activities, these parents usually view the participation as demeaning and the activities as insignificant. As suggested by Banks (1988), to combat such feelings of prejudice, teachers need to explain the details of their curriculum and its rationale and to ensure that parent involvement activities are significant.

Research by Parra and Henderson (1982) indicates that at least some groups of Latino parents are dissatisfied not only with teacher attitudes but also with the academic skills which are taught in our schools. Latino parents want teachers to instruct their students in the *basics* and are puzzled when their children's teachers introduce games and puzzles.

Many Latino parents also feel that by not taking their children's cultural background into consideration, the school shows a lack of responsibility for their social and emotional development. Unlike many Asian parents, Latino parents do not send their children to

Saturday or heritage schools where children are given instruction in culture and language. Most Latinos are very proud of both their language and their cultural heritage and want their children to maintain their first language and culture. The inclusion of family values in the educational program is recognized for successfully teaching these children. There is a need to promote Latino children's positive identity with their cultural heritage so that an alliance is created between home and school.

Although there is not a strong history of volunteer work in schools among Latino families, the Latino community is a supportive one. Many Latinos work very actively in their communities. The concept of a community-organized after-school program, for example, has long been known throughout the Southwest as an *escuelita* (little school). The escuelita is organized by volunteers from the community who provide tutorial, language and cultural experiences to young children (Padilla 1982).

Table 9–2 summarizes incongruities between mainstream American teachers' and Latino parents' expectations.

In the preceding discussion, I pointed out differences in the cultural assumptions of middle-American teachers and language minority parents. The generalizations made pertain to specific groups of

Table 9–2
Incongruities between Mainstream American Teachers' Expectations and Latino Parents' Expectations

Mainstream American Teachers' Expectations	Latino Parents' Expectations
Students should participate in classroom activities and discussion.	Students should be quiet and obedient, observing more than participating.
Students should be creative, free to respond to requirements in their own ways.	Students should be shown what to do but allowed to organize the completion of the task creatively.
Students learn through inquiry.	Students learn through observation.
Students should do their own work.	Students should help one another.
Critical thinking is important. Analytical thinking is important too.	Factual information is important; fantasy is too.
Goals are important.	People are important.
Children should state their own opinions, even when they contradict the teacher's.	Teachers are not to be challenged.
Students need to ask questions.	Students should not ask a lot of questions.

parents, namely recent arrivals to the United States who now reside in urban areas and who come from China, Vietnam and Mexico. It should be pointed out that thousands of immigrants enter the United States each year and the concerns faced by each group of immigrants are more similar than different. As Berger (1981) points out, children everywhere, though culturally different, are all children.

> Children are like snowflakes
> At first they appear to be alike
> But on closer examination they are
>   all different
> Focus on their similarities
> But understand their differences.
>
> (Berger 1981, p. 94)

It is beyond the scope of this book to discuss the parental expectations of all cultural groups. However, for information concerning other groups, see Chapter Ten.

Given the language minority parents' expectations regarding their involvement in schools, the following means of encouraging language minority parent involvement are suggested.

1. Orientation Programs.   It is useful to provide both language minority students and their parents with orientation workshops about the school system in the United States (Olsen 1988). In these workshops, parents can be given translations of essential school information. In addition, they can be given information concerning community agencies which provide interpreters and support to families in dealing with the schools. During orientation sessions, parents can also be informed of the many ways in which they can participate in their children's schooling. (Refer to the appendix for useful resources.)

Teachers can help language minority parents understand and accept their instruction by informing them about the curriculum and its rationale. This is particularly important since language minority parents often question "the legitimacy and relevance of the educational program if learning is not taking place in a manner in which they were taught or with which they are familiar" (Grant 1981, p. 130).

During the orientation session, parents can also be informed of *after-school* or *extracurricular* activities, such as nature clubs, musical organizations, science clubs, art and drama groups, language clubs, or athletic groups which may impact their children's learning. As Baker (1983) points out, there is a need to involve students in those extracurricular activities and sports in which students have not been encouraged to participate. Many language minority students do not participate in swimming, tennis, and skiing, primarily because the facilities needed for these sports are not available in their communities. Other language minority students are discouraged from participating in extracurricular activities because their parents do not understand their value. One student complains:

> My parents will not let me stay after school to play soccer. They say I have to study. I study and I study and I study. That is what they believe I need to do. If I don't have homework, I still study. They make me do it over and over again. They really want me to do well, but they don't understand about the schools here.
> 10th grade Cambodian boy, immigrated at age 9 (reported in Olsen 1988, p. 82).

Some schools show parents slides or videotapes to introduce parents to the school program. These media are particularly useful for *orienting* language minority parents who often need to enroll their children in schools during the middle of the school year when teachers and administrators have little time to discuss their school programs and curriculum. (A description of programs successfully using videotapes is included in the appendix.)

Handbooks are another useful means of providing parents and students information about schools. They can be prepared in advance in the languages of the students and given to parents when they enroll their children in school. (Berger 1981, makes many practical suggestions for writing handbooks.)

2. Initial Contacts. Although most middle-American teachers feel that both parents and teachers are responsible for initiating parent/teacher interaction, teachers must take the initiative with language minority parents. Grant (1981) suggests that all parents or guardians be systematically contacted by phone or in person at the beginning of the school year. If you do not speak the native languages of your students, it is wise to make the first contact with a parent volunteer from your class or with someone from the school parent-teacher organization who speaks the student's home language. Such a person may be willing to call other parents to help you to obtain help for your parent involvement program.

It is essential to respect and use your students' home language so that students are taught to feel proud of the communication which takes place in their homes. Teachers must never encourage parents to switch to English in their homes. Research shows that native language development contributes to English language development, while first language loss contributes to a lessened self-esteem. (See Chapter Two.)

3. Home Visits. As Cazden (1986) points out, most teachers fail to visit their language minority students' homes, but such visits can provide them with valuable information about their students. Grant (1981) suggests that when teachers make home visits they make an appointment ahead of time, keep the visit short (20 minutes to a half hour), and avoid asking prying questions (some language minority students are in the United States illegally and fear deportation). He gives this advice to teachers who do not speak their students' home languages:

> If you are not bilingual and are planning to visit a student's home where English is not spoken by the parents, it is helpful to send a note home in the parents' language telling them of your lack of ability with their language and desire to make the visit. If your student can serve as interpreter, this will be a good opportunity for her to see the advantage of knowing two languages and to feel *important* by assisting two people who are very important in her life. If the student is unable to serve as interpreter, invite a trustworthy person to serve. Finally, make certain the parents do not feel *put down* because of their inability to speak your language (Grant 1981, p. 135).

In many cultures, home visits are only done when students require reprimanding. This is the case with many Chinese, Korean, Japanese and Vietnamese groups. In most Latino cultures, home visits are highly valued, particularly when teachers have something positive to say about their children's progress. Bear in mind, however, that some language minority parents have had such negative experiences with the schools that any home visits might be met with suspicion.

What should you accomplish during these home visits? Encourage active parent participation! Just inspiring a parent to read aloud to students daily (in any language) has a significant effect on children's learning. Lapides (1980) recommends that teachers provide parents with ideas for enhancing their children's first as well as second language development (refer to Chapters 2 and 3; see also the appendix of this chapter). As discussed in Chapter 5, you might also encourage parents to share with you the ways they have observed that their own children learn best. Berger (1981) gives many additional suggestions for making home visits successful.

4. Parent Conferences. You might want to hold a parents' meeting during the first month of school at a time convenient for most parents. There, you can discuss your curriculum and channel parent involvement in several concrete ways. Again, it is important to provide flexible scheduling of parent conferences and arrange childcare. Also, unless you inform language minority parents in advance of the importance of these conferences, they will probably not attend. This means that you will need to contact parents in advance and, when necessary, use parent volunteers to encourage language minority parents and guardians to attend parent conferences. There are a number of excellent resources which discuss structuring parent conferences. (See Berger 1981 and Lombana 1983.)

5. Parent Involvement in Classes. The inclusion of parents of diverse cultures as volunteers in your classrooms is important because such inclusion is a sign of approval. When the volunteers are monocultural, this subtly communicates to students that other groups are not significant enough to be included. This exclusion encourages racist beliefs.

Parents can provide valuable assistance in many classroom activities. For example, they can help students at a learning center, work with students individually on class projects or serve as group leaders during field trips. They can also read aloud to small groups. Enright and McCloskey suggest that "if you have several students from the same language group, find a parent who will read or tell stories to them in their native language" (p. 263). To foster multicultural education, teachers can invite native English speakers to join in these reading groups. In this way, they inform native English-speaking students that diverse languages are valued.

Unfortunately, parents regularly find themselves having too much to do to volunteer time working in their children's classes. This is particularly the case with language minority parents (Phenice, Martinez and Grant 1986). Again, it is important to provide flexible time-scheduling for volunteers; teachers may even need to schedule parts of their curriculum around parent schedules. Volunteers may need to work for limited time periods. For example, parents may be willing to work once a week for a month, but cannot commit their time for the entire school year. Language minority parents may also be unaccustomed to working in middle-American schools and will not know what they are expected to do when working with groups. In some cases, they may be illiterate. Teachers will need to provide language minority parents with training sessions. It is essential that language minority parents who are able to volunteer be given significant tasks (for example, working with reading groups, not cleaning paint brushes). In addition to this, teachers need to understand when parents are too busy to volunteer in their children's classes and avoid giving preferential treatment to those students whose parents have time to do such volunteer work.

Language minority parents can gain considerably through parent involvement programs. According to Enright and McCloskey (1988), the best programs "operate in multilingual schools where second language learners' parents (who often are also still learning the new language and culture) help out in the classrooms, cafeteria, library and playground and by doing so help both their children and themselves" (p. 263).

6. *Events.* "The easiest way for parents to find their way into your classroom is to help you celebrate something. Plays and programs always provide a good draw; parents enjoy seeing their own children perform" (Enright and McCloskey 1988, p. 262). A sure way to provide parties that take into account the kinds of music, dancing, and games that your students are familiar with is to include parent representatives from as many different cultural groups as there are in your class. However, these celebrations should not be the only cultural parts of your curriculum. Separating cultural content from other parts of the curriculum can have the effect of perpetuating stereotypes and myths based on discriminatory practices. Baker

(1983) contends that "teaching multicultural content in an integrated fashion can serve to help children better understand, value and live in our culturally diverse society" (p. 47).

In addition, greater attention needs to be placed on publicizing these events. Grant (1981) suggests that posters be placed in local supermarkets and neighborhood stores advertising school events and the need for volunteers. School activities can also be advertised through organizations which are active in the community. For example, some schools work with churches to encourage parent and community participation. School announcements can be read at church services or placed in church bulletins. Grant notes that this kind of cooperation between school and church has been very successful in areas where the influence of the local clergy is very significant.

7. *Parent Talks.*   Parents or other people who represent a particular profession or have an interest in a special topic can be invited into the classroom to talk with the students. They can "give talks and answer questions about their native countries, their occupations, their hobbies and their favorite stories" (Enright and McCloskey 1988, p. 262).

The teacher should ensure that there is diversity among parents who give talks. For example, if parents talk about their occupations, care must be taken "to locate a male nurse when young children are learning about career choices. Likewise, special effort must be made to invite a female telephone installer or minority or female physician, dentist or banker to talk to the class." (Baker 1983, p. 89)

8. *Homeroom Advisers.*   In some high schools, parents serve as homeroom advisers who help teachers and students with problems relating to attendance, job opportunities, personal careers and school credits. In elementary schools, homeroom advisers plan special events such as class parties and picnics. Again, the inclusion of parents of diverse cultures is important in that it conveys the message to students that language minority parents are significant enough to play major roles in the classroom.

9. *Informal Contacts.*   Informal contacts with parents provide teachers with a means of monitoring their language minority students' progress on an on-going basis. There are several ways of maintaining these contacts. It is common to send home notes which are carried home by the student. Many schools use *Glad Notes*, postcards which pass along good news about students. One advantage of *Glad Notes* is that they can be written in advance in various languages. Some elementary and secondary teachers phone two parents every evening in order to contact each student's family regularly. Others contact only the parents of students who would most benefit from the call. Others send multilingual newsletters home with their students which the students themselves write. Some, who send letters home to parents who are illiterate in English, put a check mark on the top of those letters which are important. This lets the parents know that they must have the letters translated. Teachers who do not

have translators sometimes make simple, easy to read, marks on their students' papers. They have translators explain the marks to the parents and use them consistently to help parents understand them.

  10. Homework.   Homework can also be used effectively to involve parents. However, the ways in which teachers plan it and parents respond to it can make it have positive or negative results. Language minority students may be prone to problems relating to homework because their parents are usually unable to give them sufficient direction.

  In view of these difficulties, McCloskey and Enright (1988) suggest that, for children, *homeWORK* be replaced with *homeFUN* activities which the student completes with his or her family. They suggest these activities:

- make a personal time line of the student's life.
- make a map of family or ancestral migrations.
- collect insults, jokes or riddles.
- study how family members use reading or writing: list the many ways in which a family member uses print in one day.
- sketch bedrooms, houses, blocks.
- make maps of routes commonly traveled, for example, at school.
- get a library card and learn how to use it.
- write down an unwritten family recipe as a family member prepares the dish.
- collect funny stories about the student's childhood.
- study a particular aspect of parents' childhood: work, housing, television, radio, segregation.
- make lists and sketches of wildlife near the home in a certain category, for example, insects, mammals, birds.
- collaborate on a cooking activity.

(Enright and McCloskey 1988, p. 266)

  11. Family Literacy Programs.   The success of family literacy programs, in which parents and children read together is well documented. Tizard, Schofield and Hewison (1982) report on a two-year project in an inner-city area of London. In this project, dramatic improvements in children's reading occurred as a simple consequence of sending books home regularly and requiring children to read these books to their parents, many of whom were non-native English speakers. The children who participated in the project made greater progress in reading than their peers who received special instruction in small groups from a reading specialist, but did not participate in the family literacy program. As discussed in Chapter 3, reading in any language develops reading ability. Ada (1986, 1988), implemented a family literacy program with Latino parents in Pajaro Valley, California. Sixty to eighty parents met each month to examine books critically and to discuss their children's writing. They were then given books to discuss with their children at home in Spanish. If the parents could not read, they could use the illustrations in the books to guide them in the discussion. After they discussed these books with their children, they encouraged their children to do their own writing which they would then share at the next monthly meeting. By the end of the project, Ada reports, the parents were so excited about the program, that they checked out nearly all the books from the public library. Although all the parents were not literate in the beginning of project, by the end all participants, parents and children alike had gained literacy skills. Interestingly, Ada held the literary sessions in the public library, a less intimidating place for the parents.

12. Parent Advisory Committees.   In addition to these means of involving parents, community participation in our schools can also be gained through parent advisory committees. In the past, however, far too often parents have been manipulated and intimidated during advisory committee meetings. Care must be taken to involve parents as partners in their children's education and to allow parents to have a *voice* in the education their children receive. They must be informed of the legal realities as well as "the activities and attitudes of the local policy makers" (Curtis 1988, p. 291). In addition, they must understand that social change normally requires long-term commitment.

Conclusion

If language minority students are to have the educational opportunities of mainstream Americans, parental involvement is imperative. By maximizing the parents' options to participate in their children's schooling, and accepting and appreciating the cultural styles of language minority parents, teachers can increase their language minority students' opportunities to succeed academically.

ACTIVITIES AND DISCUSSION QUESTIONS

1. Consider the following letter from Dear Diane: Letters from Our Daughters.

Dear Diane,
I'm a high school senior, and like with many of my friends, my main problem is my parents. They accept nothing except straight A's from me. Last report card I got a B in English and they immediately asked me why I only got a B, and why couldn't I have gotten a higher grade. They're so critical of me. I can't remember a single time when they have told me they were proud of me or that I did a good job. I'm getting so discouraged. What can I do to get them to change? DISCOURAGED STUDENT

(Wong 1983, p. 1)

If you were *Diane*, how would you answer this student's letter?

What types of information would you give to Asian parents at parent education workshops?

2. Describe several ways to encourage language minority parents who are illiterate in both their first and second language to participate in school events. In what specific ways would you make these parents feel comfortable at the events?

3. Many Asian parents aren't used to praising their children for their achievements. In some traditional Asian cultures it is even considered bad luck to praise children as this might draw attention to them and cause the Gods to envy and even steal them. Do teachers have the right to encourage Asian parents to praise their children for their academic advancements? Is such praise beneficial?

4. Some language minority students are embarassed when their parents come to school because their parents dress and behave as they would in their homelands. How can you help these language minority students overcome their embarrassment?

5. Interview a few parents of language minority students. Ask them to discuss their concerns about their children's schooling.

RECOMMENDED READING

ASHWORTH, M. 1985. *Beyond Methodology: Second Language Teaching and the Community.* New York: Cambridge University Press. Provides teachers with many ideas for gaining the support of the community and utilizing its resources.

DAVIES, D. (ed.) 1981. *Communities and their Schools.* New York: McGraw-Hill. Contains essays which examine critical issues affecting schools and communities.

GRIFORE. R. J. and BODER, R. P. (eds.) 1986. *Child Rearing in Home and School.* New York: Plenum Press. Primarily intended for elementary school teachers, the book discusses strategies for improving home and school relations. Contains chapters pertaining to both native and non-native English speaking children.

LOMBANA, J. H. 1983. *Home-School Partnerships: Guidelines and Strategies for Educators.* New York: Grune and Stratton, Inc. Gives useful ideas for developing better communication with parents and families.

APPENDIX

Resources

Building stronger relations between language minority parents and the schools involves both a community thrust and school initiated efforts. Many districts are beginning to offer parent materials in the languages of the families. The following examples go beyond that important translation step to active involvement of parents.

The Hacienda/La Puente Project

The Hacienda/La Puente School District [in California] shows movies in a variety of languages to draw parents to the school site in the evenings. The movies are followed by native language speakers on topics such as the educational system in the United States, and issues facing children in the community. These evenings are regularly offered to the Korean, Chinese, and Spanish speaking parents.

Contact
Anthony Guerro
District Specialist
1600 Pontenova Drive
Hacienda Heights, California 91745

Center for Southeast Asian Resettlement

Operating in San Francisco, Marin, and Santa Clara Counties, the Center for Southeast Asian Resettlement provides translation, mediation and support for parents to participate in teacher/family conferences and other meetings with schools. In addition, their Language Bank makes translators available to both schools and parents.

Contact
Vu-Duc Vuong, Executive Director
CSEARR
975 O'Farrell Street
San Francisco, California 94109
(415) 885-2743

La Escuela de la Raza Consumer Language Program

The La Escuela de la Raza Consumer Language Program is a collaborative project of UCLA and Los Angeles Unified School District. The consumer education program provides workshops on weekday evenings and Saturdays for immigrant parents at Lincoln High School. The course is taught by UCLA student volunteers, and covers basic survival skills, an opportunity to practice situational English, awareness of consumer products and agencies, preparation for the GED, processes for registering children in school and an orientation to the school system. The UCLA contact with parents and presence on the school campus also enhances the recruitment of students to the university.

Contact
La Escuela de la Raza
Consumer Language Program
Community Programs Office
University of California at Los Angeles
MG 102
Los Angeles, California 90024
(213) 825-7843
(from Olsen 1988, p. 83)

CHAPTER TEN

Appreciating Cultural Diversity in the United States

Underlying Principle 9 is the notion that teachers must understand the cultural values and behaviors of their students. This chapter provides teachers with information concerning some of the diverse cultural groups they are likely to find in their classrooms. However, before turning to this discussion, a word of warning is in order. "Issues involving ethnicity and education invariably evoke strong emotional responses" (Sue and Padilla 1986, p. 36). Stereotyping is a problem and cautions against cultural stereotyping must be taken seriously. We all know middle-Americans who love raw fish, eat dinner at 3:00 p.m. and never offer compliments. We also know Japanese who hate rice, speak loudly, and compliment effusively. Behaviors change over time, from individual to individual, and from situation to situation. For example, as language minority students acculturate, they sometimes take on the values of mainstream Americans. Thus, language minority students who have completed their entire educations in the United States commonly acquire many typical middle-American *school values.* A different problem associated with making judgments about groups is that these judgments often reflect the mainstream-American perspective and give less credit to minority group perception. Also, cultures are dynamic and changing. Concepts such as *Asian culture* imply an unchanging, monolithic culture which is misleading. Keep these concerns in mind as the discussion turns to diverse cultural groups. The term *cultural group* is used here interchangeably with the term *ethnic group* to refer to a group which shares "a common ancestry, culture, history, tradition, and sense of peoplehood and that is a political and economic interest group" (Banks 1988, p. 8).

To avoid confusion, it might be useful to review the labels I use to refer to various cultural groups. The term *language minority student* refers to non-native English speaking students who lack full proficiency in English. The term *Latino* is used as a cover term in reference to individuals of Spanish-speaking origin. Latinos who live in the United States include:

(1) *Mexicans.* Those individuals who identify themselves as *Mexicans* usually relate more to the cultural norms of Mexico than they do to those of the United States. They tend to be recent arrivals of the United States who are not citizens.

(2) *Mexican-Americans.* Those who identify themselves as Mexican-Americans are individuals of Mexican heritage who reside in the United States. They do not identify with the Chicano movement which takes as its primary goal the attainment of political, economic, and educational equity in the United States.

(3) *Chicanos.* Those who identify themselves as Chicanos are individuals of Mexican heritage who reside in the United States and who support the Chicano movement.

Asian refers to persons who have recently immigrated to the United States from Asian countries, while *Asian American* refers specifically to those individuals of Asian heritage who are citizens of the United States. Finally, *middle-American* and *mainstream American* are used interchangeably to refer to anyone in the United States of any race or religion who shares middle class values and traditions.

Middle-Americans

Before discussing the rich cultural values of the language minority students participating in our classrooms, it is helpful first to examine middle-class, mainstream American values. When examining values, educators must realize that all values are abstract, generalized principles which influence behavior (Banks 1988). While each country has its own national values that are to some extent shared by its members, it also has other values which distinguish its subcultures. It should also be mentioned that individuals can have strong or weak identification with a cultural group, and this determines the extent to which individuals follow cultural values.

The information on the various cultural groups is not intended to be complete. Rather, it is intended to whet the appetite of teachers so that they will read more about cultural groups and observe the language minority students in their classrooms more keenly. Teachers will need to evaluate all information pertaining to cultural groups *critically* so that they will avoid forming false stereotypes about individuals.

Cantoni-Harvey (1987) characterizes middle-class, mainstream Americans as follows:

> The American middle-class culture plans and organizes time, cherishes change and novelty, and gives prominence to the young, rather than to the elderly. It is characterized by competitiveness and upward mobility, and encourages individual accomplishment. It also assumes that natural problems can be overcome by technology and ingenuity, and views people as neither good nor evil but perfectible. (p. 6)

Damen (1988), based on references in Stewart (1972) and Condon and Yousef (1975), identified general value orientations of middle-Americans in contrast to an opposite orientation. (See Table 10–1 below.) For Damen (1988), the Contrast American column does not describe any particular culture, but merely represents an opposite orientation. She states, "Of course, the American profile is drawn in broad strokes and describes the mainstream culture; ethnic diversity is of necessity blurred in this sweeping treatment" (p. 195).

Thus, according to Damen (1988), middle-class, mainstream-Americans generally believe that they can control their environment and that change is good and should be encouraged. They believe in equality, which in their opinion is linked to individualism and informality. Their achievement orientation reflects the so-called *American Dream* or Horatio Alger orientation. They are oriented to the future and plan future goals carefully. Rather than approaching problems using a consensus-seeking approach in which group harmony is

Table 10–1
Some Implicit Cultural Assumptions

Middle-American (USA)	Contrast Middle-American
Personal control of environment	Man dominated by nature
Change inevitable and desirable	Change non-existent; tradition favored
Equality of opportunity	Class structure dominant, hierarchical (social hierarchy determines opportunities)
Individualism valued	Interdependence but individuality
Future orientation	Present or past orientation
Action orientation	"Being" orientation
Directness and openness	Suggestive, consensus-seeking; group orientation
Practicality, pragmatism, rationality	Feeling orientation; philosophical attitude
Problem-solving orientation	Inactive, enduring, seeking help from others
Cause-and-effect logic	Certainty and knowledge
Individual competition	Group progress
Do-it-yourself approach to life	Dependence upon intermediaries for success

(Adapted from Damen 1988, p. 195)

valued, they approach problems directly and openly, confronting others if necessary. Many middle-Americans view things in terms of black and white and cause and effect. They have a competitive, do-it-yourself approach to life. Other cultural groups have different values.

The challenge in educating language minority students is to create educational programs which will enhance the educational achievement of all students. Diverse cultural and linguistic groups are a national resource, not an obstacle. Simple knowledge of a student's culture may not create educational equity for that student. As Robinson (1985) points out, the teacher can never step into the shoes of a student, but will forever contend with the trappings and implicit biases of personal experiences. Yet, understanding other cultures can help our own cultural repertoires expand.

This section provides brief descriptions of the values of many major cultural groups in the United States. Included are descriptions of Asian Americans (such as Cambodians, Chinese, Filipinos, Koreans, Laotians, and Vietnamese) and Latinos (such as Mexicans and Puerto Ricans). While other cultural groups could be included here, the groups discussed are among the largest populations of language minority students and are the groups with whom I am most familiar. The brief descriptions of the groups below are intended as samples of the type of information which is needed for all the cultural groups represented in our classrooms. Useful references pertaining to some major cultural groups not discussed are listed in the suggested reading at the end of this chapter.

Asians

While it is attempted here to draw a composite picture of what is Asian, readers should be aware that not everyone fits neatly into this composite. Asians are divided into numerous cultural groups.

Background. In 1940, the Asian population in the United States was about 250,000; in 1969, the number was 900,000. However, by 1980, the Asian population had grown to nearly 3.5 million, and in 1985 the number of Asians living in the United States approached an estimated 5.1 million (Kitano and Daniels 1988). The amendment of the Immigration and Nationality Act in 1964 gave an annual quota of 20,000 immigrants from each country and a total annual quota of 170,000 immigrants for Asian countries. Under this act, a complicated system was created that favored persons who had close relatives in the United States or who had professional skills. Those who have derived the most benefits from the preference provisions of the 1965 law have been Asians, especially Chinese, Koreans, Indians, Filipinos and Southeast Asian ethnic groups.

Asians have been alternately welcomed and ostracized in the United States. Discrimination against Asians has been evident since their earliest days of immigration to the United States. However, by the early 1980s, the American media were noticing the substantial achievements of many Asians. In 1982, *Newsweek* printed a flattering report: "Asian-Americans: A *Model Minority.*" This has become a popular expression and a stereotype. Yet, Asian Americans have faced discrimination, educational handicaps, language barriers, and difficult citizenship requirements. (Kitano and Daniels 1988; see also Wing 1972). A report from the United States Department of Commerce (1983) points out that:

> . . . even in the case of Asian Americans, who perform well on measures such as college graduation and SAT mathematics subtest scores, a rather mixed picture emerges. Although they have succeeded in higher education, they paradoxically have over four times the proportion of persons failing to have any education whatsoever, compared to whites. In addition, they appear to be underrepresented at levels of middle and upper management compared to the level of educational attainment of those who successfully graduate from universities.

How is it possible to reconcile problems of poverty and educational inequality with the stories about *model minorities?* It is possible because Asians are divided into numerous ethnic groups with diverse acculturation patterns. Asians themselves often speak of the dissimilarities between American-born Asians and fresh-off-the-boat or plane (FOB) immigrant Asians (Kitano and Daniels 1988).

Chinese

Background. Chinese immigrants began to arrive in the United States in about 1847. Discrimination against the Chinese, especially by middle-American workers who were experiencing economic difficulties, and various attempts to curtail Chinese immigration and rights, culminated in the passage of the Exclusion Acts in 1882. Later immigration acts such as the Displaced Persons Act of 1948 and the Immigration and Nationality Act of 1952 increased the number of Chinese immigrants. Immigration of Chinese between the years 1944 to 1965 was selective, however, favoring the most highly educated professional and technically skilled. The number of Chinese immigrants has increased dramatically due to the Immigration Act of 1965, the admission of a large number of refugees from Southeast Asia, particularly after the fall of Saigon, and the influx of Chinese students from Taiwan.

Chinese students from Taiwan represent a large ethnic group in the United States who, by and large, come from middle and upper middle-class families that are highly urbanized. Recently, the Taiwanese have been sending their male children alone to the United States on temporary student visas to live with established United States residents in order to avoid compulsory military service at home. The Taiwanese have also been sending their children to American universities because of limited space and difficult entrance requirements in Taiwanese colleges.

One other group of Chinese is now coming to the United States:

Hong Kong Chinese. According to Cheng (1987), "many Chinese from Hong Kong have come to the United States because they fear the consequences of the Communist takeover of Hong Kong in 1997" (p. 22). Hong Kong, a colony ceded to Britain after the Opium War, will remain under British rule until 1997, when it will revert to China. Many Chinese are now trying to leave Hong Kong. The recent immigration reform of 1986 increased the quota for Hong Kong from 600 to 5,000 each year (Public Law 99-603, November 6, 1986), and we can expect to see a rise in the number of immigrants from Hong Kong in the coming decade (Wong 1988).

After the Cultural Revolution (1964–1974), many Chinese scientists and students from the People's Republic of China came to the United States to study. Cheng (1987) reports that the ten year cultural revolution damaged Chinese educational institutions, research, and scholarship. "Educational facilities were damaged; public monuments defaced; teachers and scholars publicly humiliated and imprisoned; books, artwork, and important documents destroyed and schools closed" (p. 22). In the last decade, efforts have been made to make up the academic ground lost by encouraging students to study in the United States and then return to teach in China. Approximately 73,000 Chinese students have received visas to study in the United States, according to official United States figures.

Another reason the Chinese from the People's Republic of China were until recently immigrating to the United States concerns our diplomatic relationship with mainland China. According to Cheng (1987):

> Since President Richard Nixon's ping-pong diplomacy, many Chinese from the People's Republic of China have applied for immigration to the United States in order to join their family members, or to study. It is estimated that there are 10,000 students from China in American institutions of higher learning.
>
> (p. 22)

Also, in 1981 "the annual 20,000-per-country quota for immigrants from China was changed to apply separately to the PRC [People's Republic of China] and Taiwan, resulting in an increase in immigrants from the two countries from 25,800 in fiscal year 1981 to 35,800 in fiscal year 1984" (Gardner, Robey and Smith 1985, p. 37).

Since the massacre of pro-democracy demonstrators in and around Beijing's Tian An Men Square, in June 1989, returning to China has been a frightening prospect for the 40,000 Chinese students studying in the United States. The extent to which Chinese students from the People's Republic of China will continue to come to the United States is, at this time, unclear.

In addition to these groups of Chinese immigrants are ethnic Chinese from areas such as Cuba, Burma, and Indo-China. Lopez (1982) estimates that as many as 100,000–200,000 of the Vietnamese refugees are ethnic Chinese.

Like other Asian groups, the Chinese at first suffered discrimination. Wong (1987) notes, "The first generation (19th century) of Chinese immigrants could not legally establish families in the United States. Also legally forbidden to socialize with non-Chinese, they saw little reason to learn Western customs or to learn more than a minimal amount of English. Calling them the *Yellow Peril* and the *Chinese menace*, United States workers wanted to force them out of the country" (p. 6). Many other examples of discrimination against Asians have been reported. For instance, the San Francisco Board of Education refused to allow a 10-year-old girl to enroll in the city's public schools because one of her parents was Chinese. In some states, intermarriage between whites and Chinese was illegal. In San Francisco, Stockton and Sacramento, Chinese immigrants were residentially segregated (Kitano and Daniels 1988).

Values. Chinese from Taiwan, Hong Kong, and the People's Republic of China vary widely with respect to values. Yet it is possible to make certain generalizations about those from these countries who come from middle-class families and who have lived in the United States fewer than ten years. It should be pointed out that not all Asians are middle-class. Although many Chinese have *made it* in the United States (see Hsia 1988), significantly more Chinese than whites still live below the poverty level (Wong 1988).

Chinese children are generally obedient. They usually respect elders and those in authority. Cheng (1987) states, "value is placed on outward calmness and on control of such undesirable emotions as anger, jealousy, hostility, aggression, and self-pity" (p. 22).

Many traditional Chinese families expect their children to do well in school and to go into fields which ensure their future employment. Children are taught to believe that the only way to succeed in life is to work hard and respect authority. Such views may be inconsistent with a philosophy promoted in the United States which emphasizes the balance between work and play. Many Chinese consider individual recreation wasteful and self-indulgent; they do not have hobbies and do not understand their importance to middle-Americans. Not surprisingly, there are relatively few Chinese athletes.

Like other groups of Asians, the Chinese respect the elderly and feel a moral obligation to support aging parents. Children generally try to repay their parents' sacrifices by being successful and supporting them in old age. Ogbu and Matute-Bianchi (1986) report that Chinese parents make great sacrifices to see that their children have the necessary education to become successful. "Their children reciprocate by working hard in school in order to succeed academically, obtain good employment, and earn good wages to fulfill their filial obligations" (pp. 103–104).

The Chinese brought a cultural tradition to the United States which stresses respect for learning as a means of self-advancement. Sung (1967) points out, "even when a college degree led to no more than a waiter's job [in America], the Chinese continued to pursue the best education they could get, so that when the opportunities developed, the Chinese were qualified and capable of handling the job'' (pp. 124–125).

In line with this, Heath (1986), in describing Chinese immigrants who have recently arrived in the United States, notes that Chinese children are expected to assume responsibilities according to their age and sex and to perform these duties independently of their personal feelings and goals. Heath suggests:

> Children must defer to adults, who determine what their children can do and tell them when they should do it. Children are encouraged to model themselves after authorities and watch what they do and practice again and again to achieve perfection. (p. 158)

Education. For many Chinese students and teachers, books contain knowledge, wisdom and truth. Maley (1986) reports that for Chinese from the People's Republic of China, "knowledge is *in* the book and can be taken out and put inside the students' heads. Hence the reverence with which books are treated, the value they are assigned, and the wish to learn by heart what they contain" (p. 102).

Heath (1986) suggests that traditional Chinese parents see their role as complementing that of the school and serve as active agents in their children's schooling. For instance, Chinese parents ". . . tell their children to listen to the teacher, to obey, and to recognize that practicing habits rewarded by the school will help ensure future job opportunities '' (p. 159). Middle and upperclass parents especially value such subject areas as English, math, and science since these subjects will help their children achieve future career goals.

Chinese schools generally do not stress creativity. In the People's Republic of China, for instance, students are not expected to discover new truths. In Civil Service examinations, essays must not be written to show originality. Wu (1982) explains that "to go against Confucius and the Classics would be like attacking the First Amendment in America now" (p. 123).

Another primary characteristic of Chinese education, in both the People's Republic of China and Taiwan, is memorization. Rather than analyzing books, it is not uncommon for the Chinese in the People's Republic to memorize parts and main points (see Chance 1987).

Reading and writing are emphasized in Chinese schools. This emphasis on reading and writing in the People's Republic of China may be traced to the ancient attempt to unify the Chinese through a common written language. Chinese are spread over a wide geographic area and speak many different dialects. Wu (1982) states:

> An individual's role in such a society was to learn the written code so as to be a member of Chinese society. The values generated from the unity in writing was respect for writing, to the extent that pieces of paper with writing on them would not be discarded. Ching-hsi tzu chih, kung-teh wu liang (To respectfully save writing and paper would accumulate unlimited merit) is a common saying. (p. 124)

Although the Chinese value group harmony and unity, there is little group work in their schools. Exams are competitive as are other classroom activities. (See Chapter 8.)

Chinese immigrants generally believe that an education in the United States offers them a means of improving their status. As one Chinese student reported in a class project (Ong 1976): "The immigrants viewed free public education of their children as the hope of the future. Education became the chief means to raise their economic status and social conditions and to get out of the Chinatown ghetto. The Chinese were motivated to use education to advance themselves" (p. 8). She then went on to add, "As a matter of fact, one of the major reasons for immigration was the quest for a better life for their children through American free education." Consequently, these Chinese immigrants "tend to exert considerable pressures on their children to study hard and succeed in school according to Anglo middle-class criteria or standards of school success" (Ogbu and Matute-Bianchi, p. 110).

"Depending on the background of an adult Chinese immigrant to America, his or her initial command of English upon entry may vary from no knowledge whatsoever to native proficiency" (Wong 1988, p. 204). Wealthy Hong Kong immigrants, who received excellent English instruction in private language institutes, often come to the United States fluent in English. On the other hand, poorer Hong Kong immigrants, who received some instruction in English since kindergarten, may be illiterate in English (Wong 1988). This is because although English has long been taught in Hong Kong, the English language instruction given in the public schools is quite poor. Even today, Chinese teachers in Hong Kong are required to teach in English even though they themselves have limited proficiency in English.

In contrast to Hong Kong schools, Taiwan schools do not teach English as a foreign language until junior high school (Kaplan and Tse 1982). However, English instruction in Taiwan is hampered by the lack of fully proficient English instructors and adequate teaching materials and approaches. In the People's Republic, there is considerable current interest in the teaching of American English. English instruction begins in junior high school; however, the quality of this instruction is often poor (Wang 1982).

Filipinos

Background. Most Filipinos have only moved to the United States within the last ten years. The recent influx of Filipinos is the result of the 1965 immigration legislation. Since 1970, the Filipino American population has tripled (Kitano and Daniels 1988). If immigration laws do not change, experts believe that Filipinos will continue to come to the United States in large numbers. One projection has estimated that by the year 2,000, Filipinos will be the largest

Asian American group, with just over two million persons, nearly double the 1985 figure (Kitano and Daniels 1988).

Filipinos have immigrated to the United States in three large waves. The first were primarily young men who sought college degrees in the United States and then returned to the Philippines. Kitano and Daniels (1988) report that the second were agricultural workers who sought work on the West Coast. In 1944, the Philippines became independent from the United States, and a tight quota was placed on immigration. Kitano and Daniels suggest that the more recent waves (since the 1965 Immigration Act) include those trying to improve their economic and educational opportunities or join family members already in the United States. A few Filipinos have come to the United States because they are political exiles from the dictatorship of Ferdinand Marcos, who ruled the Philippines from 1965 to 1986. Despite the political reformation and the government of Corazon Aquino, the same lack of economic opportunity for educated persons that led hundreds of thousands of Filipinos to emigrate in past years continues. Many Filipinos come with advanced college degrees. A few obtain jobs commensurate with their educational backgrounds, but many others encounter licensing difficulties and discrimination (Azores 1987). As Cheng (1987) points out, "Filipino lawyers may find work as clerks; teachers as secretaries; dentists as dental aides; and engineers as mechanics" (p. 57). Still, a low-paying job in the United States often pays more than a more prestigious position job in the Philippines (Cordova 1973).

Using the 1980's census, Cabezas, Shinagawa and Kaguchi (1987) analyzed the standard of living of Filipino Americans. They found that, compared to other Asians and middle-Americans, Filipinos remain in a subordinated position.

Values.   The Filipinos place a great value on education. In fact, Cheng (1987) reports that in many Filipino communities, Filipinos sell family property in order to send their children to school. There is competition to get into Filipino schools since there are not enough schools in the Philippines to admit all qualified students. This explains why many Filipinos come to the United States to improve the educational opportunities of their children.

Filipino children are often taught to respect their elders very early in life. Cheng (1987) states:

> They learn not to talk unless they are addressed, not to interrupt a conversation, and not to volunteer information. Looking down is considered a sign of respect. Conversely, eye contact with elders is viewed as a sign of defiance. Children also learn that they should not even walk in front of an elder. (p. 58)

Traditional Filipinos generally believe that emotions should not be expressed freely. Cheng (1987) explains:

> Although they may appear calm and collected, they may be very

unhappy and angry. Because of the emphasis on interpersonal relationships and the need for affiliation and cooperation, Filipinos attempt to get along with their companions at all costs in order to maintain self-esteem and social acceptance. (p. 58)

To the Filipino, self-esteem comes by saving face in interactions with others. Thus, being shamed is an extremely humiliating experience for most Filipinos. "The personal relationship style of Filipinos is markedly different from that of Americans. A favor done for someone must be repaid or remain forever a *debt*. A person who does not return a favor loses face and may become forever shamed." (Cheng 1987, p. 60)

Perhaps because of their former colonial relationship with the United States, Filipino Americans are often considered the most *Westernized* of the Southeast Asians (Cabezas, Shinagawa and Kawaguchi 1987; see also Galang 1988). Many Filipino Americans have assimilated to life in the United States, acquiring middle-American norms and values while simultaneously losing Filipino ones.

Education. The education in the Philippines can be characterized as strict in discipline, with tightly structured long school days, and a reliance on lecture and rote memorization (Olsen 1988). In the Philippines, English is the language of instruction in the schools and children begin to study it in their first year. Galang (1988) explains that in 1974, language policy was implemented such that Pilipino [one of many languages spoken in the Philippines] became "the medium of instruction in social studies/social science, character education, work education, health education and physical sciences, and English was used to teach science, math and related areas" (p. 240). Approximately 45% of the population of the Philippines were able to speak English in 1977; however this percentage has since declined (Beebe and Beebe 1981). There are several varieties of English used by Filipinos today. According to Galang (1988), "If an indigenized or Filipinized variey of English is the one in which a Filipino immigrant has been the most comfortable, upon emigration to the United States, his or her adaptation to the all-English environment may be more similar to that of speakers of nonstandard American dialects than to that of ESL learners" (p. 240). For the most part, Filipinos are familiar with the English script, and this aids their transition to our schools.

Koreans

Background. Koreans are among the fastest growing of the ethnic groups in the United States. Numerically, the Korean population already surpasses that of Chinese communities in Los Angeles and San Francisco (Kitano and Daniels 1988). According to the United States Bureau of the Census, approximately 700,000 Koreans lived in the United States in 1983. Most Korean students come from middle and upper-middle class families. "Although there are exceptions, recent Korean immigrants are primarily highly educated, professional, technical or managerial workers settling here to improve their standard of living and provide their children with good educations." (Olsen 1988, p. 19; See also Choy, 1979, Kim 1977, and Patterson and Kim 1976.) Since 1975, all Korean immigrants have come from South Korea (Cheng 1987).

The current immigration is mostly of families and thus includes a large proportion of women and children. According to Kim (1988),

> The extensive exposure to and contacts with the United States through the Korean conflict and subsequent U.S. aid and exchange programs have meant that many South Koreans view the United States in a positive light. Thus, when the 1965 Immigration and Naturalization Act went into effect Koreans were ready to take advantage of the increased immigration opportunities to the United States. (p. 255)

Immigrant expectations include economic success in the majority culture, retention of aspects of the Korean culture, rapid flight to more *desirable* housing in the suburbs, and the development of ethnic business districts. Other expectations include permanent residence, a good education for their children and American citizenship.

Occupational adjustment for the Korean immigrant generally means downward mobility (very few are able to gain jobs of equal status to those that were held at home), segregation from the mainstream (the small businesses are often in Koreatowns or other minority areas), and general isolation from middle-American communities (Kitano and Daniels 1988). According to Kim (1988), "it is not uncommon to find college-educated Korean immigrants working as filling station attendants or as seamstresses in garment factories" (p. 258).

Korean immigrants are, for the most part, Christian. Sixty percent are Protestant, 10 percent are Catholic, and approximately 8 percent are Buddhist (Kim, Sawdey and Meihoefer 1980). Religious institutions play important roles in Korean communities since they serve as social networks, and provide information about the United States and a variety of services which help Koreans adapt to the United States (Kim 1988).

Values.   Koreans come from a traditional culture, where tasks and roles are clearly divided. Korean immigrants to the United States "display qualities of hard work, rugged individualism, adaptability, self-confidence and strong faith in the American dream of unlimited opportunity for all" (Kim 1988, p. 259).

Middle-American values, stressing individuality, autonomy and competition, are often in conflict with traditional Korean values of family centeredness, interdependence, and cooperation. "The Chinese have had a strong influence of Korean culture. In fact, the prevailing themes of Korean culture are similar to those on Chinese culture, namely harmony, filial piety, reverence for elders, and the importance of social order and family. All the Korean family names are derived from Chinese family names." (Cheng 1987, p. 67)

Values which are often attributed to Koreans include sentimentalism, the reluctance to state an opinon strongly, the desire to maintain face and indirectness. Koreans are sometimes considered the most friendly in Asia. According to Rutt (1987), "they have a keen sense of humor, are quick to laugh but also quick to show anger in a somewhat Irish manner" (p. 33). But a sensitive dimension also lurks beneath the pathos of the so-called *Irish of Asia.*

The reluctance to state one's opinion strongly also seems closely tied to Korean values. Stating one's opinion too strongly is usually considered arrogant to Koreans. By mitigating personal opinions, Koreans save others' *face* as well as their own. Saving face is a very important part of Korean values. Korean children are often taught to control their emotions and behaviors so as not to embarass others. "A well-behaved Korean child generally does not talk back, does not ask many questions, thinks twice before answering a question, and is embarrassed when given attention" (Cheng 1987, pp. 67–68).

Kim (1980) suggests that many Korean immigrants continue to feel a strong sense of attachment to the Korean culture but also desire to learn the ways of the new culture. Korean parents are generally positive about their life in the United States. They want their children to learn English and to attain success in middle-American society.

Education. Korean education is divided into six-year elementary schools, three-year middle schools and three-year high schools. Undergraduate programs in colleges and universities are four years (Korean Overseas Information Service 1986, 1987). In Korea, teachers are highly respected and usually sit or stand at an elevated desk at the front of the classroom. The number of students varies from 50 to 70, depending on the schools. Schools are in session from six to nine hours daily, Monday through Friday and four to five hours on Saturday. The academic year starts the first week in March and ends toward the last of February. The schools permit students to stay after school to study in special rooms. Hyun (1987) states:

> There are also private study halls and libraries in the cities for students to study in the evenings. Most students take this opportunity to study harder and usually do not return home until late evening. Even during the summer and winter vacations, many students spend most of their time at these study halls.
>
> (Hyun 1987, p. 67)

English is required throughout junior high school and high school. However, the focus of this English instruction is on grammar rather than communication.

Students are not accustomed to non-authoritarian teachers. Oral exercises are rare and discussions non-existent. Note-taking occupies a great deal of the older Korean student's time. "Oral exercises are mostly used by the teachers who ask questions by calling on students to answer or by permitting volunteers to do so" (Lee 1982, p. 110). All class activities are decided by the teacher who has the final authority in classroom situations. Students are never responsible for choosing class activities or courses.

Emphasis in the primary grades is on both reading and writing. Students in the lower grades learn mechanical rules of writing such as spelling and punctuation, but rarely do any writing themselves in the classroom. Considerable homework is given to children. This includes a daily journal and required reading. In addition to this homework, parents often encourage, or force, their children to complete daily worksheets and to read a special daily newspaper designed for school children.

Southeast Asians

Southeast Asians who have entered the United States as refugees include the Cambodians (Kampucheans), the ethnic Chinese, Hmong, Laotians, and Vietnamese. The government has defined a refugee as a person who flees his or her native country for safety. Few refugees return home, though many harbor the hope of returning. The Population Reference Bureau estimated that in 1985 there were 634,200 Vietnamese, 218,400 Laotians, and 160,800 Cambodians living in the United States, the majority on the West Coast. California has the most Southeast Asian refugees (135,308), followed by Texas (36,198) and Washington state (16,286) (Kitano and Daniels 1988).

The first wave of Southeast Asian refugees arrived immediately after the fall of Saigon in 1975. Many were military personnel, civil servants, teachers, farmers, fishermen and employees of Americans who feared that their lifestyles would not be compatible with those of a communist regime (Kitano and Daniels 1988). Educational attainment of this first group was generally higher than that of more recent waves of refugees.

The second wave started in 1978 as a result of the conflict between Vietnam and China. As many as 40% of all those who left Vietnam at this time were Chinese. They left because the Vietnamese government put into practice "a discriminatory harassment policy that sought overtly to encourage emigration of Chinese Vietnamese residents from different localities in Vietnam" (Chung 1988, p. 277). The Vietnamese, disturbed by the increased hostilities on the border between China and Vietnam, feared economic domination by ethnic Chinese Vietnamese, a people who traditionally occupied the middleman class and have long been a focus of resentment. This second wave of refugees consisted primarily of blue collar workers and farmers with little formal education. Although in the first wave, 48.8 percent had attended more than four years of college, only 29.1 percent had attended college in the second wave (Kitano and Daniels 1988). Those who came later had considerably less experience with city life, and were sometimes unfamiliar with such institutions as schools, factories and public hospitals.

In 1982, the third wave of Vietnamese refugees came to the United States. This wave was preceded by the Refugee Act of 1980 in which the word *refugee* was defined and objectives were established for refugee programs. It also coincided with the development of the *Orderly Departure Program*, in which many Vietnamese refugees were allowed to join their relatives in the United States. Presently, however, the number of refugees has subsided and the quota set for the current year (1989) has been greatly restricted. (Refer to Chung 1988.)

Many Southeast Asians spent years in refugee camps before arriving in the United States. Some went to camps in Thailand, Malaysia and the Philippines, where they experienced pain and suffering. Vicious attacks on helpless boat people from Vietnam by Thai pirates have been well-documented; some 80 percent of all boats were apparently attacked at least once and women were often raped (Tien, Phuc and Thuy 1981).

Initially, Southeast Asian refugees were sponsored by individual families and churches. In their first months in the United States, they were in loose contact with middle-American families. Strong tendencies both to accept guidance from those among their own groups who know English and to work cooperatively to share resources have enabled many of the refugees to build stable supportive communities (Olsen 1988). Most Southeast Asian groups have little or no hope of returning to their homelands, and they are thus driven by their desire to build a new life in the United States.

The Vietnamese

Although stereotypes abound in the literature, little empirical research documents the values of the various groups of Southeast Asians living in the United States. What follows is a discussion of those values which pertain to lower-middle-class Vietnamese who have arrived in the United States within the last ten years.

Middle-Americans often equate material wealth with success. Traditional Vietnamese, on the other hand, influenced by Buddhism and Taoism, look down on material gain, and instead value *enlightenment*. For the Vietnamese, the wisdom which comes through enlightenment opens channels of social and political power. "Power and influence is not the goal of enlightenment, it is just a by-product of it. Material gain is an obstacle to gaining true wisdom; it is a burden on the person who aspires for enlightenment." (Erickson and Cucelogu 1987, p. 29).

Hoskins (1971) observes that "a Vietnamese's honor lies in not giving or receiving embarrassment or shame" (p. 1). The Vietnamese emphasis on harmony may create stress in the competitive environment of the United States.

Although middle-Americans value self-reliance very highly, Southeast Asians do not. Children are trained to rely on the family, which is the first loyalty of the Vietnamese,

... And the family consists not only of the living, but of the spirits of the dead as well as those who have not yet been born. Anything a man does, he does out of family consideration rather than for himself as an individual. (*A Guide to Two Cultures* 1975, p. 10)

In almost all circumstances, the Vietnamese evaluate a person's action with respect to whether this action brings shame or pride to their families. To think of oneself first goes against the very fundamentals of Confucian thinking (Erickson and Cucelogu 1987, Phap 1980).

Many Vietnamese believe that they are responsible for their own actions in life since these behaviors will establish their status in the next. This might explain why some Vietnamese do not value altruism. (Phap 1980).

The Vietnamese respect old age and particularly value the advice given by elderly people. A popular Vietnamese saying states that "The seventy-year-old should listen to the seventy-one-year-old" (Phap 1980, p. 5).

The Vietnamese are often wary of *strangers*. There is a Vietnamese saying that translates roughly to: "Just as the length of a road is known only by actually travelling on it, the qualities of a man are known only by living with him for a long time" (*Indochinese Refugees Education Guides* 1980, p. 2).

Centuries of foreign domination, particularly the long struggles with the Chinese, have further increased the mistrust of strangers. Hoskins (1971) explains,

Distrust of strangers is a part of Vietnamese training. A typical children's folk story, *The Man with the Gold Coin*, illustrates this point. Once there was a man who was so kind he sometimes helped people who were not even his relatives. He was so wise the Emperor asked him to oversee the interests of the people in a certain region of Vietnam. He went out once a year to resolve problems and advise the people in his care. In one village, he noticed a boy who seemed to want to ask a question. "What is it, my boy?" asked the wise man. "I have a gold coin a foreigner gave me, but I cannot spend it at the store. Tell me, oh wise man, has it any value?" asked the boy. "You have guessed rightly," replied the wise man, "If you can buy nothing with it, it is of no value, so I would trade it for an ordinary copper one." The boy traded, thanked him and went away happy. A friend and companion of the wise man was troubled and finally when he could contain himself no longer said, "You are noted for your honesty and yet you know the value of the gold coin. The boy may not know now, but when he grows up he will know you cheated him." "Ah ha!" replied the wise man, "You have found the point of my teaching. When he grows up and finds out about the coin, he will learn something worth much more than the money he lost. He will have learned that you cannot trust anybody! . . ." The traditional Vietnamese attitude of distrust of outsiders has been heightened during the many decades of war. (p. 6)

Like most other Asians, traditional Vietnamese do not normally seek professional counseling for their personal problems. They are used to seeking help from family members. This creates a problem for teachers who want to advise Vietnamese students. If the teachers are successful, the Vietnamese students will treat them as family members, who can be contacted at any time of the day, asked for any type of help and be expected to be personally involved (Erickson and Cucelogu 1987).

Education. Most of the children who arrived in the United States with the first wave of Vietnamese in 1975 have fared very well. These youngsters "did not undergo extended school interruption since they left at the end of April, 1975 . . . . and came with their entire families intact" (Chung 1988, p. 280). The schooling of Vietnamese students who arrived with the second and third waves of Vietnamese has been disrupted because of war, and many of them have had to live for at least some time in refugee camps. Students rarely received adequate instruction. Most of the camps had few books and few trained teachers. Only some provided English instruction. Those Vietnamese who came in the third wave (after 1982) also experienced a change from one educational system to another since the Communist government "required nonacademic activities such as street maintenance, political meetings and political educational sessions" (Chung 1988, p. 281). The schooling of third-wave Vietnamese has often been interrupted by resettlement camps. Chung (1988) explains:

> As early as 1980, refugee resettlement workers started to see, among incoming immigrants, young adolescents arriving from Southeast Asia without their parents or accompanying relatives. Classified as unaccompanied minors, these young adolescents came with little preparation, little education and many adjustment problems. They came from both urban and rural areas and shared similar experiences such as constant displacement during the war, interruption in schooling, and for those who lived far away from urban areas, little preparation for living in a technological society. Without family support and supervision, they ran into trouble with schools and sometimes law enforcement agencies due to their survival-type behavior. (p. 281)

Differences in classroom expectations can contribute to the Vietnamese student's difficulties. As Chung (1988) puts it:

> While the typical American classroom often involves dynamic interaction and exchanges between students and teachers, the typical Vietnamese classroom promotes receptive or passive learning. In Vietnamese classrooms, the teacher is viewed as the giver of knowledge and the student as the receiver of this knowledge.

Vietnamese students are generally not used to engaging in extended questions and answers but are more ready to repeat drills and copy down the new vocabulary to memorize. Hence, many [Vietnamese] students may find it difficult to meet the expectations of their teachers, particularly when these expectations involve a good deal of active participation. (p. 283)

Most formal schooling in Vietnam has stressed memorization and repetition. Analytical thinking, a kind of one-step-at-a-time approach (see Chapter 6), which is highly valued by middle-Americans, is not valued by the Vietnamese. Erickson and Cucelogu (1987) explain that in Buddhist thinking, after receiving enlightenment, one has the ability to intuitively understand an idea without analyzing its separate elements. Textbooks are unavailable to students, and so students rely principally on the teachers' lecture. However, students are often reluctant to ask any questions of their teacher, so they depend on one another to obtain a complete set of notes. This cooperation among classmates is consistent with Vietnamese customs emphasizing reliance on one another. The following Vietnamese saying summarizes this custom: "Learning from the teacher is not better from learning from friends" (Burmark-Parasuraman 1982, p. 45).

Cambodians (Kampucheans)

The Khmer, the majority group in Cambodia, constitute about 85 percent of the population. In 1962, Pol Pot took over the leadership of Cambodia. His leadership was followed by a reign of terror which ended in the murder of an estimated two million Cambodians in a country of seven million (Olsen 1988) and the relocation of 33,000 Cambodians to Thailand and 150,000 to Vietnam (Kitano and Daniels 1988). Pol Pot's primary targets were the intellectuals, government officials and city people, but Cambodians of all classes suffered. During the years of the Pol Pot regime there were no schools in the country, and children were separated from their families and sent to work farms. In 1978, Vietnam invaded Cambodia and replaced the Pol Pot regime with a new government. The invasion was followed by another exodus from Cambodia. An estimated 100,000, fearing war between the Khmer and the Vietnamese, escaped to Thailand. Continued disease and starvation, along with Vietnamese warfare, drove nearly 500,000 Cambodians to refugee camps along the Thai border. One student describes his experience in war-torn Cambodia:

The tragedy during the war hurts inside when I remember what happened in the past. I try to not think about it, but at night I dream and see my brother who they killed. I dream about him trying to find us. I dream they keep shooting him and shooting him until I wake up.
10th grade Cambodian boy, immigrated at age 12 (reported in Olsen 1988, p. 22)

The Hmong

Approximately 60,000 Hmong now reside in the United States. The Hmong are natives of China who lived in the hills of Laos, Thailand and Vietnam early in the 19th century. They date back as far as 3,000 years. Speaking their own language and wearing special clothing seen nowhere else in Southeast Asia, they are considered independent, hard-working and peace-loving. "Between 1960 and 1975, thousands of Hmong were recruited by the Central Intelligence Agency (CIA) to conduct clandestine maneuvers in the region against the Viet Cong and the Communist Pathet Lao . . . After the fall of Vietnam in 1975, approximately 100,000 fled to escape retaliation for these activities." (Cheng 1987, p. 49; see also Walker 1985). The fall of Vietnam and the departure of the American forces resulted in thousands of Hmong fleeing Laos. At first, resettlement programs tended to disperse the Hmong across the United States, but then the Hmong relocated. In 1985, an estimated 20,000 were reported as living in the San Joaquin Valley, with approximately 15,000 living in Fresno. A group of about 10,000 settled near Minneapolis (Kitano and Daniels 1988).

Many of the Hmong had little or no experience with written forms of their own language. In fact, only in the past thirty years have there been written forms of their languages. Perhaps as a consequence, the Hmong have a rich oral tradition of legends and folk stories which have been passed down from generation to generation (Bliatout, Downing, Lewis and Yang 1988).

"The Hmong, organized through a traditional clan membership, have preferred agricultural occupations and have worked as cooperative groups to secure large blocks of land to establish their own farms from Minnesota to California" (Kitano and Daniels 1988, p. 163).

Many of the Hmong have difficulty adjusting to the United States. In an investigation of the Hmong living in the United States, Meredith and Cramer (1982) found that 92% of those interviewed suffered from stress-related diseases. Of the Hmong interviewed by Smalley (1984), 65% said that living in the United States was not preferable to living in Southeast Asia, and 86% said they would return to Southeast Asia if they could.

Other Asian Groups

Other Asian groups include the Japanese, Hawaiians, Guamanians and Micronesians. I have limited my discussion to the more numerically significant groups above. (However, refer to suggested readings for information pertaining to Asian groups not discussed.) Before turning to the section on Latinos, it is important to reiterate that, as Asians become acculturated their values often change; stereotypes rarely hold.

Latinos

Background. Like the Asian population, the Latino population is growing quickly. There are numerous groups of Latinos, having different attitudes and approaches toward acculturation and assimilation (Montgomery and Orozco 1984). The term *Latino* is used here to refer to individuals of a Spanish-speaking heritage. The term *Hispanic* is sometimes used for this purpose; however, some Latinos prefer the word *Latino,* since it is itself a Spanish term, whereas *Hispanic* is an Anglo term. I use the term *Mexican* to refer to individuals who identify themselves as Mexicans and who tend to relate more to the cultural norms of Mexico than they do to those of the United States. I use the term *Mexican-American* to refer to those individuals of Mexican heritage who identify themselves as Mexican-Americans and who do not identify with the Chicano movement which takes as its goal the attainment of political, economic and educational equality in the United States. Finally, I use the term *Chicano* to refer to those individuals of Mexican origin who support the Chicano movement. I will be referring to two groups of Latinos living in the United States — Mexicans and Puerto Ricans. (For information pertaining to other Latino groups, please refer to the suggested readings.)

Mexicans

Mexicans are a highly heterogeneous group. As Buriel (1984) puts it, a randomly drawn sample of Mexican and Mexican Americans in the United States will yield individuals who differ on a variety of cultural characteristics such as the ability to speak Spanish, generational status, ethnic identity and appreciation for cultural values, holidays, and traditions" (p. 96).

Mexican immigration patterns differ from Asian for historical, political, and geographical reasons. The 2,000 mile border between Mexico and the United States almost ensures a continuous migration between these two countries (Buriel 1984). The perennial first generation of Mexican immigrants sustains the vitality of Mexican-American culture. According to Buriel (1984), other ethnic groups who were separated from their homelands by thousands of miles of ocean, have assimilated quickly to the United States. "By contrast, the proximity of Mexico to the United States has reinforced not only Mexican-American culture, but also the stereotype that Mexican-Americans are foreigners" (Buriel 1984, p. 99).

Although there is a centuries-long history of Mexican immigration to the United States, large-scale Mexican immigration really began in the 1940s when the Bracero Program was created (Portes and Bach 1985). During the Bracero period, most immigration was seasonal as guest workers came north to work during planting and harvesting periods and then returned to Mexico. The largest wave of Mexican immigration has been since the mid-1960s with a growing number of Latinos settling permanently (Portes and Bach 1985).

Estimates of the number of undocumented Mexicans suggest that between five and ten million people live illegally in the United States (Wallerstein 1983). Testimony before the Senate Judiciary Subcommittee in Fall 1981 suggested that 250,000 to 500,000 undocumented persons enter the United States each year. Fear of deportation prevents many undocumented students from registering in schools.

The Immigration Reform and Control Act of 1986 was introduced to curb the number of undocumented immigrants by imposing civil penalties and fines for employers who knowingly hired undocumented workers. The act also included an amnesty program that allowed a large number of undocumented workers (primarily from Mexico) who lived in the United States to obtain legal status if they could prove that they had been living in the United States since January 1, 1982. Wallerstein (1983) suggests that many of the undocumented would apply for permanent residence through the Amnesty Program (established in 1988) if it were not for the backlog of paperwork at the Immigration and Naturalization Service.

For the most part, Mexicans initially leave their homeland because of poverty and the belief that economic conditions in the United States will be better than those in Mexico. The majority come to find work (in factories or the service industries) in urban areas. Many others come to join family members already here.

Until United States annexation in 1848, the Southwest (including, Texas, New Mexico, Arizona and California) belonged to Mexico. Mexicans born in the United States before the Mexican-American War of 1848 were guaranteed full rights of United States citizenship under the Treaty of Guadalupe Hidalgo. Parodoxically, the offspring of these citizens are still considered immigrants, however. The treaty was supposed to have assured that the Southwest would remain bilingual and bicultural. It stated, for example, that "Mexicans would have special privileges derived from their customs, language, law, and religions." In fact, however, these stipulations have rarely been honored (Rivera 1970). Until recently, statutes prevented Mexican-American children from speaking Spanish at school. Cortes (1986), for instance, describes the punishment of one student.

> *I will not speak Spanish at school,* wrote the young Mexican-American boy. The words increasingly covered the chalkboard, as he repeated and repeated the teacher-imposed penance. The punishment: to write that sentence 50 times after school. The crime: having been caught speaking Spanish with his Latino classmates during recess. Such was the process known as *Spanish Detention,* once a hallowed type of traditional retribution aimed at imposing conformity on Hispanic students. (p. 3)

Many Mexican working-class families live in poverty with chronic unemployment and malnutrition. Despite a long history in the United States, they are still subject to discrimination. The exploitation that Mexicans have suffered has included unequal access to housing, education, political power and economic resources (see, for example, Carter 1970, Ramirez and Castañeda 1974 and Ogbu and Matute-Bianchi 1986). The persistent academic failure of some groups of Mexican immigrants has been documented extensively. (For a review of the research, see Trueba 1989.) Many Mexican students do not believe they have the same opportunity to succeed as their middle-American peers. Even though Mexican parents may tell their children to work hard at school and study conscientiously, society may tell these children differently, resulting in their mistrust of mainstream Americans and of the schools themselves (Ogbu and Matute-Bianchi 1986).

Today, most Mexicans live in California, Arizona, New Mexico, Colorado and Texas, but there are large concentrations also in Illinois, Michigan, and Kansas. While most Mexican communities are located in the cities of Los Angeles, El Paso, San Antonio, and Chicago, some Mexicans also live in rural areas (Crandall, Dias, Gingras and Harris 1981).

Values. As Carter (1970) points out, educators have promoted rather inaccurate, negative stereotypes about Mexican students which simply have no basis in reality. Sanchez (1983) notes:

> No one has defined precisely what generalized Mexican culture is. Often the phrase evokes superficial notions of food, music, charro dress, macho men and legends. Some traditionally mentioned characteristics, like large families, authoritarian father image, virginal women are in reality the product of rural family units, where children function as farm hands to ensure survival and subsistence and the father functions as foreman to maintain discipline in the field without incurring additional maintenance burdens. (p. 21)

As mentioned earlier, once stereotypes are formed they are difficult to change. This is unfortunate. Mexicans differ widely in terms of their diverse historical, social, and cultural roots. In response to the great diversity of Mexican communities in the United States. The discussion which follows focuses only on working-class Mexicans of fairly recent arrival (less than ten years) in the United States who continue to use Spanish in the home. Central to their values are traditional notions of family, responsibility, authority, respect, and pride in their Mexican heritage and language. Since immigration to the United States is motivated by a desire for change and upward mobility, an achievement orientation is another core value of Mexican immigrants.

For most Mexicans, the family is central and takes precedence over individuals (Heath 1986). Family members are obligated to help one another. For Mexicans, questions about the family are polite; yet for many middle-Americans, such questions may be discomfiting, since they may seem too personal. The unwillingness of many mainstream Americans to engage in extensive small talk about the family only confirms for some Mexicans that middle-Americans are cold and insensitive.

Mexican children are generally taught and expected to be responsible in various ways at an early age (Laosa 1984, Levine and Bartz 1979). Mexicans often emphasize authority and in the home delegate authority on the basis of sex and age with males and elders holding positions of authority (Alvirez, Bean, and William 1982). Children are taught to respect authority and are "reminded to listen attentively to their elders, to obey them, to help if they need it and to honor them" (Phenice, Martinez and Grant 1986, p. 81). Although children are given considerable responsibilities in the home, they are often given the freedom to choose how they are to accomplish tasks. In such a way, both independence and creativity are encouraged (Delgado-Gaitan 1987).

Many Mexican families take pride in their Mexican heritage and want their children to become fluent in Spanish. Buriel (1984) suggests that for many Mexican immigrants, Spanish is a symbol of "ethnic and cultural loyalty" (p. 101).

Mexicans in the United States are not exactly the same as Mexicans in Mexico. The very fact that they immigrated to the United States from Mexico indicates a desire for change, "which they share with all other immigrants, and which distinguishes them from other persons who remained in Mexico" (p. 119). According to Buriel, these immigrants are more likely to come from the most productive sectors of the Mexican population, have more self-confidence in their survival capabilities, and more pride in themselves as Mexicans. He states, "Perhaps as a consequence of their achievement-oriented personalities, Mexican immigrants complete more years of schooling prior to immigrating than the national average for the Mexican population," and, in addition, "the proportion of illiterates among immigrants is approximately seven times less than for the Mexican population" (p. 121). He also adds that among those who begin their employment history in the United States as farmworkers, the majority move into non-agricultural work and also make certain that their children do not work in agriculture (see also Cornelius et al., 1982).

Unfortunately, the culture of Mexicans in the United States has sometimes been used as a convenient (though inaccurate) explanation for the reason many Mexicans do so poorly in our schools. Their culture has allegedly discouraged achievement motivation (Demos 1962), while encouraging aggression (Heller 1966) and other negative values. This next section challenges negative stereotypes.

Machismo is sometimes said to affect negatively all aspects of Mexican life. This is an erroneous stereotype. Among some Mexicans, males are considered adults earlier on in life than their middle-American peers. In families of low economic status, male adolescents may quit school before graduating to help support their families. To assist their families, while in high school, these males will sometimes work after school in a variety of low-paying jobs (washing dishes in fast-food restaurants, working in gas stations, and doing construction work). High school educators who genuinely want to help these students would do well to assist them in obtaining jobs, such as tutoring positions, which develop academic skills.

Another inaccurate stereotype related to *machismo* is the idea that Mexican girls value working in the home. While family and home-life are values of Mexicans, Mexican girls of low socioeconomic level frequently stay home to take care of siblings and clean house because their mothers are working.

Yet another stereotype is that Mexicans do not value education. This, again, is false. Mexicans have high expectations of their children and want them to advance themselves (Wong-Fillmore 1983). Nonetheless, they do not always know the specific steps their children should take to go onto college or go into a specific field. They often expect teachers to provide their children with accurate information concerning college and careers (Delgado-Gaitán 1988). (See Chapter 8.) Mexican parents generally respect teachers and expect them to take primary responsibility for teaching their children (Delgado-Gaitán 1988). They believe that the schools have their students' best interests in mind. According to Phenice, Martinez and Grant (1986), many Mexican parents, particularly the poor, generally do not deliberatedly engage in intellectual tasks with their children. "The teachers and the school are considered the authority on intellectual matters and the cultural value of respect for authority dictates that the home respect the school" (p. 81).

In line with this false stereotype is that which holds that Mexicans do not want to improve their standard of living. Mexicans came to the United States to improve their economic position in life and have struggled for economic equality for generations. The majority of Mexican immigrants who come to the United States have little formal education, few skills and no understanding of English. Not only do they face the immediate necessity of providing their families with income, but they also face discrimination. As Buriel (1984) states,

> . . . those [Mexican-American] individuals who have achieved oc-
> cupational success have done so primarily because they pos-
> sessed the ambition to exploit even the most meager opportunities
> in their environment. Hence, it is hypothesized that the motive to
> achieve is inherent in traditional Mexican-American culture, and
> it expresses itself in proportion to both its strength and the extent
> to which opportunities are available in the person's environment.
> (p. 108)

A different myth about Mexicans concerns violence. Mexicans are often portrayed on television and in the news media as gang members and degenerates. Yet, gangs are not a part of Mexican culture. Buriel (1984) states, ". . . it is precisely among recent immigrants where there is the least amount of gang activity. This is not to deny that gangs composed of Mexican-American youths do not exist, [sic] but rather to make the point that the origins of gang activity are not to be found in traditional Mexican-American culture." (p. 115)

A massive study, reported by Grebler et al. (1970) was based on in-depth interviews with a large representative sample of urban Mexican-Americans in Los Angeles and San Antonio. The major conclusions reached by Grebler et al. suggest other false stereotypes about Mexicans and Mexican-Americans:

1. Only three to four percent of the urban families lived in extended-family households, disproving the notion that Mexican-Americans are familistic enough to establish joint households in an urban setting.

2. There was little difference between Mexican-American and other families with respect to the degree of familial help given to its members.

3. A high proportion of single-parent homes existed. Almost one-third of the sample respondents stated that they had been reared by one parent.

4. There was significant variation in decision-making in the family. In some families the fathers made the important decisions, in other families the mothers made decisions and in others decision-making was a collaborative effort.

5. A close study of parents' attitudes revealed that there was no significant difference in the educational goals parents held for boys and girls.

6. Parents expected that a good education was one of strict discipline.

7. Machismo was not a salient characteristic of Mexican American family life.

Recent research tends to confirm these findings. (See Griswold del Castillo 1984.)

Education. Current Mexican school structure includes several basic levels kindergarten until age six, followed by six years of elementary school, secondary school, and higher education. Students are promoted by examination at all levels of schooling. Although primary education through the sixth grade is officially compulsory, only 15% finish a sixth grade education in rural areas (Olsen 1988). Nonetheless, the literacy rate is quite high, currently 83%. The Mexican teacher is an authority figure. Strict discipline is maintained within the classroom. In general, students are expected to obey their teachers, and teachers are expected to monitor the complete academic progress of the students. Teachers may call on parents for support, but they do not seek input from parents on academic matters.

It is important to point out that many Mexicans consider the Southwest part of their homeland; "the existing domination [by the United States] is perceived as an usurpation and unjust fact. Further, the historical legacy means that the Anglo is not only an imperialist, but also an historical enemy; to acculturate is not merely to exercise a culture preference but to go on the other side." (Quiñones, 1973, p. 10) Chicanos who have lived in the United States for generations are continuously struggling against discrimination. Some have suffered cultural and identity loss, while others are consciously seeking to acquire or reacquire their culture and identity. Chicanos, Mexican-Americans, and Mexicans in the United States all benefit from schooling which acknowledges the richness of their cultures.

Puerto Ricans

According to the United States census, over two million Puerto Ricans lived in mainland United States in 1980. Nearly half are under age seventeen (Zentella 1988). Although Puerto Rico is not independent from the United States, it is not a state; it is a *Free Associated State.* Puerto Ricans are citizens of the United States; this enables them to move freely back and forth between the United States and Puerto Rico (a three and a half hour air flight). Today, one third of all Puerto Ricans live on the mainland of the United States; half were born here. In 1970, 62% of Puerto Ricans living in the United States lived in New York City. However, today this percentage has dropped to 43%. While one part of the population has achieved a measure of economic success, the other has slipped into poverty. The high school drop out rate is now 60%. 40% of all young adult Puerto Ricans in the United States are unemployed.

Puerto Ricans come to the mainland for many reasons, including uncertainty of political status, economic difficulties, the population explosion on the islands, and the absence of legal or political restrictions on migration. Skilled professionals such as lawyers, engineers and accountants as well as unskilled blue collar workers who cannot obtain employment on the island continue to come to the mainland.

Although Puerto Ricans are Latinos, they differ from other Latino groups in being a composite of several different cultural groups, including the Jibaros (the indigenous People of Puerto Rico) and descendants of African slaves. After the United States occupied Puerto Rico in 1898, Spanish was banned from the schools and courts for fifty years (Zentella 1988). Nowadays, there is a trend towards bilingualism (Spanish/English) with ESL programs within the schools. However, Spanish is the official language of the schools and courts.

Values. Most Puerto Ricans respect the family. Individuals are perceived in relationship to others in the family. Like other Latino groups, Puerto Ricans have a deep sense of family obligation. One's primary responsibilities are to families and friends. Persons in important positions help their friends and family members.

The role of the woman has greatly changed in recent times. The influence of the mother over the son is particulary strong, and women play important political roles as mayors and professors.

In contrast to the individualism that focuses on the individual's ability to compete with others for better wages, the Puerto Ricans' individualism tends to focus on the inner importance of a person, emphasizing those qualities that constitute the uniqueness of a person and his or her goodness or worth. All persons are expected to be treated with dignity. Puerto Ricans are often more sensitive than middle-Americans to anything that appears to be personal insult or disdain. Many do not take practical jokes lightly or enjoy making jokes in which people make fools of themselves.

Many Puerto Ricans value bilingualism highly and hope that the schools will teach their children both Spanish and English. As Fitzpatrick (1987) puts it,

> . . . when Puerto Ricans ask for bicultural programs, they are asking, on a much simpler level, for sensitivity to themselves and their way of life, respect for the background from which they come; the cultivation of pride in their background among their children; and a curriculum that teaches the children who they are and what they come from by adequate courses taught by competent staff in Puerto Rican history, music, art, literature, spiritual and religious values, and so forth. It is the neglect, often crude, that aggravates Puerto Rican parents and results in a failure of the schools to provide an environment in which Puerto Rican identity would be fostered while children prepare to make their way in American life. (pp. 154–155)

Zentella (1988) makes the following recommendations to teachers based on her experiences working with Puerto Rican children. First, Zentella suggests that we accept the varieties of Spanish and English Puerto Rican children might speak. The varieties of Puerto Rican Spanish and English used by Puerto Ricans in the United States are often considered inferior dialects. Zentella recommends that teachers respect these varieties and add to them rather than attempt to take them away. Although first generation Puerto Ricans speak English with varying degrees of proficiency and first language interference, Zentella suggests that teachers keep in mind that the language they hear Puerto Ricans speak in their communities may be two varieties of nonstandard English, Puerto Rican English and vernacular English. Some Puerto Ricans acquire a variety of English which is indistinguishable from that spoken by some blacks. It is also important to remember that many Puerto Ricans speak two varieties of Spanish. Crandall et al. (1981) explain:

> Those [Puerto Ricans] who have recently arrived from the island speak a Spanish similar to that spoken on the island. Those who have been here for some time, or who have acquired Spanish here, speak a heavily English-influenced Spanish. (p. 8)

Second, Zentella (1988) suggests that teachers allow their students to code-switch (that is, alternate between the languages which they speak) since the Puerto Rican community values code-switching. As Zentella (1988) puts it, "classroom norms may be in conflict with community norms if students are never allowed to code-switch in any part of a lesson or school day" (p. 158).

Finally, Zentella suggests that teachers be alert to changing values and norms of Puerto Rican communities. She points out that the *va-ven* (*go-come*) migration has caused values and norms to change.

Teachers need to be aware of the changes and respond to them sensitively.

Conclusion

The challenge in educating language minority students is to create programs which will enhance the educational achievement of students of all cultural backgrounds. This chapter has primarily provided teachers with information about the homelands which language minority students left. To a lesser extent, it has considered the cultures of students who have acculturated. It is important to keep in mind that as language minority students live in the United States, they take on new cultural values and beliefs. (Refer to Chapter 2 for a discussion of some of the factors which affect an individual's adaptation to the United States.) Teachers must appreciate the cultures of their students both outside of and within the United States. And, they must interact with students as individuals rather than as stereotypical members of cultural groups. In this chapter, due to space limitations, I provided only basic information concerning the rich cultures of some of the language minority groups in our classrooms. For additional references, refer to the suggested reading listed at the end of this chapter. Teachers need to critically assess this reading and question stereotypes.[1] In the following chapter, I will suggest some specific strategies for creating classrooms which take advantage of the language and cultural experiences of language minority students.

ACTIVITIES AND DISCUSSION QUESTIONS

1. These expressions are frequently heard in the United States today. What specific values underlie them? Are these values unique to mainstream Americans? Do you know people other than middle-Americans who share these values? If so, how do you explain this?

   - Actions speak louder than words.
   - Stand on your own two feet!
   - Do your own thing!
   - Look out for Number One.
   - You get what you give.
   - Time is money.
   - Don't just stand there. Do something.
   - The sky's the limit.

2. Consider the following letters to *Dear Diane: Letters from Our Daughters.* They are written by Asian-American high school students to a reader who offers advice. If you were *Diane* how would you respond to the letters?

Dear Diane:

Because I find it more comfortable to speak Korean, I like to hang around other Korean friends. I know that my English and knowledge of American ways won't improve unless I try to mix with non-Korean students, too. So now, I'm trying to spend some time with both groups.

My problem is that these two sets of friends never mix. I'm just about the only person that each group has in common. My Korean friends think that I'm getting stuck up, or drifting away from my roots; my non-Korean friends think that I'm being too cliquish.

The pressure from the groups grows each day, but I still don't know what to do. Got any advice? (Wong 1983, p. 25)

Dear Diane:

After living at home for the first year of college, my folks finally agreed to let me move to a dormitory. As part of the bargain, though, they made me promise to come home every weekend and on holidays. I'm trying my best to live up to this promise, but sometimes it's hard.

There are times when I would prefer just to stay in the dorm with my friends. If I have to keep going home every week, I'm still just like a kid who hasn't left home. My friends are more independent and only go home on special occasions. How can I convince them to loosen the ties?

(Wong 1983, p.27)

Dear Diane:

I'm pretty quiet in my math class. I don't want to let others know that I'm not that smart. My teacher thinks that because I'm Asian and quiet, I'm doing all right. The farther behind I get, the more I'd just like to skip school and hang out.

What can I do to let her know that I'm lost, and may need some extra help? It'd be so easy just to chuck this whole thing.

(Wong 1983, p. 47)

3. A difficult problem of many young immigrants who enter elementary schools in the United States is loneliness. Consider, for instance, the examples below in which two immigrants describe their first few days in the United States:

> A Vietnamese lady at my school helped me. She is not a teacher, but it was very lonesome without her and I smiled on the days she came. She was the only person who helped me to learn. No one else spoke my language. She would read the book with me and try to figure out what it meant. Sometimes she didn't know either. The rest of the time I drew pictures because I couldn't understand what was going on.
> 7th grade boy, immigrated at age 8 (reported in Olsen 1988, p. 61)

> I started in 7th grade and had trouble looking for classes. In Mexico we stay in the same place all day. I went to the first class because that is where I was taken. It was over so soon and I didn't know to go to

another class, so I went home. I got in trouble. They should have told me, and had someone walk me to my classes at first. I didn't know. Mexican boy, immigrated at age 12 (reported in Olsen 1988, p. 71)

In the absence of translators, what can we do to help our students feel more comfortable when they first enter our classrooms?

4. Patterns of prejudice, conflict and social isolation are said to increase as students reach adolescence. Language minority students often come to school anxious to make friends. Yet this enthusiasm is killed when they meet with discrimination. What can be done to reduce prejudice in our schools? Interview several language minority students to obtain their suggestions.

5. In Olsen's study involving in-depth interviews with 360 immigrant school children, she found that the immigrant children frequently expressed "the desire to obtain an American friend to guide them and show them how things are done" (Olsen 1988, p. 37). How can teachers help immigrant students make such friends?

RECOMMENDED READING

The following are only intended as a starting point for interested educators. Some of the articles and volumes cited contain information about the native homelands of language minority students, while others contain information about the histories, values, and cultures of language minority students in the United States.

Asians and Latinos in the United States

McKay. S. and Wong, C. (eds.) 1988. *Language Diversity: Problem or Resource?* Cambridge: Harper and Row. Provides a social and educational perspective on contemporary immigrant language minorities in the United States. Intended for pre-service and in-service teachers of English as a Second Language, it addresses language policy, language heritage and current linguistic composition, and examines the demographic, sociocultural and linguistic characteristics of the Vietnamese, Filipinos, Chinese, Koreans, Mexican-Americans, Puerto Ricans and Cubans living in the United States.

Asians

Cheng, L. - R. 1987. *Assessing Asian Language Performance: Guidelines for Evaluating Limited-Proficiency Students.* Rockville, Maryland: An Aspen Production. Provides information about the cultural and linguistic characteristics of diverse Asian cultural groups including the Chinese, the Indochinese (the Vietnamese, Laotians, Hmong and Cambodians), the Filipinos, Koreans, Japanese, Hawaiians, Guamanians, and Micronesians. Although primarily designed for speech therapists interested in assessing limited English proficient students, the book has broad implications for content-area and ESL teachers.

Brazilians

WIDGER, R. 1977. *Brazil Rediscovered*. Philadelphia: Dorrance and Co. Includes useful information concerning the everyday life of a middle-class Brazilian family.

Chinese and Chinese Americans

Bilingual Education Office, California State Department of Education. 1984. *A Handbook for Teaching Cantonese-Speaking Students*. Sacramento, California: California State Department of Education. Provides useful information concerning the values and learning styles of Cantonese-Speaking students.

Tsai, S. H. 1986. *The Chinese Experience in America*. Bloomington: Indiana University Press. Provides an excellent overview of the Chinese experience in the United States.

Cuban-Americans

BOSWELL, T. and CURTIS, J. 1983. *The Cuban-American Experience: Culture, Images and Perspectives*. New Jersey: Rowman and Slanheld. Provides an overview of the history, traditions and values of Cuban-Americans.

The Filipinos and Filipino Americans

BEEBE, J. and BEEBE, M. 1981. The Filipinos: A special case. In Ferguson, C. A. and Heath, S.B. (eds.) *Language in the United States*. Cambridge: Cambridge University Press. 322–338. Describes the ways in which Filipino Americans are similar to and different from other Asian minorities in the United States.

Hmong

BLIATOUT, B. T., DOWNING, B. T., LEWIS, J. and YANG, D. 1988. *Handbook for Teaching the Hmong*. Rancho Cordova, California: Southeast Asia CRC. Covers the traditions, values and beliefs of the Hmong, gives useful guidelines and suggestions for working with Hmong students.

Indochinese

RUBIN, J. 1981. *Meeting the Educational Needs of Indochinese Refugee Children*. Washington D.C.: National Institute of Education. ES 212 699. This report discusses cultural and linguistic characteristics of Indochinese ethnic groups and makes practical recommendations for implementing educational programs which serve Indochinese students.

Iranians

BRASWELL, G. W. JR. 1977. *To Ride a Magic Carpet*. Describes the customs, values, and religions of Iranians.

Japanese

REISCHAUER, E. O. 1977. *The Japanese.* Cambridge, Massachusetts: Belkap Press of Harvard University. Discusses Japanese values and traditions.

Koreans and Korean-Americans

California State Department of Education, Office of Bilingual and Bicultural Education. 1983. *A Handbook for Teaching Korean-Speaking Students.* Los Angeles: Evaluation, Dissemination and Assessment Center, California State University, Los Angeles. Describes Korean history, immigration patterns and culture with a focus on teaching Korean immigrant students in mainstream American schools.

KIM, H. K. (ed.) 1980. *Studies on Korea: A Scholar's Guide.* Culture, history and religion, Honolulu, Hawaii. A reference volume covering diverse aspects of Korean, containing chapters written by specialists in each field.

Malaysians

LENT, J. (ed.) 1977. *Cultural Pluralism in Malaysia: Policy, Mass Media, Education, Religion, and Social Class.* DeKalb, Illinois: Northern Illinois University. Distributed by the Cellar Book Shop, Detroit, Michigan. Each chapter addresses diverse aspects of Malaysian life.

Mexicans, Mexican-Americans and Chicanos

MARTINEZ, J. L. and MENDOZA, R. H. (eds.) 1984. *Chicano Psychology.* New York: Academic Press. Chapters by experts in their fields cover the Chicano experience in the United States, schooling, assessment, and acculturation patterns.

PORTES, A. and BACH, R. 1985. *Latin Journey: Cuban and Mexican Immigrants in the United States.* Berkeley, California: University of California Press. Discusses the acculturation experiences and immigration patterns of Cubans and Mexicans in the United States.

Native Americans

WAX, M. L. 1971. *Indian Americans: Unity and Diversity.* Englewood Cliffs, New Jersey: Prentice-Hall. Commentary on situations and problems of Native Americans. An extensive survey of anthropological and ethno-historical literature.

Puerto Ricans and Puerto Rican Americans

FITZPATRICK, J. 1987. *Puerto Rican Americans: The Meaning of Migration to the Mainland.* Englewood Cliffs, New Jersey: Prentice Hall. Focuses on Puerto Ricans in the United States with special emphasis on those in New York City. It discusses the dynamics of their migration, the Puerto Rican family, education, religion, and problems of poverty and drug abuse.

Saudi Arabians

PATAI. R. 1973. *The Arab Mind.* New York: Charles Scribner's Sons. An overview of Arab child-rearing practices, religion, language and traditions.

Vietnamese

California State Department of Education. 1982. *A Handbook for Teaching Vietnamese Speaking Students.* Los Angeles, California: Evaluation and Dissemination Center, California State University, Los Angeles. Provides valuable background information on the history, values and education of Vietnamese immigrants, includes many useful suggestions for teaching Vietnamese elementary and secondary school children.

COOKE, D. C. 1968. *Vietnam, the Country, the People.* New York: W. W. Norton Co., Inc. Discusses how the Vietnamese differ from Westerners, from the perspective of a Vietnamese village family.

NOTES

1. I urge the readers to take great caution when interpreting any information about cultural groups, including the information contained in this chapter.

CHAPTER ELEVEN

Incorporating Your Students' Languages and Cultures

For Cummins (1989), the extent to which the language minority students' primary languages and home cultures are incorporated into the school curriculum constitutes a significant predictor of academic success.

> In programs where minority students' L1 [first language] skills are strongly reinforced, their school success appears to reflect both a solid academic foundation and also the reinforcement of their cultural identity. In addition to the personal and future employment advantages of proficiency in two or more languages, more subtle educational advantages also result from continued development of both languages among bilingual students. (p. 60)

Cummins (1989) also emphasizes:

> We must understand that children who are culturally and linguistically different, and therefore prime candidates for the label, *learning disabled*, need learning environments that encourage the use of native language and culture as a means to continue the learning process started at home. Use of the native language also encourages a smooth transition from the home to the school. (p. 25)

This need to maximize the language minority students' linguistic and cultural talents is addressed by Principle 10: *Incorporate your students' languages and cultures.* Before discussing this principle, it will be helpful to describe two different approaches to minority instruction: multicultural education and critical pedagogy.

Multicultural Education

Following Grant, Sleeter and Anderson (1986), I describe multicultural education here as follows:

Multicultural Education

Purpose: To reduce social stratification and assimilation by promoting knowledge and appreciation of America's cultural diversity.

Assumptions: Assimilation is undesirable; standard school curricula and practices are biased; all aspects of schooling should reflect diversity, which will eventually lead to reduction in prejudice and to social structural change.

Practices: Re-write curricula to reflect ethnic, gender, social class, and handicap diversity; promote diverse learning styles; promote use of more than one language; provide nontraditional staffing patterns. (p. 48)

In this view of multicultural education, language minority students need not give up their home cultures when acquiring middle-American cultural behaviors, since the cultures of all students are respected. Traditional standard curriculum is broadened so that it includes not only middle-American perspectives, but also cultural minority ones. While our standard, traditional curriculum often does an outstanding job of presenting middle-American perspectives, it often reinforces a sense of middle-American superiority and degrades the image of cultural minorities. As Trueba (1989) puts it:

> . . . textbook language is often the tip of a foreign culture for many children, including those who are losing their home language more rapidly than they are acquiring English as a second language. Textbooks are composed by the mainstream speakers of English, by adults attempting to communicate with children, holding cultural assumptions peculiar to middle-class mainstream members of American culture and their interpretation of how children talk and think. The characters of the stories may be children themselves, but the voices and cognitive structures are those of adults. In this ethnocentric adult world of textbooks, the message (conscious and/or unconscious) is conformity and submission. (p. 143)

Language minority students seldom find their own experiences or histories reflected anywhere in our classrooms. This may diminish their self-esteem, creating "a sense of unreality and unimportance about their past" (Olsen 1988, p. 68; see also Skutnabb-Kangas and Cummins 1988 and Fishman 1989).

A major goal, then, of multicultural education is to increase our students' cultural repertoires. To do this, teachers must create educational environments in which the experiences of a wide range of groups are valued. Among others, these groups include females, handicapped persons, immigrants who have recently arrived in the United States, and long-term residents and citizens of the United States of diverse cultural and first language backgrounds. Mainstream American and language minority students will benefit from multicultural education, since both groups expand their perspectives in creating a new vision of the cultural heritage of the United States. All students, including middle-American, develop "tolerance and skills for living in a diverse world" (Olsen 1988, p. 68). A multicultural classroom does not have to be one that is characterized by students of multicultural backgrounds; a multicultural class may consist of pre-dominantly middle-American or Latino students.

Multicultural classrooms promote cultural pluralism. As Ovando and Collier (1985) cogently explain, "Cultural pluralism characterizes a society in which members of diverse cultural, social racial, or religious groups are free to maintain their own identity [sic] and yet simultaneously share a larger common political organization, economic system, and social structure" (p. 110).

Thus, in multicultural classrooms, the study of culture is incor-porated into *daily* classroom activities. As Cortes (1974) so eloquently puts it:

> This does not mean just reading about so-called Spanish Califor-nia in the fourth grade, or having a unit on Mexico as a foreign culture in the sixth grade, or setting up a couple of high school classes in Mexican-American Studies. These may be steps in the right direction, but they can only be termed tokenism if the rest of the educational process remains ethnocentrically Anglo . . . (p. 332)

Multicultural classrooms include the continuous study of di-verse cultures and their contributions to the United States. For exam-ple, in multicultural high school and college history and literature classes, the study of all cultural groups is successfully integrated throughout the curriculum. In multicultural elementary school classes, the students learn about the experiences and contributions of diverse cultural groups in the United States from day one, and they continue their study of cultural diversity throughout grade school.

According to some, multicultural classes can purge education of its prejudice-producing ethnocentrism. Davidson and Davidson (1989) characterize such classes by the following:

1. There is a major emphasis placed on ensuring that individual students, as well as various cultural groups, have equal, or nearly equivalent, opportunity to learn in the school setting. This typically involves the establishment of new financial, personnel, pedagogical, and staff development and evaluation practices;

2. There is an emphasis on maximizing the academic success of individual students, as well as the academic success rates of various cultural groups in the student population;

3. There is adept collection and interpretation of sociocultural data performed by teachers of individual students;

4. There is treatment of all parents and students as *valued cli-ents*, and the cultural and religious values and requests of

those parents and students are respectfully received, evaluated, and positively acted on when these requests do not undermine the public school curriculum;

5. There is emphasis on home-school cooperation and cultural continuity;

6. There is development by students of new self-confidence, skills, and the historical and cultural knowledge which will allow them to function effectively as culturally literate citizens within their own communities, as well as a range of domestic and overseas cultures.

7. There is a selection of both content and instructional strategies for the social science, science, language arts, music art, and physical education curriculum which is informed by a *multicultural perspective*. This perspective allows a teacher to recognize that culture, race, sex, religion, socio-economic level and exceptionality are potent variables. In addition, when we are discussing the selection of content and instructional strategies, a multicultural perspective leads curriculum developers and teachers to content which makes it clear to students that art, music, language(s), history, ethics and political life of the people of the United States have been significantly influenced by a wide range of individuals and cultural groups. A multicultural perspective also leads teachers to focus on the achievement of greater amounts of cross-cultural understanding and harmony, as well as other equity-oriented objectives. (Adapted from Davidson and Davidson 1989, pp. 5–6)

(For excellent discussions of multicultural education, see Banks 1988, Bennett 1986, Craft 1984, Garcia 1982, Gollnick and Chinn 1986, Kendall 1983 and Tiedt and Tiedt 1986. For a useful review, see Grant, Sleeter and Anderson 1986.)

Critical Pedagogy

The inherent problem with the multicultural education approach to minority instruction, noted by Cummins 1989, Darder 1989, and Skutnabb-Tove and Cummins 1989, is that it fails to emphasize the fundamental inequalities that exist in the United States. Related to this problem, multicultural education also fails to accentuate the necessity of critically evaluating the existing social, historical, cultural, economic, and political reality.

Most, if not all, curricula in our schools strongly mirror middle-American values, attitudes and biases — they therefore perpetuate the values and power relations which legitimize dominant mainstream groups at the expense of minority groups. Schools, with their concern for consensus and conformity, sustain mainstream American culture through a *hidden curriculum*.

Aronowitz and Giroux (1985) explain how this hidden curriculum functions:

> . . . the dominant school culture functions not only to legitimate the interests and values of dominant groups; it also functions to marginalize and disconfirm knowledge forms and experiences that are extremely important to subordinate and oppressed groups. This can be seen in the way in which school curricula often ignore the histories of women, racial minorities, and the working class . . . (pp. 147–148)

An example of the hidden curriculum is illustrated in the work of Anyon (1980), who found that the social studies books used in public schools are dominated by trends that confirm middle-American values. These trends include: (1) an over-emphasis on social harmony, social compromise, and political consensus, with very little said about social struggle and class conflict; (2) an intense nationalism; (3) an exclusion of labor history; and (4) a number of myths regarding the nature of political, economic, and social life.

In contrast to the multicultural education approach, a critical pedagogical approach takes advantage of the students' own histories by delving into their biographies. Students become aware of the validity of their own perceptions and are made conscious of their own capabilities to change their lives. Critical pedagogy requires reflection, new constructive forms of thinking, and action.

The following section examines some principles for incorporating the language minority students' cultures into the curriculum which are consistent with critical pedagogy.

(1) *Avoid cultural invasion.* Teachers may unwittingly impose mainstream culture on their students. This is what Freire (1970) calls *cultural invasion,* an action which sustains the social, political, and economic oppression of minority groups. He describes *cultural invaders* as follows:

> . . . invaders penetrate the cultural context of another group, in disrespect of the latter's potentialities; they impose their own view of the world upon those they invade and inhibit the creativity of the invaded by curbing their expression. . . . In cultural invasion . . .the invaders are the authors of, and actors in, the process; those they invade are the objects. The invaders mold; those they invade are molded. The invaders choose; those they invade follow that choice — or are expected to follow it. The invaders act; those they invade have only the illusion of acting through the action of the invaders . . . All domination involves invasion . . . a form of economic and cultural domination (p. 150)

(2) *Encourage critical dialogue.* Critical pedagogy calls for genuine dialogue between students and teachers. For Freire (1970), "dialogue is a moment where human beings meet to reflect on their reality as they make and remake it . . . through dialogue, reflecting together

on what we know and don't know, we can act critically to transform reality" (pp. 98–99). A pedagogy which employs critical dialogue necessitates "guidance and facilitation rather than control of student learning by the teacher, and the encouragement of student/student talk in a collaborative learning context" (Cummins 1986, p. 28). Freire and Macedo (1987) point out that educational practices which prevent dialogue silence students and ultimately hinder those students' critical capacities. As a result, the students do not develop the understanding necessary to help them struggle effectively toward empowerment.

Darder (1989) suggests that *minority* educators should serve as guides and role models and that *middle-American* educators should recognize their own limitations and enter into dialogue with respect for the knowledge that the students bring into the classroom. Easier said than done. It is difficult for middle-American teachers to acknowledge their limitations because to do this they must relinquish the power associated with holding authority and let their students instruct them (Freire 1970). Dialogue requires that teachers share power more equitably and, in so doing, empower their students.

(3) *Allow the student to shape the curriculum.* Teachers must become partners in their students' educations. Teachers should encourage their students to write their own educational scripts, with their collaboration. As Cummins (1989) puts it, "those who defend the sacredness of curricula and the untouchable character of certain teaching practices seem to view both children and teachers as empty vessels who need to be given digested pieces of knowledge that neatly fit a mold" (p. 28). Teachers need to be empowered to create curricula and use teaching methods that they perceive as the most appropriate for language minority students. This means expanding their power for decision-making.

In a similar vein, Enright and McCloskey (1988) point out:

> Your second language learners bring to the classroom an already-developed knowledge about the people, places, objects, and events in their families and in their native cultures. They often bring a rich experience with the discourse traditions of their native cultures; their peoples' ways of conversing; their ways of behaving appropriately in various social settings (including school); their ways of using reading and writing; and even their ways of presenting information and telling stories. These resources, rather than being ignored or remediated, can be studied and used to enrich their owners' learning and the learning of the entire class. (p. 208)

(4) *Challenge the status quo.* McLaren (1988) believes that, above all, critical pedagogy must encourage an unwavering commitment to empower the powerless and to transform existing social inequities and injustices. Thus, students must be able to find opportunities to participate freely with others as they learn the forms of knowledge, values, and social practices necessary for them to under-

stand how society works, where they are located in it, and what inequities it harbors (Giroux 1988). By carefully considering the social and cultural conflicts and contradictions they experience in their classrooms and in their communities, language minority students can be encouraged to develop their political and social voices and to use them for their own empowerment. They can learn to question oppression and dismantle conditioned definitions of who they are in our society.

Critical educators believe that all people are capable of making meaning of their lives and of resisting oppression, but the capacity to resist is limited and influenced by such issues as class, race and gender. Fay (1987) explains that many students resist seeing themselves as oppressed and are willing to maintain social practices which perpetuate their subordinate position. This means that teachers need to encourage students to question prevailing attitudes, beliefs, values, and practices.

Freire (1970) suggests the use of problem-posing. In this approach, teachers might initially ask such questions as: "How did we come to be what we are?" and "How could we change?" The problem-posing approach enables students to become critics of the world in which they live (Fay 1987). For Freire (1987), problem-posing leads to *conscientization*, the process by which students achieve a rich awareness of the sociopolitical and economic realities which shape their lives and their ability to influence them.[1]

(5) *Develop curricula and pedagogical practices around the community traditions, histories and forms of knowledge that are often ignored within middle-American schools.*We should teach all content-areas from minority perspectives, not primarily from the perspective of middle-Americans. Banks (1988) illustrates how this can be done in a history course, for example:

> When studying a period in U.S. history, such as the colonial period . . . the course does not end when students view the period from the perspectives of mainstream historians and writers. Rather, they ponder these kinds of questions: Why did Anglo-American historians name the English immigrants colonists and the other nationality groups immigrants? How do American-Indian historians view the colonial period?

Similarly, Banks (1988) suggests that when studying World War II, diverse perspectives of the internment of Japanese Americans be given. He states:

> There is no one perspective of the internment of Japanese Americans during World War II and no one Japanese-American view of it. However, accounts written by people who were interned, such as Takasha's powerful *A Child in Prison Camp*, often provide insights and perspectives on the internment that cannot be provided by people who were not interned. Individuals who viewed the internment from the outside can also provide us with unique

and important perspectives and points of view. Both perspectives should be studied in a sound multiethnic curriculum. (p. 180)

Teachers must acknowledge and incorporate their students' cultures in a variety of subject areas in daily classroom activities and everyday curriculum. Rather than presenting separate units on specific cultural themes, it is better to incorporate a multicultural point of view to whatever content area you are studying. Enright and McCloskey (1988) suggest, for example, that rather than presenting a unit on the contributions of immigrants, "your everyday study of history (or science or literature) can consistently make students aware that among the important figures in North American history, many were immigrants or came from minority ethnic groups" (p. 219). Cultural diversity should also be reflected in bulletin boards and displays and audiovisual aids. Books, films, filmstrips, slides, charts and other audiovisual aids must be multicultural. Guest speakers representing a wide variety of occupations and cultural backgrounds should be invited to class, and field trips should be planned so as to expose students to greater cultural diversity.

In searching for content to include in the teaching of social studies or in a reading activity at the elementary level, Baker (1983) suggests incorporating poems, stories, books on myths, and fables that stimulate writing activities and that focus on cultural differences and similarities. She states, "encouraging children to write stories and poems about themselves is a multicultural activity because it is an opportunity for them to express their own feelings and to share with others something about themselves" (p. 98). Language minority students can enrich their classroom social studies lessons by discussing their own traditions and critically investigating issues of their own choice, the more controversial the better, since culturally neutral issues are non-existent.

As Baker (1983) explains, a teacher who includes books about a variety of cultures in the classroom library, book corner, or interest center conveys a message to the students about the acceptability of cultural diversity. (The appendix of this chapter lists appropriate pleasure reading books for young children.) Baker states, "creating corners where children can read and view filmstrips and slides that are multicultural will teach them about diversity and help reinforce reading and observation skills" (p. 88).

Exemplary means of incorporating the cultures of language minority students into the curriculum which are consistent with the principles described here are cooperative learning, learning centers, dialogue writing and critical literacy. Many of these are discussed by Cummins (1989).

Cooperative Learning

Cooperative learning has been successfully used to incorporate the language minority students' perspectives into the curriculum. In cooperative learning, classes are structured so that "students work together in small, cooperative teams" (Kagan 1986, p. 231). Groups can be formed in such a way that students are encouraged to speak their primary languages and share cultural insights with one another.

> In the cooperative classroom most content-related student talk occurs either in pairs within teams or in the small group. Team members are supportive, hoping their teammates will perform well. If there is correction, it is in the process of negotiation of meaning not in the process of evaluation. In such a situation, talking is adaptive — it leads to content and language acquisition. And to the thing which means most to most students — peer support and recognition. (Kagan 1989, 3:7)

Kagan (1989) provides teachers with many useful suggestions regarding ways to easily incorporate cooperative learning into many classroom situations. Cooperative activities provide forms of socializing which draw upon and improve the interactional abilities that students have already acquired. In addition to developing new language skills, cooperative learning has been shown to improve relations among different cultural groups (Slavin 1980, 1983).[2] Kagan (1989) states that "in classes which use integrated student learning teams, positive race relations among students increases — students choose more friends from other races" (2:10). It should be pointed out, however, that cooperative learning is not necessarily consistent with the principles of critical pedagogy. It needs to be employed in such a way that it fosters students' critical thinking and creates opportunities for students to use this thinking for immediate learning and personal advancement.

Learning Centers

Learning centers are another excellent way to provide students with opportunities to utilize their cultural knowledge. In learning centers, students work together without teacher supervision. These centers permit students to work individually or in small groups. (See Waynant and Wilson 1974 for useful suggestions for setting up these centers.)[3] It is important that the activities introduced in learning centers be an integral part of the curricula. A Mexican center featuring *sombreros* and *piñatas* is more likely to trivialize than legitimitize Mexican culture. Cultural themes must be integrated into daily classroom activities. The long-range effects of isolating and trivializing cultural themes are detrimental and can prevent students from developing the notion that minority groups are critical components of the school curriculum. "The danger of negative learning occurring is greatly increased when the types of experiences are isolated and are not integral parts of the total curriculum" (Banks, p. 176).

Dialogue Journal Writing

Dialogue journal writing, in which the participants converse in writing, is a natural way for language minority students to communicate with each other and to share their personal experiences. Garcia and Garcia (1988) highlight the role of journal writing in validating the students' language and sociocultural experiences. In a recent study, Flores and Hernandez (1988) report that a bilingual kindergartener named Jesús gained literacy skills through his use of daily transactions with his teacher within the communicative context of dialogue journals. Flores and Hernandez (1988) state, "Jesús learned to read and write alphabetically in both Spanish and English. Both his teacher and parents were amazed" (p. 3). Dialogue journal writing can promote bilingualism and learning with older students just as well as it can with younger.

Critical Literacy

Ada (1988 and Ada and de Olave 1986) describes a pedagogical approach which involves critical thinking, reading, and the personal experiences of language minority children. She outlines the following four stages of what she terms the *creative reading act*: Students move from a descriptive phrase (in which they learn what the text says) to a personal interpretive phase (in which they relate information to their own experiences and feelings). They then move to a critical phase (in which they compare and contrast what is presented in their reading with their own personal experiences and begin to critically analyze the issues discussed in the text). In the final phase, they discuss what actions can be taken to resolve problems posed in the text.

Ethnic Traveling Treasure Chests/Kaleidoscope Collections

Some school districts make available ethnic traveling *treasure chests* or *kaleidoscope collections* which include approximately 25 artifacts of a culture that are often displayed in plexiglass or which can be touched and/or manipulated. These artifacts are exhibited and travel among schools. The items are often controversial and elicit discourse on human relations and stereotypes. The treasure chests cultivate respect for the many different ways people can contribute to society and are generally incorporated into the state frameworks in language arts, social science, science, math, and visual and performing arts. (One such treasure chest has been produced by the Historical and Cultural Foundation of Orange County, California.)

Other activities which can be used to incorporate the students' perspectives into the curriculum include simulation, role-playing, and socio-drama as well as process-oriented writing.

The activities described can be used to change the school so that it respects and legitimizes the cultures of students in our classrooms; these educational activities build on our students' experiences, letting us appreciate their diverse learning styles. In addition, they can be used to raise the consciousness of students and teachers about society and to help all to develop a commitment to obtaining social, economic, political and educational equity.

Incorporating the Languages of Your Students into the Curriculum

The primary languages as well as the cultural backgrounds of language minority students must be recognized. Teachers who wish to act as advocates for language minority students encourage those students to develop their first language proficiency even where bilingual education programs are unavailable (Cummins 1989). New Zealand educators give the following suggestions for reinforcing language minority students' languages and cultures in the school program:

- Reflect the various cultural groups in the school district by providing signs in the main office and elsewhere that welcome people in the different languages of the community;
- Encourage students to use their L1 [first language] around the school;
- Provide opportunities for students from the same ethnic group to communicate with one another in their L1 where possible (e.g., in cooperative learning groups on at least some occasions);
- Recruit people who can tutor students in their L1;
- Provide books written in the various languages in both classrooms and the school library;
- Incorporate greetings and information in the various languages in newsletters and other official school communications;
- Display pictures and objects related to the various cultures represented at the school;
- Create units of work that incorporate other languages in addition to the school language;
- Encourage students to write contributions in their L1 for school newspapers and magazines;
- Provide opportunities for students to study their L1 in elective subjects and/or in extracurricular clubs;
- Encourage parents to help in the classroom, library, playground and in clubs;
- Invite second language learners to use their L1 during assemblies, prizegivings, and other official functions;
- Invite people from ethnic minority communities to act as resource people and to speak to students in both formal and informal settings. (Adapted from New Zealand Department of Education 1988, reported in Cummins 1989, p. 61.)

According to Cummins (1989), telecommunication systems also provide a means of incorporating the primary languages of your students into your curriculum. Cummins reports that one of the major educational uses of computer networking is the *Computer Chronicles Newswire* (described by Mehan et al. 1984, 1986; Riel 1983). This networking connects students in San Diego with classes across the world. Computer networking has also been used to link language minority students with countries where their native languages are spoken (see, for instance, Rosa and Moll 1985, and Sayers and Brown 1987). For example, Latino students from San Diego were linked with native Spanish speakers in Madrid in the Rosa and Moll project. The largest network designed for Latino students in the United States is *De Orilla a Orilla, From Shore to Shore.* (For useful discussion, see Sayers 1986 and Sayers and Brown 1987.) Cummins (1989) reports that a primary goal of the *Orillas* project has been to promote Spanish and English literacy through children's writings in both languages. Through the *Orillas* project, children from Puerto Rico, Connecticut, San Diego and Tijuana have been communicating with classes nearly on a daily basis.

Interactive Videodisc

Videodiscs "like no other medium, bring together the emotional, affective power of television with the processing power of the computer" (Findley 1986, p. 10). The system is relatively inexpensive, requiring a videodisc player and a computer setup that includes a monitor, keyboard, and a microcomputer. Videodiscs provide learners with meaningful input, and teach the listening skills necessary for academic success (Richard-Amato 1988). Excellent bilingual videodiscs are now available which allow students to switch easily from one language to another. For example, "The Living Textbook—Life, Physical Science and Earth Science Interactive Multimedia Library" series produced and distributed by Optical Data Corporation has been successfully used in the Santa Ana Unifed School District in California. This series combines "real world" texts, graphics, animation, still frame slides, moving video segments and separately assessible sound tracts in both Spanish and English. It enables monolingual English-speaking teachers to teach their students difficult concepts in their students' first language, Spanish, and has the potential to create a multisensory environment that addresses the learning levels, speeds and modality strengths of different students.

Finding Out/Descubrimiento

Another example of a project which successfully incorporates the child's first language into the curriculum is the *Finding Out/Descubrimiento Project.* Originally developed by De Avila and Duncan, this program provides elementary children with small group math and science instruction. Materials, currently grouped around seventeen groups or units, are available in both Spanish and English. The children (grades 2–5) engage in activities "in which reading, writing, and computation are integrated with higher order thinking skills" (Kagan 5:13). Evaluations of this highly successful program demonstrate its success in teaching Spanish and English literacy as well as math and science concepts (see Cummins 1984, Kagan 1989).[4]

Pen-pals.

Penpals offer yet another activity which utilizes the primary languages of language minority students. As Enright and McCloskey (1988) note:

> Having students edit and add punctuation marks to their letters because their penpals in a bilingual school in another country will be able to understand them better is an intrinsically useful and supportive way of correcting writing that no amount of red correction marks on a student's writing assignment can ever produce. (pp. 24–25)

Classroom Correspondence

Classroom correspondence also promotes the students' primary languages. Enright and McCloskey (1988) suggest that teachers set up a bulletin board where students can leave messages for one another and encourage joke or riddle exchanges. They can also exchange views on controversial topics of their own choice.

Conclusion

Teachers must be sensitive to the needs of their language minority students and legitimize and respect their primary languages and home cultures. These students are not responding well to traditional educational procedures used in our schools. Every year the gap between mainstream American student academic progress and minority student progress grows wider. Kagan (1989) states:

> Each year non-white students fall farther behind white students: while there is little or no difference in achievement scores at or near entry to school, by the end of elementary school non-white students are about half a grade behind white students in math and a full grade behind in reading. By the end of junior high school, the gap has doubled so that white students score a full grade higher in math and two full grades higher in reading. Beyond that, it is impossible to get accurate comparison figures because there are differential drop-out rates — non-white students begin dropping out of the educational pipeline much earlier than do white students . . . . The education drop-out rates are staggering. (2:8–2:9)

In the introduction, I outlined the following eleven principles for providing language minority students with successful instruction in the multicultural classroom:

1. Know your students.
2. Understand language development.
3. Make your lessons comprehensible.
4. Encourage interaction.
5. Appeal to diverse learning styles.
6. Provide effective feedback.
7. Test fairly.
8. Encourage minority parent participation.
9. Appreciate cultural diversity.
10. Incorporate your students' languages and cultures.
11. Reduce prejudice.

These principles address the major problems which language minority students encounter in our schools (outlined in Chapter 1). Informed educators will need to be sensitive to the issues described in this volume if they are to make equal education possible for all students.

ACTIVITIES AND DISCUSSION QUESTIONS

1. List all those activities of a school day that might be unfamiliar to a student from another culture. Ask students from other cultures to describe those aspects of school which were particularly difficult for them when they first came to the United States.
2. Interview a language minority student and outline all the areas in which the student could contribute to your classroom curriculum.
3. Interview some language minority students who have been in the United States more than a year. Ask each student what would have made life easier when he or she first entered school in the United States.
4. Collect resources about a specific culture represented by the students you teach, have taught, or would like to teach. Include books, magazine articles, etc.
5. Restructure a specific classroom activity in such a way that you incorporate your students' languages and cultures.

SUGGESTED READING

Multicultural Education

APPLETON, N. 1983. *Cultural Pluralism in Education: Theoretical Foundations.* New York: Longman.

BAKER, G. C. 1985. *Planning and Organizing for Multicultural Instruction.* Reading, Massachusetts: Addison-Wesley Publishing Company.

BANKS, J. A. 1988. *Multiethnic Education.* Boston: Allyn and Bacon, Inc.

BENNETT, C. I. 1986. *Comprehensive Multicultural Education: Theory and Practice.* Newton, Massachusetts: Allyn and Bacon, Inc.

CRAFT, M. 1984. (ed.) *Education and Cultural Pluralism.* Philadelphia, Pennsylvania: The Falmer Press.

GARCIA, R. L. 1982. *Teaching in a Pluralistic Society.* New York: Harper and Row.

KENDALL, F. E. 1983. *Diversity in the Classroom: A Multicultural Approach to the Education of Young Children.* New York: Teachers College Press.

LYNCH, J. 1986. *Multicultural Education: Principles and Practice.* London: Routledge and Kegan Paul.

TIEDT, P. L., and TIEDT, I. M. 1986. *Multicultural Teaching: A Handbook of Activities, Information and Resources.* Massachusetts: Allyn and Bacon.

WILLIAMS, L. R., and DE GAETANO, Y. 1985. *A Multicultural, Bilingual Approach to Teaching Young Children.* Reading, Massachusetts: Addison-Wesley Publishing Company.

NOTES

1. In a similar vein, Banks (1988) suggests that teachers need to help all students develop the ability to make reflective political decisions, to gain and exercise political power effectively, and to struggle for political, social and educational equality. He suggests that teachers provide numerous concrete examples of how "previously excluded and politically powerless minority groups in history have attained power and how certain non-reflective actions and inactions can result in further exclusion and victimization" (Banks 1988, p. 185). Students can then better understand how they have been victimized and how myths contribute to their feelings of inferiority and powerlessness. Banks argues:

> They [students] must develop a sense of political efficacy and be given practice in social action strategies that teach them how to get power without violence and further exclusion. In other words, excluded ethnic groups must be taught the most effective ways to gain power. The school should help them become both effective and reflective political activists. (p. 187)

2. Enright and McCloskey (1988) give these suggestions for developing cooperative goals and activities:

How to Develop Cooperative Goals and Activities

1. Set up rules and procedures that promote cooperation, collaboration and multicultural understanding. At the beginning of the year:

- Establish a supportive environment that provides for students' safety and information needs.
- Involve students in writing a classroom constitution that promotes class goals.

- Involve students immediately in collaborative, cooperative activities that help them learn about one another and about the cultures represented in the classroom.

2. Build cooperation into the learning tasks students perform by creating must-cooperate tasks. Include such activities as:

- Cooperative projects. Have peer groups conduct investigations and create products to show what they have learned; use jigsaw to create situations in which everyone is an expert on some part of a task. [In jigsaw activities, each student in a group has information the other students in the group need. This creates an information gap which stimulates discussion, since in order to complete jigsaw activities, all students must share their information.]
- Peer conferences. Help students learn to use brainstorming and feedback conferences with peers.
- Cooperative Games. Use games that are cooperative, and adapt competitive games of the cooperative model.
- Learning Centers. Provide students with opportunities for many kinds of discourse in a situation in which they work independently, without direct supervision.
- Classroom correspondence: Provide students with opportunities for real written discourse with one another, with the teacher, and with others outside the class.

3. Consider three other factors:

- Resources: Use materials and supplies in ways that foster collaboration and cooperation.
- Student roles. Use various roles for students which are matched to their needs, including equal roles, differentiated roles, and self-selected roles. [See Kagan 1989.]
- Student characteristics. Group or disperse students in accordance with expertise, interest, social style, and language proficiency to promote collaboration and language learning. [Kagan 1989 offers very practical guidelines for grouping students.]

3. Enright and McCloskey (1988) make the following suggestions for setting up interest centers:

1. *Directions should be appropriate for independent use.* When introducing the new center, review all center activities. Give instruction to the full group by demonstration and explanation and also provide directions at the center itself. Directions can be provided in several languages.

2. *Centers should include a number of different activities in various languages and learning levels.* Vary them according to difficulty level. Let beginning second language learners experience success.

3. *Provide some hands-on activities as well as pencil-and-paper tasks.* Student inventions can be inspired by real machines displayed in the center.

4. *Centers should provide a way for students to evaluate themselves while they participate or afterwards.* Enright and McCloskey suggest that teachers use self-evaluation, charts, class-lists, student record forms to help students evaluate themselves. (pp. 234–235)

4. For further information about *Finding Out/Descubrimiento*, contact either D. Edward De Avila, Linguametrics Group, PO Box 3495, San Rafael, California 94812 (415) 459-5350 or Dr. Elizabeth Cohen, School of Education, Stanford University, Palo Alto, California 94306 (415) 723-4661.

APPENDIX

Recommended Pleasure Reading Books for a Multicultural Elementary Classroom

Caribbbean (Jamaica, Trinidad, Haiti)
ERROL. L. 1978. *Nini at Carnival.* London: The Bodley Head Ltd.

KIRPATRICK. O. 1979. *Maja the Snake and Mangus the Mongoose.* Garden City, New York: Doubleday.

SINGER, Y. 1976. *Little Miss Yes Yes.* Toronto: Kids Can Press.

WOLKSTEIN, D. 1981. *The Banza.* New York: Dial Books, E. P. Dutton, Inc.

Asia (People's Republic of China, Korea, the Philippines, Taiwan, and Vietnam)
ARUEGO, J., and ARUEGO, A. 1972. *A Crocodile's Tale.* Toronto: Scholastic-TAB.

BISHOP. H., and WIESE, K. 1938. *The Five Chinese Brothers.* New York: Coward McCann Inc.

HAMADA, H. 1967. *The Tears of the Dragon.* New York: Parents Magazine Press.

HEAPS, L. 1984. *A Boy Called Nam.* Toronto: MacMillan of Canada.

MAHOOD. K. *The Laughing Dragon.* Longon: Collins.

Maiden of Wu Long and the Axe and the Sword, The. 1978. Told by F. Ling, and M.-S. Lau, Toronto: Kids Can Press.

MARQUAND, J., and BENDER. P. 1969. *Chi Ming and the Lion Dance.* London: Dennis Dobson.

POTTER. D., and NEEN, S. 1977. *The Best Time of the Year.* Oklahoma City, Oklahoma: The Economy Co.

WALLACE, I. 1984. *Chin Chiang and the Dragon's Dance.* Toronto: Douglas and McIntryre.

YASHIMA. T. 1958. *Umbrella.* New York: Viking Press.

North American Native American (Canada, New Mexico)
CLEAVER, N. 1973. *How the Chipmunk Got Its Stripes.* Toronto: Scholastic-TAB.

DEWDNEY, S. 1980. *The Hungry Time.* Toronto: James Lorimer and Co.

Nanabush and the Rabbit. 1971. Retold by D. H. Odig, Toronto: Ginn and Co.

PERRINE, M. 1968. *Salt Boy.* Boston: Houghton Mifflin.

East Indian

SAVITRI. K. 1968. *Two Little Chicks.* New Delhi: Children's Book Trust.

Seventh Daughter in the Sun, retold by T. Thapar, 1977. India: Thompson Press.

SHIKUMAR, S. 1966. *The Crow.* New Delhi: Children's Book Trust.

African

AARDMA, V. 1960. *Tales from the Story Hat.* New York: Coward, McCann.

AARDMA, V. 1975. *Why Mosquitoes Buzz in People's Ears.* Toronto: Scholastic-TAB.

ACHEBE, C. 1977. *The Flute.* Enugu, Nigeria: Fourth Dimension Publishing. (Reprinted with permission of Dorman Publishers and Heald-Taylor. From Heald-Taylor 1989, pp. 43–44)

Latino

IZENBERG. J. 1976. *Great Latin Sports Figures: The Proud People.* New York: Doubleday. (English)

LA LUZ (eds.) 1969. *Bedtime Stories in Spanish.* Skokie: Illinois: National Textbook Company. (Spanish and English)

MISTRAL. G. 1972. (adapted by Dana, D.) *Crickets and Frogs: A Fable in Spanish and English.* New York: Atheneum. (Spanish and English)

NERUDA. P. 1965. *Bestiary/Bestiario.* New York: Harcourt. (Spanish and English)

WILLIAMS, L. 1979. *The Tiger!/El Tigre!* Englewood Cliffs, New Jersey: Prentice-Hall.

Books read in Ada's (1986, 1988) creative reading project, developed under the auspices of the Bilingual Program of the Pajaro Valley School District: *

ADA, A. F. and DE OLAVE, M. 1975. *Maravillas.* Lima, Peru: Ed. Brasa.

BALSOLA, A. 1984. *Munia y el Cocolilo Naranja.* Barcelona: Destino.

BALSOLA, A. 1984. *Munia y la Señora Piltronera.* Barcelona: Destino.

BROGER. A., and KALOW, G. 1978. *Buenos Días, Querida Ballena.* Barcelona: Juventud.

BROGER, A., and KALOW, G. 1978. *El Cucuyo y la Mora.* Caracas, Venezuela: Banca del Libro (Ediciones Ekare).

HUECK. S. 1982. *El Poni, el Oso, y la Manzano.* Barcelona: Juventud.

LIONNI. L. 1982. *Nadarin.* Barcelona: Lumen.

LIONNI. L. 1982. *Frederick.* Barcelona:Lumen.

LOBEL. A. 1977. *Sopa de Ratón.* Madrid: Alfaguara.

LOOF. J. 1974. *Historia de una Manzana Roja.* Valladolid: Minon.

LOOF. J. 1974. *Mi Abuelo es Pirata.* Valladolid: Minon.

LOOF. J. 1971. *La Paloma y la Hormiga.* Barcelona: La Galera.

TURIN, A. and BOSNIA. N. 1984. *Arturo y Clementina.* Barcelona: Lumen.

TOMIE, P. DE. 1984. *La Virgen de Guadalupe.* Madrid: Ediciones Ecuentro.

STEADMAN, R. 1972. *El Puente.* Valladolid: Minon.

WILLIAMS, L. and VENDRELL SOLE, C. 1984. *Que hay destras del árbol?* Barcelona: Hymsa.

*This list is reprinted with the permission of Alma Ada and Multilingual Matters from: Ada, A. 1988. The Pajaro Valley experience: Working with Spanish-speaking parents to develop children's reading and writing skills through the use of children's literature. In T. Skutnabb-Kangas, and J. Cummins (eds.) *Minority Education.* Clevedon, England: Multilingual Matters. For additional information on the creative reading methodology used by Ada (1988), refer to A. Ada, and O. Del Pilar, 1986. *Hagamos Caminos.* Reading, Massachusetts: Addison-Wesley. Also, note that many of the books listed above are now available for purchase through the Santillana Publishing Company, located in San Diego, California.

Glossary

ACCULTURATION. Process of adapting to a new culture, entailing an understanding of cultural patterns.

ADDITIVE OR ADHESIVE ACCULTURATION. A type of cultural adaptation in which certain aspects of the new culture are added to the immigrants' traditional culture (from Huhr and Kim 1984).

ADJUNCT ESL CLASSES. Classes generally adjoined to regular college courses designed to give ESL students additional practice in and exposure to the particular language uses of a specific course (such as psychology, economics or history).

ANALYTICAL THINKING. Linear step-by-step processing of information.

ANOMIE. State in which students begin to adapt to the target culture [the United States], while often simultaneously losing some of their native culture.

ASIAN. A person who has recently immigrated to the United States from an Asian country.

ASIAN-AMERICAN. Individual of Asian heritage who is a citizen of the United States.

ASSIMILATION. Complete absorption of the characteristics and the behaviors of the other culture.

BICS. Basic interpersonal communication skills (from Cummins 1981); the aspects of language proficiency strongly associated with basic fluency in face-to-face interaction.

BILINGUAL EDUCATION. An educational program in which two languages are used in the instruction.

BILINGUAL EDUCATION ACT. The federal statute passed in 1968 as Title VII of the Elementary and Secondary Education Act which provided federal support for bilingual education programs.

BILINGUALISM. The use of two languages by the same person or group.

CALP. Cognitive academic linguistic proficiency; the aspects of language strongly associated with literacy and academic achievement (Cummins 1981).

CHICANO. Individual of Mexican heritage who resides in the United States and who supports the Chicano movement.

CHICANO MOVEMENT. A movement which takes as its primary goal the attainment of political, economic, and educational equity in the United States.

CODE-SWITCHING. The alternating use of two languages; for example, switching from Spanish to English in a discussion.

COGNITIVE STYLE. Manner of processing and organizing information.

COMPREHENSIBLE INPUT. Input which the learner understands (see input).

CRITERION-REFERENCED TESTS. Tests in which the students' performance is not compared to others, but is expressed in terms of actual skills of tasks performed.

CULTURE FAIR TESTS. Tests which are reported to be free from cultural bias (for example, Cattell's Culture Fair Intelligence Test, Raven's Progressive Matrices).

CULTURAL PLURALISM. The view that different ethnic groups play unique roles which can enrich the United States.

CULTURE SHOCK. Feelings of disorientation often experienced in instances of contact with other cultures.

CUP. Common underlying proficiencies of first and second languages (Cummins 1981).

DEVELOPMENTAL INTERDEPENDENCE HYPOTHESIS. The hypothesis which states that the level of second language competence which a bilingual child reaches is partially a function of the type of competency the child has developed in the first language at the time when intensive exposure to the second language begins (Cummins 1979).

DIALECT. A regional or social variety of a language which is characterized by specific linguistic features (such as pronunciation, grammar, and discourse features).

ENRICHMENT MAINTENANCE BILINGUAL PROGRAM. A program which provides instruction which aids the development of advanced primary language skills; also called maintenance bilingual program.

ESL. English as a second language.

ESP. English for special (specific) purposes. Classes in ESP are designed to give students expertise in specific content areas.

ETHNOCENTRISM. Belief in the inherent correctness of one's own cultural values and behaviors.

FEEDBACK. The response to the learners' efforts to communicate.

FIELD DEPENDENCE. A means of processing information, field dependents are hypothesized to operate holistically.

FIELD INDEPENDENCE. A means of processing information; field independents are hypothesized to operate analytically.

FOB: FRESH-OFF-THE-BOAT (OR PLANE). Term used to describe recent arrivals to the United States.

FOREIGNER TALK. The simplified speech native English speakers use when speaking to foreigners.

FOSSILIZATION. The permanent cessation of second language acquisition.

GLOBAL THINKING. Spacial, relational and intuitive thinking.

HERITAGE CLASSES. Classes that provide students with instruction in their native languages and cultures.

HOME/SCHOOL CULTURE DISCONTINUITIES. The notion that the language and cultural differences of the schools in the United States and the language minority students' home culture are so great that they prevent the students from attaining academic success.

IMMERSION PROGRAM. A program designed to provide minority language students with comprehensible input and instruction geared to their current language proficiency levels.

INPUT. The language (either written or heard) to which the learner is exposed.

INPUT AT THE I + 1. Input which is just a little above the learners' current level of second language proficiency (Krashen 1982).

INTAKE. The language input which is processed and becomes part of the learner's acquired competence (Corder 1981).

LANGUAGE ATTITUDES. Evaluative reactions toward language (such as *French is the language of romance; English is the language of business*).

LANGUAGE DISTANCE HYPOTHESIS. The hypothesis that states that learners transfer from similar languages to a greater extent than they transfer from dissimilar ones.

LANGUAGE MINORITY STUDENT. A student who has not acquired full proficiency in English.

LATINO. A cover-term in reference to all individuals of Spanish-speaking origin.

LAU VERSUS NICHOLS. A decision of the United States Supreme Court in 1974 which found that the Board of Education of San Francisco did not provide equal access to education to Chinese-speaking students who were enrolled in English-only classes they did not understand.

LEP. Limited-English proficient. A student who is not fully proficient in English and speaks a language other than English at home.

LINGUISTIC PREJUDICE. The habit of arriving at conclusions about a person's social status on the basis of his or her speech.

MAINSTREAM AMERICAN. Anyone in the United States, regardless of gender, religion, or socioeconomic level, who has United States middle-class values; used interchangeably with the term middle-American.

MAINSTREAMING. Placing ESL students in courses designed for native English-speaking students.

MAINTENANCE BILINGUAL PROGRAM. A program which provides instruction which aids the development of advanced primary language skills; also called enrichment maintenance bilingual program.

MELTING POT. Assimilationist belief that ethnic groups in the United States would mix to form a new, superior national character; the term was coined in the play, *The Melting Pot*, written by Israel Zangwill and performed in New York City in 1908.

MEXICAN. An individual of Mexican origin; individuals in the United States who identify themselves as Mexicans are usually recent arrivals to the United States who relate more to the cultural norms of Mexico than they do to those of the United States.

MEXICAN-AMERICAN. An individual of Mexican heritage who resides in the United States and who does not identify with the Chicano movement.

MIDDLE-AMERICAN. Anyone in the United States, regardless of gender, religion, or socioeconomic level, who has United States middle-class values; used interchangeably with the term mainstream American.

MOTHERESE. The simplified speech many middle-American mothers use when they talk to their babies.

MULTICULTURALISM. An approach to cultural diversity emphasizing tolerance.

NATURAL ORDER HYPOTHESIS (Krashen 1981). The hypothesis which predicts that second language learners acquire grammatical structures in their second language in predictable sequences, such that one linguistic structure is acquired before another.

NEP. Non-English proficient.

OPTIMAL INPUT. Input which best aids English language development.

OUTPUT. Speech or writing.

PREJUDICE. A unified, stable and consistent tendency to respond in a negative way toward members of a particular cultural group.

PULL-OUT CLASSES. Classes in which students are withdrawn from their regular subject classes for one or more periods a week for special English language instruction in small groups.

RATE OF ENGLISH LANGUAGE ACQUISITION. How fast the learner develops English language proficiency.

Semilingualism. Partial loss of a student's first language while not yet having acquired a second.

SENSORY MODALITY STRENGTH. The extent to which learners depend on various sources of sensory input (visual, auditory, and tactile-kinesthetic) for information.

SES. Socioeconomic status.

SHELTERED ENGLISH CLASSES. Sometimes referred to as transition or bridge classes; in these classes, students cover the same content offered in classes in which native English proficiency is assumed; the language component of these classes is adapted to suit the language minority students' English proficiency levels.

SILENT PERIOD. The time period in which limited English proficient students need to observe others prior to communicating in English themselves (hypothesized by Krashen 1982).

SOCIO-AFFECTIVE FILTER. The filter which governs how much input goes through to a language processing mechanism (proposed by Krashen 1981).

SPOTLIGHTING. Singling out a student and asking this student to perform before others.

STANDARD LANGUAGE. A standard language is one which has been codified in dictionaries and grammars, is used in a variety of contexts and has numerous functions.

SUBMERSION PROGRAM. A program in which language minority students receive no special instruction designed to help them acquire English of content areas; also called *sink-or-swim* approach.

SUP. Separate underlying proficiencies of the learner's first and second languages (Cummins 1981).

THRESHOLD HYPOTHESIS Cummins (1979). Proposes the existence of two different thresholds of language acquisition; the upper threshold is reached when the language minority student develops high levels of age-appropriate skills in both languages; the lower threshold represents inadequate skills in the language minority learner's first language.

TOTAL PHYSICAL RESPONSE (TPR). A technique for teaching ESL and foreign languages proposed by Asher (1965, 1966) which entails giving commands to students.

TRANSITION BILINGUAL PROGRAM. A program which provides some instruction in the language minority students' native language to help them keep up in their school subjects while they study English in programs designed for limited English proficient students.

WAIT TIME. The amount of time students prefer to take before answering teacher questions.

WHORFIAN HYPOTHESIS. The hypothesis, formulated by Benjamin Whorf, that the grammar of a language affects thought.

Bibliography

ABOUD, F. 1988. *Children and Prejudice.* Oxford: Basil Blackwell Ltd.

ACTON, W. 1979. *Second Language Learning and the Perception of Difference in Attitude.* Unpublished doctoral dissertation, University of Michigan.

ADA, A. F. 1986. "Creative Education for Bilingual Teachers." *Harvard Educational Review*, 56, 386–394.

ADA, A. F. 1988. "The Pajaro Valley Experience: Working with Spanish-speaking Parents to Develop Children's Reading and Writing Skills in the Home through the use of Children's Literature." T. Skutnabb-Kangas, and J. Cummins, (eds.) *Minority Education: From Shame to Struggle.* Clevedon, England: Multilingual Matters.

ADA, A. F. and M. DE OLAVE. 1986. *Hagamos Caminos.* Reading, Massachusetts: Addison-Wesley.

ALBERT, R. D. 1983. "The Intercultural Sensitizer or Culture Assimilator." D. Landis and R. Brislin, (eds.) *Handbook of Intercultural Training.* New York: Pergamon Press.

ALVIREZ, E., F. D. BEAN, and D. WILLIAMS. 1982. "The Mexican-American Family." C. H. Mindel and R. W. Habenstein, (eds.) *Ethnic Families in America.* New York: Elsevier Science Publishing Company.

d'ANGLEJAN, A. 1978. "Language Learning In and Out of Classrooms." J. Richards, (ed.) *Understanding Second and Foreign Language Learning.* Rowley, Massachusetts: Newbury House Publishers.

ANYON, J. 1979. "United States History Textbooks and Ideology: A Study of Curriculum Content and Social Interests." *Harvard Educational Review*, XLIX, 49–59.

ARCHER, C. M. 1986. "Culture Bump and Beyond." J. D. Valdes, (ed.) *Culture Bound: Bridging the Cultural Gap in Language Teaching.* Cambridge: Cambridge University Press.

ARONOWITZ, S. and H. GIROUX. 1985. *Education under Siege.* Boston: Bergin and Garvey.

ARREOLA vs. Board of Education. 1968. (Orange County, California). No. 160 577.

ASHER, J. 1965. "The Strategy of Total Physical Response: An Application to Learning Russian." *International Review of Applied Linguistics* 3: 292–9.

ASHER, J. 1966. "The Learning Strategy of Total Physical Response: A Review." *Modern Language Journal* 50: 79–84.

ASHER, J. 1969. "The Total Physical Response Approach to Second Language Learning." *Modern Language Journal* 53: 3–28.

ASHER, J. 1982. *Learning Another Language Through Actions: The Complete Teacher's Guidebook.* Los Gatos, California: Sky Oaks.

ASHTON-WARNER, S. 1963. *Teacher.* New York: Bantam Books.

ASHTON-WARNER, S. 1979. *I Passed this Way.* New York: Knopf.

ASHWORTH, M. 1985. *Beyond Methodology: Second Language Teaching and the Community.* Cambridge: Cambridge University Press.

AU, K. 1980. "Participation Structures in a Reading Lesson with Hawaiian Children: An Analysis of a Culturally Appropriate Instructional Event." *Anthropology and Education Quarterly.* 11 (2), 91–115.

AU, K. and C. JORDAN. 1981. "Hawaiian Americans: Teaching Reading to Hawaiian Children: Finding a Culturally Appropriate Solution." H. T. Trueba, G. P. Guthrie and K. Au, (eds.) *Culture and the Bilingual Classroom - Studies in Classroom Ethnography.* Rowley, Massachusetts: Newbury House Publishers.

AZORES, T. 1987. "Educational Attainment and Upward Mobility: Prospects for Filipino Americans." *Amerasia Journal* (13) 1:39–52.

BAILEY, C. 1987. "Cultural Factors Evolving From the Notional-Functional Approach." C. Cargil, (ed.) *A TESOL Professional Anthology: Culture.* Lincolnwood, Illinois: National Textbook Co.

BAKER, G. C. 1983. *Planning and Organizing for Multicultural Instruction.* Reading, Massachusetts: Addison-Wesley.

BANDURA, A. 1977. *Social Learning Theory.* New Jersey: Prentice-Hall.

BANKS, J. A., (ed.) 1981. *Education in the 80's: Multiethnic Education.* Washington D.C.: National Education Association.

BANKS, J. A., 1987. *Teaching Strategies for Ethnic Studies.* Boston: Allyn and Bacon.

BANKS, J. A. 1988. *Multiethnic Education: Theory and Practice.* Boston: Allyn and Bacon, Inc.

BARNES, D. 1976. *From Communication to Curriculum.* Harmondsworth: Penguin.

BARRON, D. 1990. "Irvine high school intergroup relations program." L. Olsen and C. Dowell, (eds.) *Bridges: Promising Programs for the Education of Immigrant Children.* San Francisco: California Today Immigrant Students Project.

BASSANO, S. K. and M. A. CHRISTISON. 1987. "Developing Successful Conversation Groups." M. H. Long and J. C. Richards, (eds.) *Methodology in TESOL: A Book of Readings.* New York: Harper and Row.

BECKER, H. J. and J. L. EPSTEIN. 1982. "Parent Involvement: A Survey of Teacher Practices." *The Elementary School Journal.* 83:2, pp. 85–102.

BEEBE, J. and M. BEEBE. 1981. "The Filipinos: A Special Case." C. A. Ferguson, and S. B. Heath, (eds.) *Language in the U.S.* Cambridge: Cambridge University Press. 322–338.

BELOUS, R. S., S. A. LEVITAN and F. GALLO, 1988. *What's Happing to the American Family? Tensions, Hopes and Realities.* Massachusetts: Johns Hopkins University Press.

BENNETT, C. I. 1986. *Comprehensive Multicultural Education: Theory and Practice.* Newton, Massachusetts: Allyn and Bacon, Inc.

BERGER, E. H. 1981. *Parents as Partners in Education: The School and Home Working Together.* Toronto: The C. V. Mosby Company.

BISSELL, J., S. WHITE and G. ZIVEN. 1971. "Sensory Modalities in Children's Learning." G. S. Lesser, (ed.) *Psychology and Educational Practice.* Glenview, Illinois: Scott Foresman and Co.

BLOUNT, B. 1977. "Ethnography and Caretaker-Child Interaction." C. Snow, and C. Ferguson, (eds.) *Talking to Children.* Cambridge: Cambridge University Press.

BOBBITT, N. and L. PALOUCCI. 1986. "Strengths of the Home and Family as Learning Environments." R. J. Griffore, and R. P. Boder, (eds.) *Child Rearing in the Home and School.* New York: Plenum Press.

BOGEN, J. 1969. "The Other Side of the Brain: Dysgraphia and Dyscopia Following Cerebral Commissurotomy." *Bulletin of the Los Angeles Neurological Society,* 34, no. 2.

BOGER, R. P., R. A. RICHTER and L. PAOLUCCI. 1986. "Parent as Teacher: What Do We Know?" R. J. Griffore, and R. P. Boder, (eds.) *Child Rearing in the Home and School.* New York: Plenum Press.

BOGGS, S. 1972. "The Meaning of Questions and Narratives to Hawaiian Children." C. Cazden, J. Vera, and D. Hymes, (eds.) *Functions of Language in the Classroom.* New York: Teachers College Press.

BRISLIN, R. W., K. CUSHER, C. CHERRIE and M. YANG. 1986. *Intercultural Interactions: A Practical Guide.* Beverly Hills: Sage Publications.

BROFENBENNER, U., (ed.) 1975. *Influences on Human Development.* Hinsdale, Illinois: Dryden Press.

BROOKS, N. 1960. *Language and Language Learning.* New York: Harcourt Brace and World.

BROWN, H. D. 1980. *Principles of Language Learning and Language Teaching.* Englewood Cliffs, New Jersey: Prentice Hall.

BROWN, H. D. 1986. "Learning a second culture." J. Valdes, (ed.) *Culture Bound: Bridging the Cultural Gap in Language Teaching.* Cambridge: Cambridge University Press.

BROWN, M. and A. PALMER. 1987. *The Listening Approach.* New York: Longman.

Bullock Report. 1975. *A Language for Life.* Report of the Committee of Inquiry appointed by the Secretary of State for Education and Science under the chairmanship of Sir Alan Bullock. London: HMSO.

BURAK, A. 1987. "Russian Speakers." M. Swan and B. Smith, (eds.) *Learner English.* Cambridge: Cambridge University Press.

BURIEL, R. 1984. "Integration with Traditional Mexican-American Culture and Sociocultural Adjustment." J. Martinez, and R. H. Mendoza, (eds.) *Chicano Psychology*, New York: Academic Press.

BURMARK-PARASURAMAN, L. 1982. *Interfacing Two Cultures: Vietnamese and American*. Hayward, California: Office of the Alameda County Superintendent of Schools.

BYERS, P. and H. BYERS. 1972. "Non-Verbal Communication and the Education of Children." C. Cazden, J. Vera, and D. Hymes, (eds.) *Functions of Language in the Classroom*. New York: Teachers College Press.

CABEZAS, A., L. H. SHINAGAWA, and G. KAGUCHI. 1987. "New Inquiries into the Socio-Economic Status of Filipino Americans in California." *Amerasia Journal* 13, no. 1:1–21.

California State Department of Education, 1984. *Studies on Immersion Education: A Collection for United States Educators*. Sacramento: Office of Bilingual Education.

CANALE, M. and M. SWAIN. 1980. "Theoretical Bases of Communicative Approaches to Second Language Teaching and Testing." *Applied Linguistics*. 1:1–47.

CANTONI-HARVEY, G. 1987. *Content-Area Language Instruction: Approaches and Strategies*. Reading, Massachusetts: Addison-Wesley.

CARBO, M., R. DUNN, and K. DUNN. 1986. *Teaching Students to Read through their Individual Learning Styles*. Englewood Cliffs, New Jersey.

CARGILL, C. 1987. "Cultural Bias in Testing ESL." C. Cargill, (ed.). *A TESOL Professional Anthology: Culture*. Lincolnwood, Illinois. National Textbook Co.

CARRILL, C. (ed.) 1987. *A TESOL Professional Anthology: Culture*. Lincolnwood, Illinois: National Textbook Co.

CARTER, T. T. 1970. *Mexican Americans in School: A History of Educational Neglect*. New York: College Entrance Examination Board.

CARTER T. T. and R. D. Segura. 1979. *Mexican Americans in School: A Decade of Change*. New York: College Entrance Examination Board.

CAZDEN, C. 1982. "Four Comments." P. Gillmore, and A. A. Glatthorn, *Children In and Out of School*. Washington, D.C.: Center for Applied Linguistics.

CAZDEN, C. 1986. "ESL Teachers as Language Advocates for Children." P. Rigg and S. D. Enright, (eds.) *Children and ESL: Integrating Perspectives*. Washington D. C.: TESOL.

CAZDEN, C. and D. K. DICKENSON. 1981. "Language in Education: Standardization Versus Cultural Pluralism." C. A. Ferguson and S. Brice-Heath, (eds.) *Language in the USA*. Cambridge: Cambridge University Press.

CAZDEN, C. and V. P. JOHN. 1971. "Learning in American Indian Children." M. L. Wax, S. Diamond and F. O. Gearing, (eds.) *Anthropological Perspectives on Education*. New York: Basic Books.

CAZDEN, C. and E. LEGETT. 1981. "Culturally Responsive Education: Recommendations for Achieving Lau Remedies II." H. Trueba, P. Guthrie and K. Au, (eds.) *Culture and Bilingual Classrooms: Studies in Classroom Ethnography*. Rowley, Massachusetts: Newbury House Publishers.

CELCE-MURCIA, M. and L. MCINTOSH. 1979. *Teaching English as a Second or Foreign Language.* Rowley, Massachusetts: Newbury House Publishers.

CELCE-MURCIA, M. 1985. *Beyond Basics: Issues and Research in TESOL.* Rowley, Massachusetts: Newbury House Publishers.

CHANCE, N. 1987. "Chinese Education in a Village Setting." G. Spindler and L. Spindler, (eds.) *Interpretive Ethnography of Education: At Home and Abroad.* Hillsdale, New Jersey: Lawrence Erlbaum Associates.

CHANG, J. 1987. "Chinese Speakers." M. Swan and B. Smith, (eds.) *Learner English.* Cambridge: Cambridge University Press.

CHENG, L.-R. 1987. *Assessing Asian Language Performance.* Rockville, Maryland: Aspen Publishers, Inc.

CHOMSKY, N. 1979. *Language and Responsibility.* Brighton, England: Harvester Press.

CHOMSKY, N. 1981. *Radical Priorities.* Montreal: Black Rose Books.

CHOY, B.-Y. 1979. *Koreans in America.* Chicago: Nelson-Hall.

CHUNG, C. H. 1988. "The Language Situation of Vietnamese Americans." S. L. McKay and S.-L. Wong, (eds.) *Language Diversity: Problem or Resource?* Cambridge, Massachusetts, Newbury House Publishers, a division of Harper and Row.

COHEN, A. 1985. "Bilingual Education." M. Celce-Murcia, (ed.) *Beyond Basics: Issues and Research in TESOL.* Rowley, Massachusetts: Newbury House Publishers.

COLE, M. 1975. "Culture, Cognition and IQ Testing." *National Elementary Principal,* 54, 49–52.

COLE, R. 1987. "Some Interactional Aspects of ESL Instruction for Preliterates." C. Cargill, (ed.) *A TESOL Professional Anthology: Culture.* Lincolnwood, Illinois: National Textbook Company.

COLEMAN, J. et al. 1966. *Equality of Educational Opportunity.* Washington D.C.: United States Government Printing Office.

COLLIER, J. 1973. *Alaskan Eskimo Education.* New York: Holt, Rinehart and Winston.

COMBS, A. W. 1979. *Myths in Education: Beliefs that Hinder Progress and their Alternatives.* Boston: Allyn and Bacon, Inc.

COMER, J. P. 1986. "Parental Participation in the Schools." *Phi Delta Kappan,* 67(6), 442–446.

Commission on Reading, National Academy of Education, 1985. *Becoming a Nation of Readers: The Report of the Commission on Reading.* Champaign, Illinois: Center for the Study of Reading. University of Illinois.

CONDON, J. 1984. *With Respect to the Japanese: A Guide for Americans.* Yarmouth, Maine: Intercultural Press, Inc.

CONDON, J. 1986. " . . . So Near the United States." J. Valdes, (ed.) *Culture Bound: Bridging the Cultural Gap in Language Teaching.* Cambridge: Cambridge University.

CONDON, J. and F. YOUSEF. 1975. *An Introduction to Intercultural Communication.* Indianapolis: Bobbs-Merrill Educational Publishing Co.

CONKLIN, N. and M. LOURIE. 1983. *A Host of Tongues.* New York: The Free Press.

CORDER, S. P. 1967. "The Significance of Learner's Errors." *International Review of Applied Linguistics* 5:161–170.

CORDOVA, F. 1973. "The Filipino American: There's Always an Identity Crisis." S. Sue and N. Wagner, (eds.) *Asian Americans.* Palo Alto, California: Science and Behavior Books.

CORNELIUS, W. A., L. R. CHAVEZ and J. G. CASTRO. 1982. "Mexican Immigrants and Southern California: A Summary of Current Knowledge." *Working Papers in U.S. - Mexican Studies.* (No. 36) La Jolla, California: Center for U.S. Mexican Studies, University of California, San Diego.

CORTES, C. 1974. "Revising the *All-American Soul Course:* A Bicultural Avenue to Educational Reform." A. Castañeda, M. Ramirez III, C. Cortes and M. Barrera, (eds.) *Mexican Americans and Educational Change.* New York: Arno Press Inc., 314–340.

CORTES, C. 1986. "The Education of Language Minority Students: A Contextual Interaction Model." *Beyond Language: Social and Cultural Factors in Schooling Language Minority Students.* California State Department of Education. Sacramento, California: Evaluation, Dissemination and Assessment Center, California State University, Los Angeles.

COX, B. and M. RAMIREZ, III. 1981. "Cognitive Styles: Implications for Multiethnic Education." J. Banks, (ed.) *Education in the 1980's.* Washington D.C.: National Education Association.

CRAFT, M. 1984. (ed.) *Education and Cultural Pluralism.* Philadelphia, Pennsylvania: The Falmer Press.

CRANDALL, J. (ed.) 1987. *ESL through Content-Area Instruction.* New Jersey: Prentice-Hall.

CRANDALL, J. A., J. DIAS, R. C. GINGRAS and T. K. HARRIS. 1981. *Teaching the Spanish-Speaking Child: A Practical Guide.* Washington, D.C.: Center for Applied Linguistics.

CRAWFORD, J. 1989. *Bilingual Education: History, Politics, Theory and Practice.* Trenton, New Jersey: Crane Publishing Co.

CULLINAN, B. and S. FITZGERALD. 1985. *Background Information Bulletin on the Use of Readability Formulae; Joint Statement of the President, International Reading Association and President, National Council of Teachers of English.* Urbana, Illinois: National Council of Teachers of English.

CUMMINS, J. 1979. "Linguistic Interdependence and Educational Development in Bilingual Children." *Review of Educational Research* 49:2, 222–251.

CUMMINS, J. 1981. "Age on Arrival and Immigrant Second Language Learning in Canada: A Reassessment." *Applied Linguistics,* 2, 132–49.

CUMMINS, J. 1981. "The Role of Primary Language Development in Promoting Educational Success for Language Minority Children." California State Department of Education, *Schooling Language Minority Students: A Theoretical Framework.* Los Angeles: Evaluation, Dissemination and Assessment Center.

CUMMINS, J. 1984. *Bilingualism and Special Education: Issues in Assessment and Pedagogy.* Clevedon, England: Multilingual Matters.

CUMMINS, J. 1984. "Linguistic Minorities and Multicultural Policy in Canada." J. Edwards, (ed.) *Linguistic Minorities, Policies and Pluralism.* London: Academic Press.

CUMMINS, J. 1986. "Empowering Minority Students: A Framework for Intervention." *Harvard Educational Review,* 56, pp. 18–36.

CUMMINS, J. 1988. "Multicultural to Anti-Racist Education: An Analysis of Programmes and Policies in Ontario." T. Skutnabb-Kangas and J. Cummins, (eds.) *Minority Education.* Clevedon, England: Multilingual Matters.

CUMMINS, J. 1988. "Second Language Acquisition Within Bilingual Education Programs." L. Beebe, (ed.) *Issues in Second Language Acquisition.* New York: Harper and Row.

CUMMINS, J. 1989. *Empowering Language Minority Students.* Sacramento: California Association for Bilingual Education.

CUMMINS, J. and M. SWAIN, 1986. *Bilingualism in Education.* London: Longman.

CURTAIN, H. A. 1986. "Integrating Language and Content Instruction." *ERIC/CLL News Bulletin,* 9(2), 1, 10–11.

CURTIS, J. 1988. "Parents, Schools and Racism: Bilingual Education in a Northern California Town." T. Skutnabb-Kangas, and J. Cummins, (eds.) *Minority Education.* Clevedon, England: Multilingual Matters.

DAMEN, L. 1987. *Culture Learning: The Fifth Dimension in the Language Classroom.* Reading, Massachusetts: Addison-Wesley.

DARDER, A. 1989. *Critical Pedagogy, Cultural Democracy, and Biculturalism: The Foundation for a Critical Theory of Bicultural Education.* Unpublished Ph.D. dissertation. Claremont.

DAVIDSON, L. and P. DAVIDSON. 1989. "Supervising with a Multicultural Perspective: Adding a New Dimension to Clinical Supervision in a Pre-Service Program." Unpublished manuscript. San Luis Obispo, California: Polytechnic State University.

DAVIES, D., (ed.) 1981. *Communities and their Schools.* New York: McGraw-Hill.

DAY, R. 1982. "Children's Attitudes Toward Languages." E. B. Ryan and H. Giles, *Attitudes toward Language Variation.* London: Edward Arnold.

DE AVILA, E. A. and S. E. DUNCAN. 1980. *Finding Out/Descubrimiento.* Corte Madera, California: Linguametrics Group.

DELGADO-GAITAN, C. 1987. "Parent Perceptions of School: Supportive Environments for Children." H. T. Trueba (ed.), *Success or Failure? Learning and the Language Minority Student.* New York: Harper and Row.

DELGADO-GAITAN, C. 1987. "Traditions and Transitions in the Learning Process of Mexican Children: An Ethnographic View." G. Spindler and L. Spindler, (eds.) *Interpretive Ethnography of Education at Home and Abroad.* Hillsdale, New Jersey: Lawrence Erlbaum Associates.

DEMOS, G. D. 1962. "Attitudes of Mexican-American and Anglo American Groups Toward Education." *Journal of Social Psychology.* 57, 249–256.

DEYHLE, D. 1987. "Learning Failure: Tests as Gatekeepers and the Culturally Different Child." H. Trueba, (ed.) *Success or Failure? Learning and
the Language Minority Student.* New York: Harper and Row.

DIAZ, S. 1983. *Cognitive Style Influence: Pervasive or Specific?* Unpublished
Ph.D. Dissertation. Harvard University.

DIAZ, S., L. MOLL and H. MEHAN. 1986. "Sociocultural Resources in Instruction: A Context-Specific Approach." In *Beyond Language: Social and Cultural Factors in Schooling Language Minority Students.* Bilingual Education Office. California State Department of Education. California State
University, Los Angeles: Evaluation, Dissemination and Assessment Center.

DOLSON, D. P. 1985. "Bilingualism and Scholastic Performance: The Literature Revisited." *NABE Journal* 10:1, 1–35.

DONOGHE, M. R. and J. F. KUNKLE. 1979. *Second Languages in Primary
Education.* Rowley, Massachusetts: Newbury House Publishers.

DREW, C. J. 1973. "Criterion-Referenced and Norm-Referenced Assessment
of Minority Group Children." T. Oakland and B. N. Phillips, (eds.) *Assessing Minority Group Children.* A Special Issue of *Journal of School Psychology,* pp. 323–329.

DULAY, H. and M. BURT. 1973. "Should We Teach Children Syntax?" *Language Learning* 23: 45–258.

DULAY, H. C. and M. K. BURT. 1977. "Remarks on Creativity in Second
Language Acquisition." M. K. Burt, H. C. Dulay and M. Finchochiaro, (eds.)
Viewpoints on English as a Second Language. New York: Regents.

DULAY, H. and M. BURT 1978. "From Research to Method in Bilingual Education." J. E. Alatis, (ed.) *Georgetown University Roundtable on Languages
and Linguistics. 1978: International Dimensions of Bilingual Education.*
Washington D.C.: Georgetown University Press.

DULAY, H., M. BURT and S. KRASHEN. 1982. *Language Two.* New York:
Oxford University Press.

DUMONT, R. V., JR. 1972. "Learning English and How to be Silent: Studies in
Sioux and Cherokee Classroom." C. Cazden, J. Vera and D. Hymes, (eds.)
Function of Language in the Classroom. New York: Teachers College
Press.

EDELSKY, C., K. DRAPER and K. SMITH. 1983. "Hookin' 'em in at the Start of
the School in a Whole Language Classroom." *Anthropology and Education
Quarterly,* 14(4): 257–81.

ELKIND, D. 1967. "Egocentrism in Adolescence." *Child Development* 38:
1025–34.

ELLIS, R. 1986. *Understanding Second Language Acquisition.* Oxford: Oxford University Press.

ENRIGHT, D. S. 1986. "*Use Everything You Have to Teach English:* Providing Useful Input to Young Language Learners." P. Rigg and D. S. Enright,
(eds.) *Children and ESL: Integrating Perspectives.* Washington, D.C.:
TESOL.

ENRIGHT, D. S. and B. GOMEZ. 1985. "PRO-ACT: Six Strategies for Organizing Peer Interaction in Elementary Classrooms." *NABE Journal*, 9(3):431–53.

ENRIGHT, D. S. and M. L. MCCLOSKEY. 1988. *Integrating English: Developing English Language and Literacy in the Multilingual Classroom.* Reading, Massachusetts: Addison-Wesley.

EPSTEIN, J. L. 1985. "Home and School Connections in Schools of the Future: Implications of Research on Parent Involvement." *Peabody Journal of Education*, 66(2), 18–41.

ERICKSON, F. 1982. *The Counselor as Gatekeeper: Social Interaction in Interviews.* New York: Academic Press.

ERICKSON, R. and F. CUCELOGLU. 1987. A report on needs assessment survey of Vietnamese students at California State University, Fullerton.

EVANS, L. 1987. "The Challenge of a Multicultural Elementary ESL Class: Insights and Suggestions." C. Carrill, (ed.) *A TESOL Professional Anthology: Culture.* Lincolnwood, Illinois: National Textbook Co.

FARR, M. and H. DANIELS. 1986. *Diversity and Writing Instruction.* New York: ERIC Clearinghouse on Reading and Communication Skills. National Council of Teachers of English.

FASOLD, R. 1984. *The Sociolinguistics of Society.* New York: Basil Blackwell.

FAY, B. 1987. *Critical Social Science.* London: Cornell University Press.

FINDLEY, C. 1986. "Interactive Videodisc: A Powerful New Technology in Language Learning. *TESOL Newsletter*, 20(1), Supplement (3), 10–11.

FINNEGAN, E. and N. BRESNIER. 1989. *Language: Its Structure and Use.* San Diego: Harcourt Brace Jovanovich.

FISHMAN, J. 1981. "Language Policy: Past, Present, and Future." C. Ferguson and S. B. Heath, (eds.) *Language in the USA.* Cambridge: Cambridge University Press, 516–526.

FISHMAN, J. 1989. *Language and Ethnicity in Minority Sociolinguistic Perspective.* Clevedon, England: Multilingual Matters.

FITZPATRICK, J. 1987. *Puerto Rican Americans: The Meaning of Migration to the Mainland.* Englewood Cliffs, New Jersey: Prentice Hall.

FLORES, B. and E. GARCIA. 1984. "A Collaborative Learning and Teaching Experience Using Journal Writing." *Journal of the National Association for Bilingual Education* 8(2), 67–83.

FLORES, B. and E. HERNANDEZ. 1988. "A Bilingual Kindergartner's Sociopsychogenesis of Literacy and Biliteracy." *Dialogue*, 5(3), 2–3.

FRECHETTE, E. 1987. "Some Aspects of Saudi Culture." C. Cargill, (ed.) *A TESOL Professional Anthology: Culture.* Lincolnwood, Illinois: National Textbook Company.

FREIRE, P. 1970. *Pedagogy of the Oppressed.* New York: Seabury Press.

FREIRE, P. 1973. *Education for Critical Consciousness.* New York: Seabury.

FREIRE, P. 1975. "Banking Education." H. Giroux, and D. Purpel, (eds.) *The Hidden Curriculum and Moral Education: Deception or Discovery?* South Hadley, Massachusetts: Bergin and Garvey.

FREIRE, P. 1983. "Banking Education." H. Giroux, and D. Purpel, (eds.) *The*

Hidden Curriculum and Moral Education: Deception and Liberation.
South Hadley, Massachusetts: Bergin and Garvey.

FREIRE, P. 1985. *The Politics of Education.* Boston: Bergin and Garvey.

FREIRE, P. 1985. *The Politics of Liberation: Culture, Power and Liberation.*
South Hadley, Massachusetts: Bergin and Garvey.

FREIRE, P. and D. MACEDO, 1987. *Literacy: Reading the Word and the World.* Boston: Bergin and Garvey.

FROMM, E. and M. MACCOBY, 1970. *Social Character in a Mexican Village.*
Englewood Cliffs, New Jersey: Prentice-Hall.

GAARDER, A. B. 1977. *Bilingual Schooling and the Survival of Spanish in the United States.* Rowley, Massachusetts: Newbury House Publishers.

GALANG, R. 1988. "The Language Situation of Filipino Americans." S. L. McKay and S.-L. Wong, (eds.) *Language Diversity: Problem or Resource?* Cambridge, Massachusetts, Newbury House Publishers, a division of Harper and Row.

GARCIA, E. E. and E. H. GARCIA. 1988. "Journals in Support of Biliteracy." *Dialogue,* 5, (3), 4–5.

GARCIA, R. L. 1982. *Teaching in a Pluralistic Society.* New York: Harper and Row.

GARDNER, R. C. and W. E. LAMBERT. 1972. *Attitudes and Motivation in Second Language Learning.* Rowley, Massachusetts: Newbury House Publishers.

GARDNER, R. W., B. ROBEY and P. C. SMITH. 1985. *Asian Americans: Growth, Change and Diversity.* Population Bulletin 40:4.

GASS, S. and L. SELINKER, (eds.) 1983. *Transfer in Second Language Acquisition.* Harper and Row: Newbury House Publishers.

GAY, G. and R. ABRAHAMS. 1983. "Does the Pot Melt, Boil or Brew? Black Children and White Assessment Procedures." T. Oakland and B. N. Phillips, (eds.) *Assessing Minority Group Children.* A Special Issue of *Journal of School Psychology,* pp. 330–340.

GIBSON, M. A. 1987. "Punjabi Immigrants in an American High School." G. Spindler and L. Spindler, (eds.) *Interpretive Ethnography of Education at Home and Abroad.* Hillsdale: New Jersey: Lawrence Erlbaum Associates.

GILES, H. 1979. "Ethnicity Markers in Speech." K. Scherer and H. Giles, (eds.) *Social Markers in Speech.* Cambridge: Cambridge University Press.

GIROUX, H. 1981. *Ideology, Culture and the Process of Schooling.* Philadelphia: Temple University Press.

GIROUX, H. 1983. *Theory and Resistance in Education.* Boston: Bergin and Garvey.

GIROUX, H. 1988. *Schooling and the Struggle for Public Life.* Minneapolis: University of Minnesota Press.

GIROUX, H. 1988. *Teachers as Intellectuals.* Boston: Bergin and Garvey.

GLASSER, W. 1969. *Schools without Failure.* New York: Harper and Row.

GLEASON, H. 1961. *An Introduction to Descriptive Linguistics.* New York: Holt, Rinehart and Winston.

GOLLNICK, D. M. and P. C. CHINN. 1986. *Multicultural Education in a Pluralistic Society.* Columbus, Ohio: Charles Merrill.

GOODENOUGH, W. 1964. *Explanations in Cultural Anthropology.* New York: McGraw Hill.

GOODENOUGH, W. 1971. *Culture, Language and Society.* Reading, Massachusetts: Addison-Wesley Publishing Co.

GOODLAD, J. I. 1984. *A Place Called School: Prospects for the Future.* New York: McGraw-Hill.

GOODMAN, K. S. 1967. "Reading: A Psycholinguistic Guessing Game." *Journal of the Reading Specialist,* 4, 126–135.

GOULD, S. J. 1981. *The Mismeasure of Man.* New York: W. W. Norton and Company.

GRANT, C. A. 1981. "The Community and Multiethnic Education." J. A. Banks, (ed.) *Education in the 80's: Multiethnic Education.* Washington D.C.: National Education Association.

GRANT, C. A., C. E. SLEETER and J. E. ANDERSON. 1986. "The Literature on Multicultural Education: Review and Analysis." *Educational Studies,* 37(2):97–118.

GRAVE, D. 1983. *Writing: Teachers and Children at Work.* Exeter, New Hampshire: Heinemann Educational Books.

GRAVES, N. B. and T. D. GRAVES. 1983. "The Cultural Context of Prosocial Development: An Ecological Model." D. Bridgeman, (ed.) *The Nature of Prosocial Development: Interdisciplinary Theories and Strategies.* New York: Academic Press.

GREBLER, L., J. W. MOORE and R. GUZMAN. 1970. *The Mexican American People: The Nation's Second Largest Minority.* New York: Free Press.

GRISWOLD DEL CASTILLO, R. 1984, *La Familia.* Notre Dame, Indiana: University of Notre Dame Press.

GUMPERZ, J., I. JUPP and C. ROBERTS. 1979. *Crosstalk: A Study of Cross-Cultural Communication.* England: National Centre for Industrial Language Training.

HAKUTA, K. 1986. *The Mirror of Language: The Debate on Bilingualism.* New York: Basic Books.

HALL, E. T. 1959. *The Silent Language.* Garden City, New York: Doubleday and Company, Inc.

HALL, E. T. 1966. *The Hidden Dimension.* New York: Doubleday.

HANVEY, R. 1979. "Cross-Cultural Awareness." E. Smith and L. Luce, (eds.) *An Attainable Global Perspective.* New York: Center for Global Perspectives.

HARRISON, P. A. 1983. *Behaving Brazilian: A Comparison of Brazilian and North American Social Behavior.* Rowley, Massachusetts: Newbury House Publishers.

HARTNETT, D. 1985. "Cognitive Style and Second Language Learning." M. Celce-Murcia, (ed.) *Beyond Basics: Issues and Research in TESOL.* Rowley, Massachusetts: Newbury House Publishers.

HATCH, E. 1983. *Psycholinguistics.* Rowley, Massachusetts: Newbury House Publishers.

HATCH, E., V. FLASHNER and L. HUNT. 1987. "The Experience Model and Language Teaching." R. Day, (ed.) *Talking to Learn: Conversation in Second Language Acquisition.* Rowley, Massachusetts: Newbury House Publishers, 5–22.

HEALD-TAYLOR, G. 1989. *Whole Language Strategies for ESL Students.* San Diego: Dormac, Inc.

HEATH, S. B. 1982. "Ethnography in Education: Defining the Essentials." P. Gilmore, and A. A. Glatthorn, (eds.) *Children In and Out of School.* Washington, D.C.: The Center for Applied Linguistics.

HEATH, S. B. 1982. "Questioning at Home and at School: A Comparative Study." G. Spindler, (ed.) *Doing the Ethnography of Schooling: Educational Anthropology in Action.* New York: Holt, Rinehart and Winston.

HEATH, S. B. 1982. "What No Bedtime Story Means: Narrative Skills at Home and at School." *Language in Society,* 11, 49–76.

HEATH, S. B. 1983. *Ways with Words: Language, Life and Work in Communities and Classrooms.* Cambridge: Cambridge University Press.

HEATH, S. B. 1986. "Sociocultural Contexts of Language Development." In *Beyond Language: Social and Cultural Factors in Schooling Language Minority Students.* California State Department of Education. Sacramento, California: Evaluation, Dissemination and Assessment Center, California State University, Los Angeles.

HEATH, S. B. and A. BRANSCOMBE. 1985. "Intelligent Writing in an Audience Community: Teacher, Students and Researcher." S. W. Freedman, (ed.) *The Acquisition of Written Language: Revision and Response.* Norwood, New Jersey: Ablex.

HELLER, C. 1966. *Mexican-American Youth: Forgotten Youth at the Crossroads.* New York: Random House.

HIRSCH, A. 1967. "Attitudinal Differences Between Vietnamese and Americans." Text of Lecture 1967 Hawaii: East-West Center Library Collection.

HODGKINSON, H. L. 1983. "Guess Who's Coming to College." *Academe* 69, 13–20.

HOSKINS, M. W. 1971. *Building Rapport with the Vietnamese.* United States Government Publication. (Reprinted by Supt. of Schools, Dept. of Education, San Diego County, California)

HSIA, J. 1988. *Asian Americans in Higher Education and at Work.* Hillsdale, New Jersey: Lawrence Erlbaum.

HSU, F. 1949. *Under the Ancestors' Shadow.* London: Routledge and Kegan Paul.

HUHR, W. M. and K. C. KIM. 1984. *Korean Immigrants in America.* Cranbury, New Jersey: Fairleigh Dickinson University Press.

HYMES, D. 1974. *Foundations in Sociolinguistics.* Philadelphia: University of Pennsylvania Press.

HYMES, D., 1981. "Ethnographic Monitoring." H. T. Trueba, G. P. Guthrie and K. Au, (eds.) *Culture and the Bilingual Classroom - Studies in Classroom Ethnography.* Rowley, Massachusetts: Newbury House Publishers.

HYUN, P., (ed.) 1987. *Introducing Korea*. Republic of Korea: Jungwoo-sa, originally published in 1967.

Interagency Task Force on Indochinese Refugees. 1975. *A Guide to Two Cultures*. Publication 8. Washington D.C.

IRA (Intercultural Relations Institute). 1982. *Take Two*. Videotape. Palo Alto, California.

IWATAKE, S. 1978. "Bridging the Asian Cultural Gap." D. Ilyin and T. Tragardh, (eds.) *Classroom Practices in Adult ESL*. Washington, D.C.: TESOL.

JACKSON, G. and C. COSCA. 1974. "The Inequality of Educational Opportunity in the Southwest: An Observational Study of Ethnically Mixed Classrooms." *American Educational Research Journal*. 10, Summer 1974:219–229.

JENSEN, A. 1973. *Educability and Group Differences*. New York: Harper and Row.

JOHN-STEINER, V. and H. OSTERREICH. 1975. *Learning Styles among Pueblo Children*. Final Report HEW: NEG-00-3-0074. Albuquerque, University of New Mexico.

JORDAN, C. 1985. "Translating Culture: From Ethnographic Information to Educational Program." *Anthropology and Education Quarterly*, 6:105–23.

JORDAN, C. et al. 1978. *A Multidisciplinarian Approach to Research in Education: The Kamehameha Early Education Project*. Honolulu: The Kamehameha Early Education Project.

JORDAN, I. 1980. "Meeting the Challenge—Serving Migrant Children." In *A Compendium of Policy Papers*. House Committee of Education and Labor. Congress of the United States, pp. 675–679.

KAGAN, S. 1977. "Social Motives and Behaviors of Mexican-American and Anglo-American Children." J. L. Martinez, (ed.) *Chicano Psychology*. New York: Academic Press.

KAGAN, S. 1981. "Ecology and the Acculturation of Cognitive and Social Styles Among Mexican American Children." *Hispanic Journal of Behavioral Sciences*. 3 (2), 111–144.

KAGAN, S. 1984. "Interpreting Chicano Cooperativeness: Methodological and Theoretical Considerations." J. L. Martinez and R. H. Mendoza, (eds.) *Chicano Psychology*, 2nd Ed. New York: Academic Press.

KAGAN, S. 1986. "Cooperative Learning and Sociocultural Factors in Schooling." In *Beyond Language: Social and Cultural Factors in Schooling Language Minority Students*. California State Department of Education. Sacramento, California: Evaluation, Dissemination and Assessment Center, California State University, Los Angeles.

KAGAN, S. 1989. *Cooperative Learning: Resources for Teachers*. San Juan Capistrano: Resources for Teachers.

KAGAN, S. and R. BURIEL. 1977. "Field Dependence-Independence and Mexican-American Culture and Education." J. L. Martinez, Jr. (ed.) *Chicano Psychology*. New York: Academic Press.

KALTON, M. C. 1985. "Korean Ideas and Values." In *Philips Jaison Memorial*

Papers. 1–116. Elkins Park, Pennsylvania: Philip Jaison Memorial Foundation.

KAPLAN, R. and J. K. TSE. 1982. "The Language Situation in Taiwan." *The Linguistic Reporter* 25:2, 1–5.

KELLERMAN, E. 1979. "Transfer and Non-Transfer: Where Are We Now?" *Studies in Second Language Acquisition* 2:37–57.

KENDALL, F. E. 1983. *Diversity in the Classroom.* New York: Teachers College Press.

KEOGH, B. K., M. F. WELLES and A. WEISS. 1972. *Field Dependence-Independence and Problem-Solving Styles of Preschool Children. Technical Report.* Los Angeles: University of California.

KIM, B.-L. 1980. *The Korean American Child at School and at Home.* Washington, D.C.: Government Printing Office.

KIM, B.-L. 1988. "The Language Situation of Korean Americans." S. L. McKay and S.-L. Wong, (eds.) *Language Diversity: Problem or Resource?* Cambridge, Massachusetts, Newbury House Publishers, a division of Harper and Row.

KIM, B.-L., M. SAWDEY and J. MEIHOFER. 1980. *Attitudes and Adaptations of Korean Immigrant Children.* Chicago: Final Report to Asian American Health Center.

KIM, H.-C., (ed.) 1977. *The Korean Diaspora.* Santa Barbara, California: Clio Press.

KIM, Y. Y. 1988. *Communication and Cross-Cultural Adaptation.* Clevedon, England: Multilingual Matters.

KITANO, H. L. and R. DANIELS, 1988. *Asian Americans: Emerging Minorities.* Englewood Cliffs, New Jersey: Prentice Hall.

KLEIN, Z. and Y. ESHEL, 1980. *Integrating Jerusalem Schools.* New York: Academic Press.

KOGAN, N. 1971. "Educational Implications of Cognitive Styles." G. S. Lesser, (ed.) *Psychology and Educational Practice.* Glenview, Illinois: Scott, Foresman.

Korean Overseas Information Service. 1986. *Focus on Korea: This is Korea.* Seoul: Samsung Moonwha Printing Company.

Korean Overseas Information Service. 1987. *Korean Handbook.* Seoul: Seoul Publishing Company.

KRASHEN, S. D. 1977. "The Left Hemisphere." M. C. Wittrock, (ed.) *The Human Brain.* Englewood Cliffs, New Jersey: Prentice-Hall.

KRASHEN, S. D. 1981. "The Fundamental Pedagogical Principle in Second Language Teaching." *Studia Linguistica.* 35(1–2) 50–70.

KRASHEN, S. D. 1981. *Second Language Acquisition and Second Language Learning.* Oxford: Pergamon Press.

KRASHEN, S. D. 1982. *Principles and Practice in Second Language Acquisition.* New York: Pergamon Press.

KRASHEN, S. D. 1983. "Newmark's *Ignorance Hypothesis* and Current Second Language Acquistiion Theory." S. Gass and L. Selinker, (eds.) *Lan-*

guage Transfer in Language Learning. Rowley, Massachusetts: Newbury House Publishers, 135–153.

KRASHEN, S. D. 1984. "Immersion: Why It Works and What It has Taught Us." *Language in Society,* (12), 61–64.

KRASHEN, S. D. 1985. *The Input Hypothesis: Issues and Implications.* New York: Longman.

KRASHEN, S. D. 1985. *Insights and Inquiries.* Hayward, California: Alemany Press.

KRASHEN, S. D. 1987. "Applications of Psycholinguistic Research to the Classroom." M. H. Long and J. Richards, (eds.) *Methodology in TESOL: A Book of Readings.* New York: Newbury House Publishers, a division of Harper and Row. Originally appeared in 1983 in C. J. James, (ed.) *Practical Applications of Research in Foreign Language Teaching.* Skokie, Illinois: National Textbook Co., 51–66.

KRASHEN, S. D. and D. BIBER. 1988. *On Course: Bilingual Education's Success in California.* Sacramento: California Association of Bilingual Education.

KRASHEN, S. D. and T. TERRELL. 1983. *The Natural Approach.* New York: Pergamon Press.

KRASHEN, S. D., M. LONG, and R. SCARCELLA. 1979. Age, rate and eventual attainment in second language acquisition. *TESOL Quarterly* 13:573–82.

KREEFT, J., R. W. SHUY, J. STATON, L. REED and R. MORROY. 1984. *Dialogue Writing: Analysis of Student-Teacher Interactive Writing in the Learning of English as a Second Language.* Washington, D.C.: Center for Applied Linguistics.

KROEBER, A. L. and C. KLUCKHOLN. 1954. "Culture: The Concept of Culture." R. Linton, (ed.) *Science of Man in the World Crisis.* New York: Columbia University Press.

LABOV, W. 1972. *Language in the Inner City.* Philadelphia: University of Pennsylvania Press.

LABOV, W. 1972. "The Logic of Nonstandard English." P. P. Giglioli, (ed.) *Language and Social Context.* London, England: Penguin Books.

LADO, R. 1964. *Language Teaching: A Scientific Approach.* New York: McGraw Hill.

LAMBERT, W. 1967. "A Social Psychology of Bilingualism." *The Journal of Social Issues.* 23:91–109.

LAMBERT, W. E. 1981. "Bilingualism and Second Language Acquisition." *Annals of New York Academy Sciences.* 379: 9–22.

LAOSA, L. M. 1982. "School, Occupation, Culture and Family: The Impact of Parental Schooling on the Parent-Child Relationship." *Journal of Education Psychology.* 74(6), 791–827.

LAOSA, L. 1982. "Sociocultural Diversity in Modes of Family Interaction." R. W. Henderson, (ed.) *Parent-Child Interaction: Theory, Research and Prospect.* New York: Academic Press.

LAPIDES, J. 1980. "Working with Parents and Preschoolers." M. J. Fine, (ed.) *Handbook on Parent Education.* New York: Academic Press.

BIBLIOGRAPHY

LARSEN-FREEMAN, D. 1986. *Techniques and Principles in Language Teach ing.* New York: Oxford University Press.

LEE, K. 1982. Students from Korea. In *Asian Bilingual Education Teache Handbook.* Cambridge, Massachusetts: Evaluation, Dissemination and As sessment, Lesley College.

LEGARRETA, D. 1979. "The Effects of Program Models on Language Acquisi- tion by Spanish Speaking Children." *TESOL Quarterly,* 13, 521–534.

LEVINE, D. 1982. "The Educational Backgrounds of Saudi Arabian and Alge- rian Students." L. Samovar and R. Porter, (eds.) *Intercultural Communica- tion: A Reader,* third edition, Belmont, California: Wadsworth.

LEVINE, E. S. and K. E. BARATZ. 1979. "Comparative Child-Rearing Atti- tudes Among Chicano, Anglo, and Black Parents." *Journal of Behavioral Sciences,* 1 (2), 165–178.

LI, G. R. 1982. *The Vietnamese: The Challenge of Sponsorship.* New York, New York: World Relief Corporation—Refugee Services Devision.

LINDFORS, J. 1987. *Children's Language and Learning,* second edition. En- glewood Cliffs, New Jersey: Prentice Hall.

LINDHOLM, K. J. 1987. *Directory of Bilingual Immersion Programs: Two- Way Bilingual Education for Language Minority and Majority Students.* Educational Report Series, No. 8.

LITTLEWOOD, W. 1981. *Communicative Language Teaching: An Introduc- tion.* Cambridge: Cambridge University Press.

LOMBANA, J. H. 1983. *Home-School Partnerships: Guidelines and Strate- gies for Educators.* New York: Grune and Stratton, Inc.

LONG, M. H. 1981. "Input, Interaction and Second Language Acquisition." H. Winitz, (ed.) *Native Language and Foreign Language Acquisition.* Annals of the New York Academy of Sciences 379, 259–278.

LONG, M. H. 1983. "Does Second Language Instruction Make a Difference? A Review of Research." *TESOL Quarterly* 17, 3, 359–382.

LONG, M. H. 1983. "Native Speaker Non-Native Speaker Conversation in the Second Language Classroom." M. A. Clarke and J. Handscombe, (eds.) *On TESOL '82: Pacific Perspectives on Language Learning and Teaching.* Washington, D.C.: TESOL.

LONG, M. H. 1988. "Instructed Interlanguage Development." L. Beebe, (ed.) *Issues in Second Language Acquisition.* New York: Harper and Row.

LONG, M. H., L. ADAMS, M. MCLEAN and F. CASTANOS. 1976. "Doing Things with Words: Verbal Interaction in Lockstep and Small Group Classroom Situations." R. Crymes and J. Fanselow, (eds.) *On TESOL '76.* Washing- ton, D.C.: TESOL.

LONG, M. H. and P. A. PORTER. 1985. "Group Work, Interlanguage Talk, and Second Language Acquisition." *TESOL Quarterly,* 19(2):207–28.

LONG, M. H. and J. RICHARDS. 1987. *Methodology in TESOL: A Handbook of Readings.* New York: Harper and Row.

LOPEZ, D. E. 1982. *Language Maintenance and Shift in the United States Today: The Basic Patterns and Their Social Implications.* Volume IV: *Asian Languages.* Los Alamitos, California: National Center for Bilingual Research, 1–28.

BIBLIOGRAPHY

'Bilingual Education and the Melting Pot: Gettting Burned." *Issues Humanities Essays:* 5. Illinois Humanities Council, , Illinois.

1987. "The Hidden Curriculum of Papago Teachers: American rategies for Mitigating Cultural Discontinuity in Early Schooling." dle and L. Spindler (eds.) *Interpretive Ethnography of Education at and Abroad.* Hillsdale, New Jersey: Lawrence Erlbaum Associates.

, A. 1987. "Xanadu *A miracle of rare device:* The Teaching of English hina." J. M. Valdes, (ed.) *Culture Bound.* Cambridge: Cambridge Uni- rsity Press.

LLER, J. P. 1929. *Cooperation and Competition: An Experimental Study in Motivation.* New York: Teachers College, Columbia University.

MCGROARTY, M. 1988. "Second Language Acquisition Theory Relevant to Language Minorities: Cummins, Krashen and Schumann." S. McKay and S. L. Wong, (eds.) 1988. *Language Diversity: Problem or Resource?* Cambridge: Harper and Row Publishers.

MCLAREN, P. 1988. *Life in Schools: An Introduction to Critical Pedagogy in the Foundations of Education.* New York: Longman.

MCLAUGHLIN, B. 1987. *Theories of Second Language Learning.* London: Edward Arnold.

MEADOWCROFT, J. and D. E. FOLEY, 1978. "Life in Changing Multi-Ethnic School: Anglo Teachers and Their Views of Mexican Children." H. La-Fontaine, B. Persky and L. Golubchick, (eds.) *Bilingual Education.* Wayne, New Jersey: Avery Publishing.

MEHAN, H. 1973. "Assessing Children's School Performance." *Recent Sociology.* 5:240–263.

MEHAN, H., B. MILLER-SOUVINEY and M. M. RIEL, 1984. "Knowledge of Text Editing and the Development of Literacy Skills." *Language Arts,* 65, 154–159.

MEHAN, H., A. HERTWECK, and J. L. MEIHLS. 1986. *Handicapping the Handicapped: Decision Making in Students' Educational Careers.* Palo Alto: Stanford University Press.

MERCER, J. 1973. *Labelling the Mentally Retarded.* Los Angeles: University of California Press.

MEREDITH, W. and S. CRAMER. 1982. "Hmong Refugees in Nebraska." B. Downing and D. Olney, (eds.) *The Hmong in the West: Observations and Reports.* Minneapolis, Minnesota: Southeast Asian Refugee Studies Project, Center for Urban and Regional Affairs, University of Minnesota.

MERCER, J. R. 1981. "Testing and Assessment Practices in Multiethnic Education." J. A. Banks, (ed.) *Education in the 80's: Multiethnic Education.* Washington, D.C.: National Education Association of the United States.

MICHAELS, S. 1981. "*Sharing Time:* Children's Narrative Styles and Differential Access to Literacy." *Language in Society* 10:423–43.

MILROY, J. and L. MILROY. 1985. *Authority in Language: Investigating Language Prescription and Standardization.* London: Routledge and Kegan Paul.

BIBLIOGRAPHY

MOHAN, B. 1986. *Language and Content*. Reading, Massachusetts: Addis Wesley.

MOHATT, G. and F. ERICKSON. 1981. "Cultural Differences in Teachii Styles in an Odawa School: A Sociolinguistic Approach." H. Trueba, 1 Guthrie and K. Au, (eds.) *Culture and the Bilingual Classroom: Studies ii Classroom Ethnography*. Rowley, Massachusetts: Newbury House Publishers.

MONK, B. and A. BURAK, 1987. "Russian Speakers." In *Learner English*. M. Swan and B. Smith, (eds.) Cambridge: Cambridge University Press.

MONTGOMERY, G. T. and S. OROZCO, 1984. "Validation of a Measure of Acculturation for Mexican-Americans." *Hispanic Journal of Behavioral Sciences* 6 (1), 53–63.

MORAIN, G. 1977. "The Cultural Component of the Methods Course." J. F. Fanselow and R. L. Light, (eds.) *Bilingual ESOL and Foreign Language Teacher Preparation: Models, Practices, Issues*. Washington, D.C.: TESOL.

MOSKOWITZ, G. 1978. *Caring and Sharing in the Foreign Language Class*. Rowley, Massachusetts: Newbury House Publishers.

MOSSE, G. L. 1966. *Nazi Culture: Intellectual, Cultural and Social Life in the Third Reich*. London: W. H. Allen.

NAKANO, F. 1982. "Asian-American Profile." In *Asian Bilingual Education Teacher Handbook*. Cambridge, Massachusetts: Evaluation, Dissemination and Assessment, Lesley College.

National Assessment of Education Progress. 1977. *Hispanic Student Achievement in Five Learning Areas: 1971–75*. Washington, D.C.: United States Government Printing Office.

National Assessment of Educational Progress. 1983. *Reading, Science and Mathematics Trends: A Closer Look. Denver: Education Commission of the States*. Washington, D.C.: United States Government Printing Office.

National Assessment of Educational Progress. 1983. *Students from Homes in which English Is Not the Dominant Language: Who are They and How Well Do They Read?* No. 11-R-50. Denver: Education Commission of the States.

The National Council of Teachers of English. 1974. Conference on College Composition and Communication.

New Zealand Department of Education. 1988. *New Voices: Second Language Learning and Teaching. A Handbook for Primary Teachers*. Wellington: Department of Education.

NINE-CURT, C. 1976. *Non-verbal Communication in Puerto Rico*. Cambridge, Massachusetts: National Assessment and Dissemination Center for Bilingual/Bicultural Education.

OCHS, E. 1983. "Cultural Dimensions of Language Acquisition." E. Ochs and B. B. Schieffelin, (eds.) *Acquiring Conversational Competence*. London: Routledge and Kegan Paul.

OCHS, E. 1986. Introduction. B. Schieffelin and E. Ochs, (eds.) *Language Socialization across Cultures*. New York: Cambridge University Press.

Office of Bilingual Bicultural Education. 1983. *Basic Principles for the Edu-*

∟age Minority Students: An Overview. Sacramento: Califor-
artment of Education.

*8. Minority Education and Caste: The American System in
ural Perspective.* New York: Academic Press.

∂87. "Variability in Minority Responses to Schooling: Nonimmi-
/s. Immigrants." G. Spindler and L. Spindler, (eds.) *Interpretive
graphy of Education.* Hillsdale, New Jersey: Lawrence Erlbaum As-
ιes.

, J. U. and M. E. MATUTE-BIANCHI, 1986. "Sociocultural Resources in
struction: A Context-Specific Approach." *Beyond Language: Social and
ultural Factors in Schooling Language Minority Students.* California
State Department of Education. Sacramento, California: Evaluation, Dissemination and Assessment Center, California State University, Los Angeles.

OLIVAS, M. 1982. "The Condition of Education for Hispanics." In *La Red/The
Net* (Report No. 56). Ann Arbor, Michigan: The University of Michigan,
Institute for Social Science.

OLSEN, L. 1988. *Crossing the Schoolhouse Border: Immigrant Students and
the California Public Schools.* San Francisco, California: A California To-
morrow Report.

ONG, C. 1976. "The Educational Attainment of the Chinese in America."
Unpublished research project. Dept. of Anthropology, University of California, Berkeley.

OVANDO, C. J. and V. COLLIER. 1986. *Bilingual and ESL Classrooms: Teaching in Multicultural Contexts.* New York: McGraw Hill.

OXFORD, R., L. POL, D. LOPEZ, P. STUPP, M. GENDELL, and S. PENG, 1981.
"Projections of Non-English Language Background and Limited English
Proficient Persons in the United States to the Year 2000: Educational Plan-
ning in the Demographic Context." *NABE Journal,* 5(3), 1–30.

PADILLA, A. 1982. "Bilingual Schools: Gateways to Integration or Roads to
Separation." J. A. Fishman and G. D. Keller, (eds.) *Bilingual Education for
Hispanic Students in the United States.* New York: Teachers College, Co-
lumbia University.

PARKER, O. D. and Educational Services Staff, AFME. 1986. "Cultural Clues
to the Middle Eastern Student." J. M. Valdes, (ed.) *Culture Bound.* Cambridge: Cambridge University Press.

PARRA, E. and R. W. HENDERSON, 1982. "Mexican-American Perceptions of
Parent Teacher Roles in Child Development." J. A. Fishman and G. D.
Keller, (eds.) *Bilingual Education for Hispanic Students in the United
States.* New York: Teachers College, Columbia University.

PATTERSON, W. and H.-C. KIM, 1976. *The Koreans in America.* Minneapolis:
Lerner Publications.

PEDERSEN, P. 1988. *A Handbook for Developing Multicultural Awareness.*
Alexandria, Virginia: American Association for Counseling and Development.

PELLOWSKI, A. 1984. *The Story Vine: A Source Book of Unusual and Easy-
to-Tell Stories from Around the World.* New York: Collier Books.

PEYTON, J. K. 1986. "Interactive Writing: Making Writing Meaningful f[o]
Language Minority Students." *NABE News*, 10(1), 19–21.

PHAP, D. T. 1980. *The Indochinese Refugees' Cultural Background*. Sa[n]
Antonio, Texas: The Intercultural Development Research Association.

PHENICE, E., E. MARTINEZ and G. GRANT. 1986. "Minority Family Agendas:
The Home-School Interface and Alternative." R. J. Griffore and R. P. Boger,
(eds.) *Child Rearing in the Home and School*. New York: Plenum Press.

PHILIPS, S. 1970. "The Acquisition of Rules of Appropriate Usage." J. Alatis,
(ed.) *Monograph Series on Language and Linguistics*. Washington, D.C.:
Georgetown University Press.

PHILIPS, S. 1972. "Participant Structures and Communicative Competence:
Warm Spring Children in Community and Classroom." C. B. Cazden, V. J.
John and D. Hymes, (eds.) *Functions of Language in the Classroom* (pp.
370–94). New York: Teachers College Press.

PHILIPS, S. 1974. "Warm Spring Indian Time: How the Regulation of Partici-
pation Affects the Progression of Events." R. Bauman and J. Sherzer, (eds.)
Explorations in the Ethnography of Speaking. Cambridge: Cambridge
University Press.

PHILIPS, S. 1974. *The Invisible Culture: Communication in the Classroom
and Community on the Warm Spring Indian Reservation*. Ph.D. Dissertation, University of Pennsylvania.

PHILIPS, S. 1983. *The Invisible Culture: Communication in Classroom and
Community on the Warm Spring Indian Reservation*. New York: Longman.

PIENEMANN, M. 1984. "Psychological Constraints on the Teachability of Languages." *Studies in Second Language Acquisition*. 6(2), 186–214.

PORTES, A. and R. BACH. 1985. *Latin Journey: Cuban and Mexican Immigrants in the United States*. Berkeley, California: University of California
Press.

QUIÑONES, J. 1973. *On Culture*. Los Angeles: UCLA Chicano Studies Publications.

RAMIREZ, A. G., E. ARCE-TORRES and R. POLITZER. 1978. "Language Attitudes and the Achievement of Bilingual Pupils in English Language Arts."
The Bilingual Review/La Revista Bilingue, 5, 190–206.

RAMÍREZ, M. A. and R. CASTAÑEDA. 1974. *Cultural Democracy, Bicognitive
Development and Education*. New York: Academic Press.

REIBEIRO, J. L. 1980. "Testing Portuguese Immigrant Children: Cultural
Patterns and Group Differences in Responses to the WISC-R." D. P. Macedo,
(ed.), *Issues in Portuguese Bilingual Education*. Cambridge, Massachusetts: National Assessment and Dissemination Center for Bilingual Education.

RICHARD-AMATO, P. 1988. *Making It Happen: Interaction in the Second
Language Classroom*. New York: Longman.

RICHARDS, J. 1980. Conversation. *TESOL Quarterly*. 14(4), 413–32.

RICHARDS, J. C. and T. S. RODGERS, 1986. *Approaches and Methods in
Language Teaching: A Description and Analysis*. Cambridge: Cambridge
University Press.

ᵧᵣ   ₁987. "Cross-Cultural Coping: Suggestions for Anglo Teach-
              ᴐ Native Americans." C. Cargill, (ed.) *A TESOL Professional*
              Culture. Lincolnwood, Illinois: National Textbook Company.

              ₃3. "The Computer Chronicles Newswire: A Functional Learning
              ₘent for Acquiring Literacy Skills." *Journal of Educational Com-*
              Research, 1, 317–337.

              . 1986. "Reading in ESL: Learning from Kids." P. Rigg and D. S.
              ght, (eds.) *Children and ESL: Integrating Perspectives.* Washington,
              ᴧ.: TESOL.

          ᴇS, W. R. 1987. "Conflicting Ideas on the Banning of Intelligence Tests:
       ᴐommentary." *Education Week,* February 11, pp. 20, 28.

    ᴨIST, R. C. 1970. "Student Social Class and Teacher Expectations: The Self-
    Fulfilling Prophesy in Ghetto Education." *Harvard Educational Review.*
    40, 411–451.

RIST, R. C. 1978. *The Invisible Children—School Integration in American*
    Society. Cambridge: Harvard University Press.

RIVERA, F., (ed.) 1970. *Mexican American Source Book.* Menlo Park, CA:
    Educational Consulting Associates.

ROBINSON, G. L. 1985. *Crosscultural Understanding: Processes and Ap-*
    proaches for Foreign Language, English as a Second Language and Bilin-
    gual Educators. New York: Pergamon.

ROMAINE, S. 1984. *The Language of Children and Adolescents.* Oxford:
    Basil Blackwell.

ROSA, A. and L. C. MOLL. 1985. "Computadores, Comunicación y Ed-
    ucación: Una Colaboración Internacional en la Intervención e Investigación
    Educativa." Infancia y Aprendizaje, 30, 1–17.

ROSENTHAL, R. and L. JACOBSON, 1968. *Pygmalion in the Classroom:*
    Teacher Expectations and Pupils' Intellectual Development. New York:
    Holt, Rinehart, Winston.

RUTHERFORD, W. and M. SHARWOOD SMITH, (eds.). 1988. *Grammar and*
    Second Language Teaching. New York: Newbury House Publishers.

RUTT, R. 1987. "Traditional literature." P. Hyun, (ed.) *Introducing Korea.*
    Republic of Korea: Jungwoo-Sa.

RYAN, E. B. and H. GILES, (eds.) 1982. *Attitudes Towards Language Varia-*
    tion: Social and Applied Contexts. London: Edward Arnold.

SANCHEZ, R. 1983. *Chicano Discourse. Socio-Historic Perspectives.* Rowley,
    Massachusetts: Newbury House Publishers.

SATO, C. 1981. "Ethnic Styles in Classroom Discourse." M. Hines, and W.
    Rutherford, (eds.) *On TESOL '81.* Washington, D.C.: TESOL.

SAVILLE-TROIKE, M. 1977. "The Cultural Component of Bilingual Education
    Programs: Theories and Practices." J. F. Fanselow, and R. L. Light, (eds.)
    Bilingual ESOL and Foreign Language Teacher Preparation: Models,
    Practices, Issues. Washington, D.C.: TESOL.

SAYERS, D. 1986, "Sending Messages Across the Classroom and Around the
    World: Computer-Assisted Language Learning." Special Supplement No. 3
    of *TESOL Newsletter,* 20, 7–8.

BIBLIOGRAPHY

SAYERS, D. and K. BROWN. 1987. "Bilingual Education and Teleco. tions: A Perfect Fit." *The Computing Teacher*, 17, 23–24.

SCARCELLA, R. 1983. "Discourse Accent in Second Language Performance. S. Gass and L. Selinker, (eds.) *Language Transfer in Language Learning*. Rowley, Massachusetts: Newbury House Publishers.

SCARCELLA, R. and C. LEE, 1988. "Korean ESL Writing Difficulties." Paper presented at the 1988 TESOL convention, Chicago.

SCHIEFFELIN, B. B. 1983. "Talking Like Birds: Sound Play in a Cultural Perspective." E. Ochs and B. B Schieffelin, *Acquiring Conversational Competence*. London: Routledge and Kegan Paul.

SCHINKE-LLANO, L. 1980. "Foreigner Talk in Content Classrooms." H. W. Seliger and M. H. Long, (eds.) *Classroom Oriented Research in Second Language Acquisition*. Rowley, Massachusetts: Newbury House Publishers.

SCHUMANN, J. 1978. *The Pidginization Process: A Model for Second Language Learning*. Rowley, Massachusetts: Newbury House Publishers.

SCHUMANN, J. 1980. "Affective Factors and the Problem of Age in Second Language Acquisition." K. Croft, (ed.) *Readings in ESL*. Cambridge, Massachusetts: Winthrop.

SCHUMANN, J. 1986. "Research on the Acculturation Model for Second Language Acquisition." *Journal of Multilingual and Multicultural Development*. 7, 379–392.

SELINKER, L. 1972. "Interlanguage." *International Review of Applied Linguistics*. X:209–30.

SEVILLE-TROIKE, M. 1979. (ed.) *Classroom Practices in ESL and Bilingual Education*. Washington, D.C.: Teachers of English to Speakers of Other Languages.

SHACKLE, C. 1987. "Speakers of Indian Languages." M. Swan and B. Smith, (eds.) *Learner English*. Cambridge: Cambridge University Press.

SIROTNIK, K. A. 1983. "What You See is What You Get: Consistency, Persistency, and Mediocrity in Classrooms." *Harvard Educational Review*, 53(1):16–31.

SKUTNABB-KANGAS, T. and J. CUMMINS. 1988. *Minority Education*. Clevedon, England: Multilingual Matters.

SLAVIN, R. E. 1980. "Student Team Learning: A Manual for Teachers." S. Sharan, P. Hare, C. D. Webb and S. Hertz-Lazarowitz, (eds.) *Cooperation in Education*. Provo: Brigham Young University Press.

SLAVIN, R. E. 1983. "When Does Cooperative Learning Increase Student Achievement?" *Psychological Bulletin*, 94, 429–445.

SMALLEY, W. A. 1984. "Adaptive Language Strategies of the Hmong: From Asian Mountains to American Ghettos." *Language Science* 7(2), 241–269.

SMITH, B. 1987. "Arabic Speakers." M. Swan and B. Smith, (eds.) *Learner English*. Cambridge: Cambridge University Press.

SMYTH, D. 1987. "Thai Speakers." M. Swan, and B. Smith, (eds.) *Learner Language*. Cambridge: Cambridge University Press.

SNOW, C., J. CHALL, J. CHANDLER, I. GOODMAN, L. HEMPHILL and V. JA-
COBS. In press. *Families and Literacy.* New York: McGraw Hill.

SNOW, M. A., D. BRINTON and M. WESCHE. 1989. *Content-Based Second
Language Instruction.* New York: Harper and Row.

SPINDLER, G. 1982. "Roger Harker and Schoenhausen: From the Familiar to
the Strange and Back Again." G. Spindler, (ed.) *Doing the Ethnography of
Schooling.* New York: Holt, Rinehart, and Winston, pp. 20–47.

SPINDLER, G. 1987. "Why Have Minority Groups in North America Been
Disadvantaged by Their Schools?" G. Spindler, (ed.) *Education and Cul-
tural Process: Anthropological Approaches.* Prospect Heights, Illinois:
Waveland Press.

SPINDLER, G. and L. SPINDLER, (eds.) 1987. *Interpretive Ethnography of
Education: At Home and Abroad.* Hillsdale, New Jersey: Lawrence
Erlbaum Associates.

SROLE, L. 1956. "Social Integration and Certain Corollaries: An Exploration
Study." *American Sociological Review,* 21, 709–716.

STATON, J. 1985. "Using Dialogue Journals for Developing Thinking, Reading and Writing with Hearing Impaired Students." *Volta Review,* 87 (5),
127–154.

STEVICK, E. 1976. *Memory, Meaning and Method.* Rowley, Massachusetts:
Newbury House Publishers.

STEWART, E. 1972. *American Cultural Patterns: A Cross-Cultural Perspective.* Chicago: Intercultural Press.

STOVER, L. E. 1962. *Face and Verbal Analogues of Interaction in Chinese
Culture.* Unpublished Ph.D. Dissertation. Columbia University.

SUE, S. 1983. "Ethnic Minority Issues in Psychology: A Reexamination."
American Psychologist, 38, 583–592.

SUE, S. and A. PADILLA. 1986. "Ethnic Minority Issues in the United States:
Challenges for the Educational System." In *Beyond Language: Social and
Cultural Factors in Schooling Language Minority Students.* California
State Department of Education. Sacramento, California: Evaluation, Dis-
semination and Assessment Center, California State University, Los Ange-
les.

SUNG, B. L. 1967. *Mountain of Gold: The Story of the Chinese in America.*
New York: McMillan.

SWAIN, M. 1986. "Communicative Competence: Some Roles of Comprehensible Input and Comprehensible Output in its Development." S. M. Gass and
C. G. Madden, (eds.) *Input in Second Language Acquisition.* Rowley, Massachusetts; Newbury House Publishers.

SWAIN, M. and S. LAPKIN, 1989. *Evaluating Bilingual Education: A Canadian Case Study.* Clevedon, England: Multilingual Matters.

TAYLOR, B. P. 1987. "Teaching ESL: Incorporating a Communicative, Stu-
dent-Centered Component." M. H. Long and J. C. Richards (eds.)
Methodolgy in TESOL: A Book of Readings New York; Harper and Row.

THOMPSON, I. 1987. "Japanese Speakers. *Learner English.*" M. Swan and B.
Smith, (eds.) Cambridge: Cambridge University Press.

THOMPSON, I. 1987. "Turkish Speakers. *Learner English.*" M. Swan and B. Smith, (eds.) Cambridge: Cambridge University Press.

TIEDT, P. L. and I. M. TIEDT, 1986. *Multicultural Teaching: A Handbook of Activities. Information and Resources.* Massachusetts: Allyn and Bacon.

TIEN, N., D. PHUC and V. T. HUY. 1981. *Pirates in the Gulf of Siam.* San Diego: Boat People S.O.S. Committee.

TIZARD, J., W. N. SCHOFIELD and J. HEWISON, 1982. "Collaboration Between Teachers and Parents in Assisting Children's Reading." *British Journal of Educational Psychology,* 52, 1–15.

TRUEBA, H. T. 1989. *Raising Silent Voices: Educating the Linguistic Minorities for the 21st Century.* Cambridge: Harper and Row.

United States Commerce, Bureau of the Census 1983. *Conditions of Hispanics in America Today.* Washington, D.C.: United States Government Printing Office.

VALDES-FALLIS, G. 1981. "Code Switching and the Classroom Teachers." *Language in Education: Theory and Practice,* 4:16, Washington, D.C.: Center for Applied Linguistics.

VALDES, G. 1988. "The Language Situation of Mexican Americans." S. L. McKay and S.-L. Wong, *Language Diversity: Problem or Resource?* New York: Harper and Row.

VYGOTSKY, L. 1978. *Mind in Society.* Cambridge, Massachusetts: Harvard University.

WALBERY, H. J., R. A. PASCHAL and T. WEINSTEIN. 1985. "Homework's Powerful Effects on Learning." *Educational Leadership,* 42 (7), 76–79.

WALKER, C. L. 1985. "Learning English: The Southeast Asia Refugee Experience." *Topics in Language Disorders,* 5(4), 53–65.

WALLERSTEIN, N. 1983. *Language and Culture in Conflict: Problem-Posing in the ESL Classroom.* Reading, Massachusetts: Addison-Wesley.

WALTERS, K. and L. GUNDERSON, 1985. "Effects of Parent Volunteers Reading First Language (L1) Books to ESL Students." *The Reading Teacher,* 66–69.

WANG, Z. 1982. "English Teaching and English Studies in China." *Language Learning and Communication.* 1:1, 5–20.

WAYNANT, L. and R. WILSON., 1974. *Learning Centers: A Guide for Effective Use.* Paoli, Pennsylvania.

WEEKS, T. 1983. "Discourse, Culture and Interaction." B. Robinette and J. Schachter, (eds.) *Second Language Learning.* Ann Arbor: University of Michigan Press.

WELCHE, F. C. and P. TISDALE, 1986. *Between Parent and Teacher.* Springfield, Illinois: Charles C. Thomas Publisher.

WELLS, G. 1982. "Language, Learning and the Curriculum." G. Wells, (ed.) *Language Learning and Education.* Bristol: Center for the Study of Language and Communication, University of Bristol.

WELLS, G. 1986. *The Meaning Makers: Children Learning Language and Using Language to Learn.* Portsmouth, New Hampshire: Heinemann Educational Books.

WHORF, B. 1956. "Science and Linguistics." J. B. Carroll, (ed.) *Language, Thought and Reality: Selected Writings of Benjamin Lee Whorf.* Cambridge, Mass.: M.I.T. Press.

WILLIAMS, J. C. 1968. *Improving Educational Opportunities for Mexican-American Handicapped Children.* Washington, D.C., Office of Education. (ED018326)

WILLIAMS, L. V. 1983. *Teaching for the Two-Sided Mind: A Guide to Right Brain/Left Brain Education.* Englewood Cliffs, New Jersey: Prentice-Hall.

WILLIAMS, T. R. 1958. "The Structure of Socialization Process in Papago Indian Society." *Social Forces,* 36, 251–256.

WILSON, L. and M. WILSON. 1987. "Farsi Speakers. *Learner English.*" M. Swan and B. Smith, (eds.) Cambridge: Cambridge University Press.

WING, L.-C. 1972. "Testimony Cited in Integrated Education Associates." *Chinese Americans: School and Community Problems* (Chicago 1972) pp. 18–28, 12–17.

WITKIN, H. and D. R. GOODENOUGH. 1976. *Field Dependence and Interpersonal Behavior. Research Bulletin.* Princeton: Educational Testing Service.

WITKIN, J. B., M. LEWIS, M. HERTZMAN, K. MACHOVER, P. B. MEISSNER and S. WAPNER. 1974. "Field Dependent and Field-Independent Cognitive Styles and Their Educational Implications." *Review of Educational Research.* (Winter) 1–64.

WOLFSON, N. 1989. *Perspectives: Sociolinguistics and TESOL.* Cambridge: Harper and Row.

WONG, S.-L. 1988. "Educational Rights of Language Minorities." S. McKay and S.-L. Wong, (eds.) *Language Diversity: Problem or Resource?* New York: Harper and Row.

WONG, S.-L. 1988. "The Language Situation of Chinese Americans." S. L. McKay and S.-L. Wong, (eds.) *Language Diversity: Problem or Resource?* Cambridge, Massachusetts, Newbury House Publishers, a division of Harper and Row.

WONG, Y.-M. 1983. *Dear Diane: Letters from our Daughters.* Oakland, California: Asian Women United of California.

WONG-FILLMORE, L. W. 1976. *The Second Time Around: Cognitive and Social Strategies in Second Language Acquisition.* Ph.D. Dissertation. Stanford University.

WONG-FILLMORE, L. W. 1983. "The Language Learner as an Individual: Implications of Individual Differences for the ESL Teacher." J. Handscombe and M. Clarke, (eds.) In *On TESOL '82: Pacific Perspectives on Language Learning and Teaching.* Washington, D.C.: TESOL.

WONG-FILLMORE, L. 1985. "When Does Teacher Talk Work as Input?" S. M. Gass, and C. G. Madden, (eds.) *Input in Second Language Acquisition.* Rowley, Massachusetts: Newbury House Publishers.

WONG-FILLMORE, L. W. 1985. "When Does Teacher Talk Work as Input?" S. Gass, and C. Madden, (eds.) *Input in Second Language Acquisition.* Rowley, Massachusetts: Newbury House Publishers, 17–50.

WU, W. T. 1982. Learning styles of Chinese children. *Asian Bilingual Educa-*

tion Teacher Handbook. Cambridge, Massachusetts: Evaluation, Dissemination and Assessment Center for Bilingual Education.

ZENTELLA, A. C. 1988. "The Language Situation of Puerto Ricans." S. L. McKay and S.-L. Wong, (eds.) Language Diversity: Problem or Resource? Cambridge, Massachusetts, Newbury House Publishers, a division of Harper and Row.

ZIMMERMAN, C. and C. WEST, 1975. "Sex Roles, Interruptions and Silences." B. Thorne and N. Henley, (eds.) Language and Sex: Difference and Dominance. Rowley, Massachusetts: Newbury House Publishers.

Index

Page numbers in italics denote information in the Notes sections.